Homeboy's Soul

Pride, Terror & Street Justice in America

An autobiography co-written by

Don Armijo and Fred Stawitz

First published in 2010 by

PUBLISHAMERICA, LLLP
Baltimore, MD

Published in 2018 by

STORYMAKERS, INC.
P.O. Box 91338
Houston, Texas 77291-1338
www.storymakersinc.com

© 2010—2018 by Don Armijo and StoryMakers, Inc.

All rights reserved.

No part of this book may be reproduced, stored in a retrieval system or transmitted in any form or by any means without the prior written permission of the publishers, except by a reviewer who may quote brief passages in a review.

The characters, conversations, and events portrayed in the book all come from Don Armijo's recollections, though they are not written to represent precise word-for-word transcripts. Rather, the authors have retold these stories in a way that evokes the sentiment of what was said and what transpired during those turbulent times. As such, this book is a work of fiction based on actual events and all characters mentioned in this work are fictitious. Any resemblance to real persons, living or dead, is purely coincidental.

Permission to print images of the individuals appearing in the photographs published in this book have been granted by those individuals.

Cover design by Fred Stawitz.

Editing by Fred Stawitz.

ISBN: 978-0-9888079-1-4

Printed in the United States of America.

Acknowledgements

I began writing *Homeboy's Soul* one day in my prison cell on a small notepad with no idea of how to write a book and nothing but the belief that it was somehow possible. Now after so many years and as many drafts, I can hardly believe that the journey has progressed so far.

I feel blessed to have had the support and assistance of so many good and talented people who were able to look past the mistakes I made in my life, to see the dream of *Homeboy's Soul* and help me to make it a reality.

Actor Danny De La Paz, who starred in the movies "Boulevard Nights," "American Me," and "Road Dogz," provided encouragement when I needed it most and has helped me believe that acting upon my faith can produce amazing results. I am thankful for the guidance he provided and his tireless assistance in helping me turn the details of my life into a coherent story.

Additionally, I want to express my appreciation and gratitude to Dolores Colunga-Stawitz who I met at a writer's conference. Many took interest in my story but Dolores took my project a step closer to success with her belief in *Homeboy's Soul*. This meeting resulted in my partnership with her husband Fred Stawitz who, as co-author, has given life to the characters in this story and has helped pry out memories and thoughts that I believed had been lost long ago.

While there are too many to mention, I want to acknowledge all the homeboys and homegirls who lived this story with me. Out of respect for their privacy, their real names do not appear in *Homeboy's Soul*. Even so, I want them to know how much I will always love them and hope they, too, are able to look past my mistakes.

Also, I want to dedicate *Homeboy's Soul* to all of the families who had to suffer the loss of their loved ones, as well as those who were victimized. I apologize for my wrongs and pray for their forgiveness.

Don Armijo

Introduction

There are moments in one's life when, upon meeting someone new, one gets the feeling that this person is somehow different, and there is a sense of purpose for this new union. It is as though a character of importance is making their entrance into the play of your life. That is how I felt when I first met Don Armijo. Something told me to pay attention to this man; that somehow our energies were to be combined toward the fulfillment of a major creative endeavor. This book is the culmination of that endeavor.

Don and I come from two totally different backgrounds. I was not raised around gangs or the gangster lifestyle. It was something my mother Margaret wanted very much to avoid when, in the mid-fifties, she very consciously moved my family from the *barrios* of East L.A. to the once-Quaker town known as Whittier.

I was born and raised in Whittier, in a middle-class neighborhood that at the time was gang free. I never had to worry about being pressured to join a gang or constantly having to deal with the reality of living in what amounted to a war zone. That is why it is so ironic that as a young actor, having been raised on the works of the finest writers in the theatre—Shakespeare, Chekhov, Saroyan, Miller—I would end up making my motion picture debut starring in the Warner Bros. feature "Boulevard Nights" as Chuco Avila, a young gangster from the streets of East L.A.

I could not have been more removed from that particular reality. Nonetheless, I found myself on the streets of East L.A., where my brothers Tony and Sonny had spent their boyhood, wearing pants that were ten sizes too big for me, with hair dyed jet black, and a small-brimmed, black felt hat atop my head, playing the very thing my mother had hoped I would not become.

In the almost three decades, as of this writing, since its release, "Boulevard Nights" has taken on icon status within the Chicano community, passed on from generation to generation. As a result, I have been thrust into icon status as well. Long after I have left this earth, I will be remembered in my community for this performance. I suppose then, that it is only fitting that Don and I should have come together on this very personal and life-affirming project.

Every homeboy has seen "American Me," or will at some time in the future. My role in that film represents what the future has in store for young, misguided men who find themselves prisoners of their own life choices. I speak to youth at risk all over the country at juvenile halls, schools, and community groups, and try to show them that with a different vision of themselves comes a different reality—that they are powerful creators with the power to change their lives, even now as they sit in front of me with their freedom taken from them.

Homeboy's Soul was written for them. They are the ones to whom this book speaks. I cannot speak from experience about the life of a homeboy, but Don can. His life is reflected back at the reader in the hope that it will have some positive affect on his or her life. Through the drama, struggles, and inner conflict, there comes a new person, forged from the pain of his past.

The problem of gangs and gang violence has roots that lie deep within the very structure of our social schematic. It is a part of our history which lives even now.

Homeboy's Soul deserves to take its place among the best literature available today on the complex and fascinating subject of what draws a promising young life to such self-destruction, and the strength it takes to break free. I am so honored to introduce *Homeboy's Soul*. I feel it can offer tremendous insight to anyone who comes to it with an open mind and a willing heart.

Peace!
Danny De La Paz

Preface

Our desire and challenge in writing *Homeboy's Soul* is to honor those who live amidst the violence and turmoil in the *barrios* surrounding East Los Angeles, while trying to offer those who have no experience with this environment a true sense of what it is like and why Don's homeboys and he made some of the choices they did. We are not trying to defend those choices as much as shed light on the circumstances that confronted Don and his homeboys and helped shape their decisions.

Homeboy's Soul provides an accurate portrayal of what life in the *barrio* is really like, from Don's first encounters with gang activities as a youngster through his rise in the ranks of one of the largest, most violent Chicano gangs on the west coast. This is Don's story and, for the most part, it is true. In the few instances where we strayed from an accurate accounting of events, we did so to minimize any additional pain that our words might inflict upon those who had been victimized so badly in the past.

Homeboy's Soul, while based on Don's personal experiences and life, also reveals something about human nature and the potential we all have for violence should we find ourselves confronted with racial and economic repression.

As you venture into the world of *Homeboy's Soul*, we invite you to confront any preconceptions or biases you may have, to free yourself to envision what you would do if you found yourself entangled in the web of poverty and oppression that characterizes life in the *barrio*. Whether you call it violence when perpetrated by homeboys doing a drive-by, collateral damage when an invading army bombs civilian populations or terror when religious fanatics fly planes into buildings, the results are the same: death and destruction. If you cannot recognize or understand the conditions that breed such violence, you will are ill-prepared to do anything to stop it.

Dig below the surface to discover the roots of violence. Find out how fear can be used as an effective tool of manipulation whether wielded by gang leaders or government officials. Human nature dictates that desperate people will use whatever means they can to preserve the illusion of security.

More soldiers, more police, and more prisons are short-sighted solutions often offered by those who profit from these Band-Aid solutions while the violence and terrorism continues unabated. *Homeboy's Soul* does not provide all the answers necessary to eradicate violence or terrorism from the surface of the earth; however, it will enlighten you to the serious challenges we face in pursuing that goal.

Homeboy's Soul invites you into the mysterious world of the most pervasive and misunderstood lifestyle in America … *gangbangers!* This provocative tale delves into the private thoughts, doubts, and fears of a normal Chicano youngster, turned killer by his choices and the circumstances of his environment.

Our hope is that by reading *Homeboy's Soul* you will develop a better understanding of the forces that drive young people to give their lives and loyalties to gangs, so that together, we can begin to push back the veil of poverty and oppression that feeds this unwelcome beast.

Don Armijo and Fred Stawitz

"Therefore, pride is their necklace;

they clothe themselves with violence."

Psalm 73:6 N.I.V

1

Riots

There it was, my ride! A pearl white banana seat perched over a jet black chassis. Sleek whitewall tires wrapped the shiny spoke rims connected to the front forks which curved out instead of in, giving my new Schwinn bicycle the long low profile of a "lowrider." Everything that could be chromed, was. Most important was the spring mounted below the handle bars, which allowed me to bounce on the front wheel. This was my ride, built and powered by me!

"Mom! I'm going outside to ride my bike with David!" I yelled to her in the kitchen as I hurried to the front door with my lowrider. It was too special to leave outside.

"Did you throw out the trash?"

Man, she was quick. One more second and I would have been out the door and out of range.

"Throw out the trash or you're not going anywhere!"

I had no choice now. I circled back through the kitchen, grabbed the bag of trash, and made a beeline for the backdoor. Outside I tossed the trash into the air. It hit inside the first of three cans lined up beside the back of the garage, like a basketball homing in on the hoop for two points.

Rather than going back through the kitchen and giving my mom the chance to find another chore for me, I opened the gate to the driveway and crept silently past the kitchen windows, down the driveway that ran along the side of the house and back in the front door without making a sound. I quietly positioned my bike in the doorway for a quick getaway. I was already moving when I shouted, "I'm leaving, Mom!"

"Be back before it gets dark, *mijo*, and be careful!"

I was off, pedaling at full speed down Mayfair Street toward David's house. We both lived on Mayfair Street which ran a short five blocks between White Avenue on the west and Park Avenue on the east. David lived closer to Park Avenue, a four-lane thoroughfare speckled with stop signs. Ours was an average neighborhood full of average one-story homes built during the housing boom of the sixties. While a few blacks and a few whites lived in this area, most of the families were of Mexican descent. Just north, where Park Avenue crossed Twelfth Street in the heart of the *barrio*, all the families were Mexican.

It was late August, 1970. I was eleven years old and enjoyed living in Pomona, California, about 30 miles east of Los Angeles.

Most people called me skinny but I preferred being thought of as thin. My light complexion, accented by black hair and brown eyes, reflected the European ancestry of my family which traced back to Spanish-Dutch on my mom's side and Spanish-Sicilian on my dad's side. All that didn't mean much to me except that I overheard my parents discussing it over dinner one evening while news of the Vietnam War blared from the TV in the other room. To me and everyone else, we were *Chicanos*, Mexicans born on this side of the border. That's how everybody else saw me and *mi familia*, and that's how I saw myself.

The Vietnam War appeared like a regular television series on the evening news. It seemed to be causing a lot of turmoil but that didn't concern me either. My world was a fun place with lots of time to play and lots of friends, each with their own special name.

Fat Joe was big and always hungry. Although his size would intimidate anyone, he was always very polite and all of the mothers around the *barrio* liked him. He was light-skinned with black hair and always seemed to be in a good mood.

Black Crow, a full-blooded American Indian, was another one of my friends. He was fluent in Spanish so he fit in with the rest of us. We gave him the name Black Crow because he was dark with jet black hair like the crows that hung out on the telephone lines which ran along the streets. Black Crow had a way of making funny comments to lighten the mood whenever my friends and I found ourselves in trouble, which seemed to be all the time. I think that's one of the reasons that he and I hit it off so well. Besides, at our age, getting in trouble was half the fun.

Nite Owl was thin and had light brown skin with black hair. He often snuck out of his house after dark to hang out with his older brothers. That must be why he seemed older than the rest of us even though we were all the same age—that and the fact that he never said much. He usually let his dark, piercing eyes say whatever he had to say. No one really knew what Nite Owl was thinking. We did know enough not to make him mad, for behind his silence lurked a danger that none of us dared unleash.

Then there were the twin brothers *Travieso* and J-Bird. Both of them were skinny and light-skinned with black hair but to look at them you couldn't really tell they were twins. J-Bird was taller and had a fuller jawbone, while *Travieso's* face was long and thin. Maybe to compensate for his narrow jaw, *Travieso*, had a nose for trouble. J-Bird got his name because whenever there was work to do around the house he always managed to disappear like a stray bird into the wind. He explained that he didn't want to be the only one left to do the chores. His mother used to say, *"Dónde esta mi pájaro?"*

Payaso, always the clown, was thin and daring and loved attention. He always seemed to have a crazy idea of something we should try, like jumping our bikes over the drainage ditch that ran behind his house. We all thought it was a great idea. Lucky for us, David, the smartest of my friends, had enough sense to question the wisdom of such reckless daring. Of course, we never let on that we appreciated David's intervention. Instead, we all called him a sissy before going on to do something equally crazy. Even so, I know that at one time or the other he saved each of us a painful trip to the hospital.

I don't know why, but David, whose hair and skin was as brown as the rest of us, didn't have a nickname like my other friends. Maybe it was because he was a shy momma's boy, except when he was saving us from our self-destructive tendencies. His dad was real cool, though. He let us hangout in the yard and even helped us fix up our bikes.

Earlier in the year, I was racing my bike down a steep hill in Ganesha Park and lost control. I crashed hard. Broke my right arm and busted out a tooth. After that, my friends started calling me *Braso*, which means the arm and would normally be spelled *"brazo,"* but like many gang tags, mine was customized with a unique spelling. I liked the sound of it, so it stuck. Guess I was lucky. I could have been stuck with the nickname *molacho*, which means "toothless," for the rest of my life.

David was already out on his bike when I arrived at his house. We hooked up with the other guys and decided to ride north on Park Avenue toward the *barrio*. The rhythmic beat of *El Chicano's "Viva Tirado"* blared from the little transistor radio David had mounted on his handlebars.

We rarely rode in a straight line. Rather, we used the entire street, swerving this way and that trying to see who would be the first to crash into the curb and tumble head first onto the grass. As we neared Grand Avenue, we noticed a lot of cars parked on the street alongside Sharkie Park.

"It's a party!" *Payaso* yelled as he raced out in front of the pack.

Not to be left behind, we all pressed hard on our pedals. The warm afternoon air blew past our faces as each of us tried to be the first to reach the corner. I had never seen a party of this magnitude. My heart raced as feelings of anticipation and excitement built within me. I wanted to be the first one there.

Then suddenly, as if by instinct, my feet hit the brakes. My ride skidded sideways to a full stop. It was as if I had entered another world and I was alone with everything happening in slow motion. Police cars blocked the intersection. *Chicanos*, young and old, were running this way and that, screaming and yelling, trying to get away from the police who were attacking them with billy clubs and flashlights. Some of the *Chicanos* fought back with bats, chains, and bumper jacks. Others stood toe-to-toe with the cops exchanging blows. It was crazy.

The crowd rolled a police car over on its side. One man threw a metal trash can through the windshield of another police cruiser. Several police officers chased him down and beat him with their clubs. Blood, gushing from wounds on his head, soaked his white T-shirt. The police handcuffed him and packed him into the back of their cruiser with nine or ten other guys who looked like sardines with their bruised and bloody faces pressed against the glass.

The *Chicanos* severely outnumbered the police and the violence was escalating. Behind me, I heard the sickening thud of a night stick crack a man's skull. As I spun my head around to look, a *Chicano* with his hands cuffed behind his back burst from out of nowhere. He raced for freedom like a rabbit trying to escape the wolves, dodging and leaping over everything in his path. A cop, his night stick swinging wildly at this side, was hot on his trail. Although exhausted and panting for air, the cop was too close to give up as he chased his quarry between two houses.

Moments later, the cop returned with a look of deep frustration. He leaned forward placing both hands on his knees, struggling to catch his breath, then he stared up at me as though I were the source of his problems. His eyes, burning with hate and anger, cut into the depth of my soul. I had never seen such a pained look before in my life. I felt as though he could reach right out and grab me at any moment, even though he was more than twenty feet away. I quickly glanced at Fat Joe. He was our strength, our power, and our protector. We relied on his size to deliver us from anyone who threatened our group, but Fat Joe sat, frozen to his bike, staring at the carnage. His knuckles clenched the handlebars squeezing out every ounce of blood until they were white. For the first time he looked small.

I could feel the danger closing in around me and pulling me into the madness. Any sense of protection I thought I had was fading very quickly.

"Let's get out of here!" I heard myself yell. It was *my* voice but it sounded distant and foreign.

Seconds later, we were all racing down the street, trying to get out of there as fast as we could. The trip home was different. *Payaso* rode in a straight line. We all did. No riding in circles. No playing chicken. *Travieso* and J-Bird kept their eyes straight ahead focused between the handlebars. Even Black Crow rode along in silence. No one made eye contact. No one spoke a word. We were all too stunned to talk.

I was glad when I finally pedaled up Mayfield Avenue and my house came into view. It was a small wood-framed house that needed a new coat of paint and some new shingles, just like the other houses on Mayfield, but at that moment, it felt like a castle that could prevent all the ills of the world from following me across the threshold.

I dropped my bike in the yard and hurried in the front door. I saw my older brother and younger sister lying on the floor watching television. The smell of fresh tortillas coming from the kitchen helped to reassure me that everything here was normal. I followed the smell and couldn't resist grabbing one from the top of the stack.

"Did you wash your hands?" my mom inquired. Too late! The tortilla was already history. "*Cochino*, go wash your hands!"

As I hurried for the bathroom, my mom caught me with another question.

"Where have you been all afternoon?"

I leaned back around the corner. "Me and my friends saw a riot at Sharkie Park."

"What!" she exclaimed. "How many times do I have to tell you not to go over there?"

"But, Mom!"

"No buts. You know better."

"At first, we thought it was a party."

"*Sí*, some party? Wait until I tell your father. Maybe next time you'll listen to me."

Man, why did I open my big mouth? My mom acted like Sharkie Park was a dirty word. As I reached for another tortilla, she intercepted my hand with a gentle swat then leaned down and gave me a kiss.

"Go wash your hands," she instructed. "*Sí*, some party."

That evening she prepared tacos for our dinner and wrapped up several extras for Dad's lunch. He worked the swing shift at a mill where they recycled used newspapers, a couple miles from our house in an industrial area framed by the 71 Freeway and Interstate 10 on the northwest side of Pomona. He liked his job and never missed work, even if he was hung over from drinking with his buddies.

After dinner, Mom loaded my brother, sister, and me into our old Chevy to deliver Dad's lunch. Instead of heading up Park Avenue which would take us past Sharkie Park, Mom swung over to Garey Avenue which runs parallel with Park. I suppose she wanted to avoid any remnants of the riot that my friends and I had witnessed earlier.

As we neared the corner of Garey and Mission, the light turned red. Something caught my eye a couple blocks over on Mission Avenue.

"*Mira!*" I climbed over my sister for a better view.

"What are all those people doing at the police station?" my mom asked rhetorically, not expecting us to know any more about what was going on than she did.

"Let's go see!" my brother and I shouted eagerly.

"Can we?" my sister chimed.

I could see a look of curiosity on my mom's face as she glanced quickly in the mirror at us. The light turned green and Mom hesitated for a moment then turned left toward the police station. At the first intersection, she turned right again and found a place to park.

"Take my hand," she said to my sister.

As we neared the police station, the sound of the crowd grew louder. Not far away, a bottle smashed to the pavement.

"I want you two to stay close," she instructed making eye contact with my brother and me. Her voice had become suddenly serious and we all knew we'd better mind her directions.

As we turned the corner and drew closer, it seemed the whole *barrio* was out in full force in front of the police station. I could see it was mostly women who were plenty angry as they chanted, "Let them go! Let our men go!" and "police brutality!"

Some of the protesters wore strange-looking brown hats that lay casually down over the top of their heads and draped over one ear. I had heard of the Brown Berets but was too young to know they were an organization started by two Episcopal priests in East Los Angeles. David Sánchez was chosen to lead the Brown Berets, a group of young *Chicanos* that promoted political and social justice as part of the *Chicano* movement. Dressed in brown berets and khaki military-style uniforms, they were our version of the Black Panthers. They worked in the fields with Cesar Chavez and in the *barrios* to help *La Raza* become more politically active and involved in community government.

Several members of the Brown Berets manned the front lines with the protesters confronting the handful of police officers that stood guard in front of the police station. Both sides seemed aware of the reporters and television cameras that watched from the sidelines waiting for someone to breach the space that separated the two sides. Tension oscillated between the groups. The policemen, who were again terribly outnumbered, looked nervous, even scared, as they each kept one hand anxiously bouncing their billy clubs against their legs.

The crowd was angry and wanted justice.

Mom pulled my brother and me close to her as we made our way through the fringes of the angry mob.

"What's going on? What are you protesting?" she asked a lady.

"It's the *juras*. They came into the *barrio* this afternoon, beat up our men, and threw them in jail for no reason at all. We're here to tell them to let our men go!" The woman turned back toward the police, pounding her fist in the air and shouting, "Let them go! They didn't do nothing to you! Let them go!"

Mom seemed satisfied with the woman's explanation.

Suddenly, a small round object bounced to rest at the feet of a policeman.

Boom! A cherry bomb exploded like the blast from a shotgun. The cop just about jumped out of his white skin. The noise startled everyone.

Mom quickly leaned down to us and said in a serious, direct tone, "Come on, your dad's getting hungry. Let's go take him his lunch."

As we hurried back toward the car, I quickly stole a glance behind me and saw that a large formation of police officers had gathered across the street. These men wore helmets with face shields and carried large clubs. They looked like they were ready for some serious business. All of a sudden, their boots pounded shockwaves into the pavement as they began marching toward the protesters. I hurried to keep up with Mom.

Again, I heard the sound of breaking glass, this time punctuated by screams as the two sides clashed. The fear I'd felt at Sharkie Park returned as my mother quickly ushered us back to the safety of our car.

That night, my mind raced as I lay in my bed. Outside, sirens and gunshots echoed through the *barrio*. Inside, anger and confusion took control of my brain. Until this day, I had thought the police were there to protect us. Now, I could see that they were to be feared.

Early the next morning, a knock at the front door awoke us. I was already peering out of my bedroom window when I heard Mom at the front door. "Who is it?"

I hurried into the living room in time to see Mark and Mary, an older couple in their mid-forties who lived across the street from Sharkie Park. With them was their son Randy, who was a teenager. They all greeted Mom, wrapped in her robe, with a friendly hug and kiss on the cheek. Mary, a short, slim, lightly complexioned woman with a pleasant looking face framed by long black hair, swept me up into her arms for a kiss on the cheek before I had a chance to escape. Mark gave me a friendly rub on the head as Mary lowered my feet back to the floor.

While Mark and Mary were about the same age, Mark looked older than Mary did. Maybe it was his dark, weathered skin or his deep-set eyes that added years to his appearance. I didn't concern myself with why, as I briefly admired the tattoo on his left arm. It showed the face of a beautiful Mexican woman with a large *sombrero* and a band of bullets looped across her shoulders. I was too young to know anything about such women, known as *Adelitas* or *soldaderas* because they fought side-by-side with the men against the repressive rule of Porfirio Diaz during the Mexican Revolution. This was quite unusual since traditionally, and in accordance with the Mexican Civil Code enacted before the revolution, women were supposed to quietly perform domestic duties in the shadow of their men.

My brother and sister got the same treatment from Mark and Mary as I did when they came running in from the bedroom dressed in their pajamas and floppy slippers. After everyone shared hugs and kisses, Mom led us all into the kitchen where she brewed a fresh pot of coffee.

"*Ay,* Elva, I'm sorry to bother you so early in the morning," Mary apologized.

"That's OK," Mom responded, placing four coffee cups on the table.

"I had to get out of the house. It's terrible what the police did. It's crazy. *O Dios mío!* The police were chasing people up and down the *calles* all night."

Just then, Dad entered, stretching his arms into a plain white T-shirt. *"Buenos días,"* he said. As he shook hands with Mark, the muscles on my dad's right forearm flexed a tattoo of a heart pierced by a dagger. Before releasing Mark's weathered hand, Dad leaned over to let Mary give him a kiss on the cheek.

"I'm sorry, we didn't mean to wake you," Mary offered apologetically.

"Don't worry about it. So what's going on?" Dad asked.

"*Ay!* It's terrible, Joey."

I never had gotten used to people calling Dad by his first name. Somehow, it didn't sound right.

"You should see the mess by our house." Mark offered. "The police chased some man into our back yard and beat him like a dog and left him there to die."

"We had to call the ambulance and they picked him up," Mary added. "They had a roadblock at the corner of the park stopping everyone."

"It's a good thing I came home on the expressway last night," Dad said as he shared a look of concern with Mom and me.

"Sí, they would have dragged you out of your car *también* and beat you," Mary stated, adding, *"Cómo un animal!"*

"What's the matter with the police? All they want to do is beat you up for no reason. The kids and I took Joey his lunch last night. We saw the crowds at the police station," Mom explained as she poured the coffee.

Like a news flash, Randy jumped into the conversation. "The *juras* marched in and it all broke loose. You should have seen how three of them beat down an old man just 'cause he couldn't move fast enough, so we had to rush out to help him. Big Joe smashed a brick in the face shield of one of the *juras*. Blood went all over the place. We held them off while some old ladies grabbed the old man and got him out of there. It was crazy!"

"They hit Jaime's wife in the stomach with a club." Anger came through in Mark's words.

"*O díos mío!*" Mom exclaimed.

"We don't know if she lost the baby," Mary added.

"She was pregnant!" Mom gasped, covering her mouth with her hand. "Don't they have any respect?"

Mark's eyes widened. "Respect? The *juras* never had respect for *La Raza!* They killed two *vatos* in East *Los* [East Los Angeles] last week. Just shot them dead! And, one of them worked for the L.A. Times."

"That's right, Ruben Salazar," Dad confirmed. "A lot of *gente* got hurt, *tambíen*."

"This was nothing," Mark railed vehemently. "In the forties, some *gavacho* sailors got drunk and raped a *ruca*, a homegirl, from our *barrio*. *Pues,* some *vatos* went into downtown L.A. and put some good beating on those sailors. One of them died. My *carnal*, who was stationed in Long Beach, told us the sailor that died was the son of a high-ranking officer."

I knew that Mark's brother was in the Navy but had only met him through the many stories that Mark had told about him.

"He said his superiors ordered him and all the *Raza* from East *Los* to come down on the zoot suiters for payback," Mark continued with anger building in his voice. "That wasn't going to happen so they got the *Raza* from up north to come in with more *gavacho* sailors and the *juras*. A lot of *vatos* got messed up."

"The Zoot Suit Riots," Dad added.

A look of disappointment befell Mark as the kitchen slipped into a respectful moment of silence which I unknowingly broke. "What's a zoot suit?"

Everyone turned to look at me. Mark laughed slightly obviously enjoying the inquiry.

"Back then we wore suits, called *drapes,* which we had tailored in the *barrio* especially for us. The pants rode high and snug at the stomach with thin suspenders to hold them in place. The legs ballooned out with razor-sharp creases which cupped in at the ankles and we always had a long shiny gold chain that looped from the waist down one leg then up into a pocket. The jacket was wide at the shoulders with a perfect fit at the waist and tails down to the knee. We wore double-soled shoes, polished to a mirror-shine. You could see your face in the reflection. We always kept our hair short and neatly combed back."

"We dressed the same way in the 50s in Pueblo, Colorado, except we called ourselves *Pachucos,*" my dad added.

I stared at Dad for a moment, seeing him in a different light.

"You old men go ahead and reminisce. Mary and I are going to fix breakfast," Mom announced as she rose setting her empty coffee cup on the counter next to the sink.

Rays from the morning sun pierced through the kitchen window as Mary joined Mom, who beat a quick series of paths between the refrigerator and the stove. Mark and my dad engaged in a conversation about their respective jobs. I excused myself and went back to my room where I lay back on my bed, staring at the mosaic patchwork of small cracks in the ceiling.

Thoughts and images of the past twenty-four hours reverberated through my mind. Everything, from the fight at the park to what Mary saw in her back yard to Randy's description of the protestors at the police station. All of that bounced around in my head along with an image of Mark in his zoot suit and his story of the Zoot Suit Riots.

There was a lot to think about, and the more I thought about it the more I wondered why the police treated Mexicans so badly. My dad was a hard-working man who provided for his family. Mom watched over my brother, my sister, and me and kept the house clean. All of my relatives and my parents' friends and the parents of my friends were the same way. *So, what was the problem?*

The more I thought about it, the more I hated the police, especially the white officers for introducing my young heart to such prejudice. In an effort to quiet my thoughts, I switched on my brother's radio, but the music didn't help so I turned it off, lay back down, and finally drifted off to sleep.

When I woke up again later that morning, I quickly got dressed and grabbed a bite to eat. As I headed for the front door, I yelled back to the kitchen, "I'm going over to David's house." In a flash, Mom appeared in the kitchen doorway.

"You're not going anywhere, today."

No matter how much I protested, Mom wouldn't back off. I was confined to the yard. Luckily, Black Crow came over to see what I had heard about the riots. It turned out that he knew just about as much as I did. He did, however, report that two of his *tios* and three older cousins had been arrested and beaten by the police. His family was collecting money from friends and relatives to bail them out of jail.

A week went by and things cooled down. I was allowed to cross the boundaries of the yard and hang out with my friends again. The riots were still on everyone's mind. I found out that Fat Joe's older brother and cousins had been arrested, as had *Payaso's* older brother and *tios*. Nite Owl's dad, his older brothers, and his *tios* were also in jail. *Travieso* and J-Bird had a couple of cousins beaten down by the police. However, the saddest news was that Jaime's wife, who had been clubbed in the stomach by the policeman, lost her baby. The death of the baby had a profound effect on everyone in our *barrio*.

In the aftermath of the riot, a series of protesters marched into East Los Angeles to focus public awareness on the Vietnam War and police brutality, as well as the social and political injustices being perpetrated against Mexican-Americans. Several of the protests evolved into riots that resulted in the destruction of many local businesses. Hundreds of people were injured. Those who were arrested were beaten down or tortured by the police. The Gestapo-style tactics of the Los Angeles County Sheriff's Deputies, who were notorious for their brutality, was common knowledge among *La Raza*.

The police even planted *Latino* undercover agents, fresh from the academy, in the Brown Berets to cause dissension amongst the ranks and to discredit the organization. This forced the Brown Berets to take their fight for equal justice underground.

I must admit that some good did come from all the violence.

Organizations, such as The National *Chicano* Moratorium, paved the way for programs like *Movimiento Estudiantil Chicano de Aztlán*, known more simply as MEChA, to rise up and serve the educational needs of the children of East Los Angeles. In addition, a curriculum that included *Chicano* history and culture gradually crept into the schools, but these changes didn't come easily.

The emerging growth and newly found strength of *La Raza* loomed as a major threat to the white political machine and multi-million-dollar real estate industry throughout Aztlán, the area of the southwestern United States that used to belong to Mexico. But in reality, *Aztlán* was more a place in the hearts of *La Raza*, a dream of prosperity that I hoped I would one day be able to enjoy, rather than a piece of American real estate or the legendary ancestral home of the Aztecs. For reasons that I fail to comprehend even to this day, the concept of sharing the American dream with *La Raza* was overwhelmed by the greed and racism inherent within the white ruling establishment. This environment was ripe for a new and tragic kind of warfare that was destined to spread like poison through the veins of our *barrios*.

Chicano youth felt powerless to stop the daily barrage of police harassment, which served only to alienate them further and to generate an attitude of rebellion against the police and the political structures that allowed such a tainted form of law enforcement to exist. Youth in the *barrios* now had a common enemy, the police.

The misunderstood qualities of *barrio* youth in the forties and fifties gave way to a new mentality in the sixties and seventies when *Pachucos* started calling themselves *homeboys*.

According to Webster, the term "homeboys" originated in the late 1890s and was adopted by the *Chicano* youth in the *barrios* of East Los Angeles in the early sixties. This one word helped forge a common identity in the struggle against the oppressive nature of the police and brought with it self-respect and the determination to survive. It embodied the warrior spirit of our Aztec and Mayan ancestors as well as the Mexican revolutionary leaders Emiliano Zapata and Pancho Villa who found a contemporary personification in the homeboys of East Los Angeles.

Despite the racial profiling, brutality, and other efforts employed by the police to weaken *La Raza*, *Chicanos* grew stronger and more distant from the prevailing form of law enforcement. A code of silence, as a passive measure to thwart police harassment, developed. Gangs, which in the forties and fifties had been populated by hoodlums and miscreants, now provided an effective vehicle for organizing homeboys as the *barrios'* only line of defense against the police.

Barrios such as White Fence, *El Hoyo Soto, Maravilla*, La Alpine, La State, 1st Street, *Alameda*, Flats, 38th Street, Punkenville, Jugtown, 22nd Street, Little T, Temple Street, La Diamond, *El Jardin*, Dogtown, Hazard, La Clover, Clantone, Watts, 7th Street, *Mateo*, and Downey had roots that traced back to the forties, perhaps even earlier. Los Angeles County alone was home to nearly three hundred different gangs in the early seventies, each representing a different *barrio*.

Our *barrio* was called Los Sharkies Twelfth Street because of the prominence of Sharkie Park and the fact that Twelfth Street transected our territory. Naturally, the shark, due to its ferocity and propensity to spread terror, surfaced as a symbol of strength and unity, essential elements of defense.

La Raza thought the police were our greatest enemy. Little did we know that a greater enemy lurked within our ranks. The mission of defending our *barrios* would become skewed to the point of fracturing the newly developing unity of *La Raza*. The primary enemy would no longer be the police. We would quickly become our own worst enemy. Our search for respect would transform from a self-empowered prophecy into a rationale for cultural genocide. Homeboys would end up killing homeboys in the name of "*barrio* pride."

What the police couldn't accomplish by force and intimidation, we would perpetrate upon ourselves. "*Barrio* pride" quickly evolved into "*barrio* warfare," embodied in violent rivalries which unleashed an evil dark side that none of us could have foreseen or were loath to admit!

# Homeboys

Fall of 1971 rolled in and with it a new school year, but this time I wasn't returning to my old school. After the riots at Sharkie Park, my parents decided to move to County Road on the south side of Pomona, which meant I had to attend a different school in an entirely different district. We didn't have any more room in the new house and it wasn't any nicer. My parents thought it would be better to get away from the violence they saw centered in the *barrio*. Needless to say, I wasn't pleased about having to leave behind all the friends I had known since kindergarten.

The thought of school starting the next day didn't make me nervous, but the idea of having to make a whole new set of friends did. As I sat on the front step enjoying the sun, a cool breeze blew in from the ocean. I began thinking about J-Bird, *Travieso*, Black Bird, and the rest of my old friends. I hated not being able to hop on my bike and cruise over to see what they were doing.

Just then, my dad drove into the driveway with some of his friends. Laughter rolled out of the car as the men spilled into the front yard. I was happy to see Dad, as the interruption prevented further thoughts about missing my friends from entering my mind. As I ran up to the car, Dad put his arm around my shoulder and introduced me to his friends. The familiar smell of the paper mill saturated his clothes, and the fragrance of beer floated on everyone's breath. The men found seats in the old lawn chairs near the front door. One of my dad's friends handed out beers from a paper bag he had carried from the car. My dad took one and rubbed the cool can on his forehead before popping the top and taking a long sip.

"I remember when me and Roy and Louie and Levi used to mix it up with the guys from North Pueblo," Dad began. Beer always opened up his memory and he liked talking about living in Colorado. "One time we went for a cruise in my '49 Ford. My younger brother Roger wanted to tag along, so we took him with us. We ran into a carload of *Pachucos* from the north side who thought they were tough and wanted to race, so I told them, 'let's go out to the highway'. On the way out there, they kept trying to run us off the road and finally sideswiped me. I decided I'd show them how to play that game. I sideswiped them right into the ditch. Roger was so scared he started crying that he wanted out. I had to take him home."

Dad loved his teenage days as a *Pachuco* in Pueblo, Colorado, and I loved hearing about it. Community lines were drawn by language and territory. For the most part, it was mostly Spanish against Italian. Having a mixture of both, Dad said he stuck with the Spanish because most of his cousins and friends spoke Spanish and they weren't involved in the gangster, mafia life-style like some of the Italians.

All the other men had their own stories to tell. I could sit out on the front step listening to them talk for hours, soaking it all up like a dry sponge in a rainstorm. Dad's friends usually stayed until the beer ran out. Somehow, Mom was always able to time dinner to be ready just as Dad and his friends were downing their last sips of beer. That afternoon I was hungry and more than happy to hear Mom announce dinner just as Dad's friends tossed their empties in the bag and headed for the car.

The next morning, I awoke early. I was excited and nervous at the same time. Today was the first day of school at my new junior high. I got dressed in a new pair of jeans and slipped into a new shirt. My parents always armed my brother, my sister, and I for school with new clothes, new notebooks, and plenty of paper and pencils. I grabbed a quick bite to eat, then hurried out the front door not knowing what to expect.

I walked to the corner and headed up Towne Avenue, another main street through Pomona, which runs parallel with Garey Avenue about eight blocks to the west. The further I walked, the more students seemed to be heading in the same direction. By the time I passed East Lexington Avenue, the sidewalks were full of kids. A couple minutes later, I reached Simons Junior High School where hundreds of kids my age gathered around a weathered one-story, red brick building.

Simons Junior High was huge. It was much larger than anything I could have imagined, and there were students everywhere all formed into small groups of boys over here and girls over there. I walked through the noisy crowd of Caucasian students trying to act as though I knew where I was going, all the time looking for a familiar *cara* and finding none. Finally, I noticed a group of *Chicanos* sitting on the benches in the outside lunch area, so I moved in that direction still hoping to recognize someone. As I approached, several of the boys turned to look at me. I couldn't believe it. There was David from the old neighborhood.

"Hey, David!"

"Hey, man. How have you been?" he asked, just as surprised to see me as I was to see him.

"Alright, but I don't like this school."

"Me neither. So your parents decided to move, too?" he smiled.

"Yeah," I said with a shrug. "What classes do you have?"

Just then, the bell rang. Everybody started moving. David and I hurriedly pulled out our class schedules and compared them. David pointed at my schedule.

"Hey, we've both got third period history. I'll see you then."

"Later," I replied.

As I watched David walk away, I felt better about my new school.

I quickly found my book locker and, with the help of a map provided by the school, I found my way to class. First and second period passed and things seemed to be going fairly well. The bell rang for third period and I headed for history class. When I arrived, I could see David with three other *Chicanos* leaning against the wall next to the classroom door.

"Hey, David!"

"So, what do you think about this school?" David asked.

"It's O.K., but I miss all the guys from the old school."

"Me too," he admitted. "But don't worry about friends around here."

David introduced me to the guys standing next to him. I could tell they were new to this school, too. Just as we started to get into a conversation, the bell rang and we all hurried into the classroom and found seats next to each other.

After third period it was time for lunch. David and I dropped off our books at our lockers and headed for the lunch area, which was divided into two parts: inside and outside. David explained that only the nerds who were considered uncool ate inside. I guess he was right because the outside area was packed. Nobody, including us, wanted the stigma of being uncool. We hurried through the lunch line and took our trays to some benches outside where I noticed that everyone at the bench David chose was a *cholo*.

When my dad was in school, these guys would have been called *Pachucos,* but times change and I guess each generation has to define itself and set its own course. This was the seventies and our generation had *cholos* with short hair, neatly combed back, dressed in Pendleton shirts with creases that traversed both breast pockets. Only the top two buttons were fastened so the sides flared out like drapes revealing a pressed white T-shirt beneath that was tucked neatly into black, blue, gray, or tan Dickies with a crisp crease running down each pant leg. Their shoes, brands such as Imperials, Buscalos, and Stacy Adams, had a mirror-like shine.

There were easily thirty to forty *cholos* in the lunch area. Even though I wasn't dressed like a *cholo*, I liked the look and felt comfortable around these guys.

Brenton Wood's "The Oogum Boogum Song" rolled out from a radio perched on the end of one of the tables as David and I finished eating.

"Hey, *Braso*. Come on, I want you to meet my *primo*," David urged.

After finishing lunch, I threw my trash into the metal can next to our table and followed David toward a group of guys standing against the wall. They were older than the *cholos* with whom we'd eaten lunch. They had a look of being in control. I could tell they had the respect of the other guys.

David led me to a tall, thin *cholo* with light brown skin and curly black hair combed straight back across his head. He was dressed to impress and it worked. The other guys showed David's *primo* a lot of respect. They all grew silent as we approached. I could feel their cold, icy stares confront me, the new kid. I tried to return a look of confidence but I had doubts about how well it came across. These guys showed no sign of a thaw until David spoke.

"*Primo*, this is my friend *Braso*."

As David's *primo* extended his hand, his eyes cut through my confidence like a knife piercing my very soul. I tried to camouflage a shiver that ran up my spine with a quick stretch of my shoulders, as if I were adjusting my shirt.

"Homeboys call me *Conejo, ese*."

I wondered why he called himself *"Conejo,"* meaning *"rabbit"* but I knew enough not to ask. His voice was slow and studied. His stare unrelenting. I reached to shake hands but my fingers immediately got lost amidst his unusual hand movements. I didn't know a thing about this handshake. Slowly a small smile tripped across *Conejo's cara* then quickly faded.

"*Dispensa, vato*, let me show you how the *Raza* do it, *ese*."

"*Sí mon,* Homes, show this youngster how it's done," echoed the *cholo* next to him with the same slow, studied manner of speaking as *Conejo*.

Conejo grabbed my hand firmly with four fingers facing up as though we were going to arm wrestle. He quickly switched to a downward motion like a normal handshake, then up again as in the first motion. Finally, he moved his hand back cupping my fingers tightly in his like a single fist with our thumbs on top. The lesson was patiently executed.

"*Órale, vato*. Now you know, *ese*," he said. "Why do they call you *Braso*?"

I explained how I lost control and broke my arm while racing my bike down a steep hill in Ganesha Park. I purposely neglected any mention of breaking my tooth. I was happy with the name *Braso* and didn't want to risk any chance of being saddled with a new name now.

"*Órale.*" *Conejo* slowly lifted his head in a half nod. Just then the bell rang. "*Ay te wacho, ese*," *Conejo* offered as he and his friends departed to their next class.

I watched with interest as *Conejo* and his friends walked away. They weren't in a hurry to get to class. They walked slowly with a self-indulgent style, almost strolling as if they owned every inch of land touched by the very soles of their shoes.

During the next several weeks, I met several more *vatos* who were my own age like *Wesos* [a name customized from the Spanish word *"huesos"* meaning *"bones"*], Wicked, *Gordo* [*"fat boy"*], Slim, Fish, and *Flaco* [*"skinny boy"*]. Gradually, I was introduced to some of the older vatos. Bad Boy, Big Jerry, Henry, *Bala* [*"bullet"*], Larry, and *Lobo* [*"wolf"*] were all fifteen and in the ninth grade.

Everybody liked and admired *Conejo*. He was a natural leader and I wanted to be just like him. Two extra years of knowledge and experience seemed like a lot to me, only a seventh grader, so I was glad when *Conejo* and the other *cholos* decided to take me under their wing and show me how to carry myself with a sense of confidence that demanded respect. Their acceptance of me was enough to get me to change my appearance and stroll with the homeboys.

All of us homeboys who hung out together at Simons claimed to be affiliated with the *Los* Sharkies Twelfth Street gang even though we no longer lived in the heart of the *barrio* and never had anything to do with the gang other than knowing some of the older members. *Los* Sharkies Twelfth Street gang had a reputation that carried respect at Simons, so we made the most of it.

Just like my family, most of the other guys used to live in the *barrio* but moved further south and east with their families after the riots. This migration didn't weaken the unity of our *barrio* but rather broadened the territory.

All in all, my first year at Simons was relatively peaceful. By the time school let out, the Sharkie Park riots were just a memory. We heard about the violence stemming from the *barrios* of East L.A. but that was thirty miles away, which made it seem worlds apart.

*   *   *

Soon the summer of 1972 was upon us. *Wesos* and I had become good friends. Homeboys called him *Wesos* because he was skinny and all bones. He lived nearby, had three sisters, two older and one younger. His dad, a former *Pachuco*, was a hard-working man who grew up in Twelfth Street during the fifties and sixties. *Wesos's* mom, like mine, worked keeping house and fixing dinner. She was always at home.

When I wasn't at home, I was usually at *Wesos's* pad listening to LPs and recording them onto cassette tapes. The only thing more important to us than music was who could make the "baddest" model car. At thirteen, *Wesos* and I were still too young to drive, so we built model cars made to look like the lowriders that cruised the *calles* of our *barrios*.

Chevrolet and Buick were the most popular makes for lowriders, especially the Chevy Impala and Caprice built between 1965 and 1972 as well as older model Chevys, from 1959 back to 1939, which we called "bombs" due to their body style and age.

The most recognizable feature of lowriders was their low clearance to the pavement, usually no more than four to five inches, while the chassis of a normal car rides six to nine inches off the ground. For me, the lower the better and if we could have figured out a way to put hydraulics on the models, we would have. Hydraulics permitted the front or back of the car to be raised or lowered separately or together.

Some systems allowed the entire chassis to rest on the ground, something called "pancaked." Some guys replaced the shock absorbers with hydraulic cylinders connected to pumps with valves controlled by solenoids, which in turn were powered by several 12-volt batteries. The more batteries, the more power!

Switches under the dash allowed the driver to control the hydraulics. Some systems, which cost upwards of a thousand dollars, could make a car jump nearly waist high if switched a particular way. Some even had beautiful murals painted on the side panels, hood, and trunk lids, while others opted for detailed pinstripe designs.

Often the interiors of the *ranflas* were specially upholstered and accented with a small diameter, chromed chain link steering wheel. Engines were immaculately clean with chromed valve covers, oil and air filters as well as spark coils. However, the picture was incomplete unless the car rested upon a set of whitewalled 5/20s wrapped around some nicely chromed, deep set rims. For me, that was the icing on the cake. This was not about transportation; this was about style. Lowriders were made to be noticed as they cruised "low and slow." It was nothing less than art on wheels.

Cholos who made that kind of investment were serious about their *ranflas* and usually joined a car club where they competed for prizes and trophies and put the cars on display, marking the beginning of some serious lowrider competition which continues today.

Membership in a car club served as low-cost insurance, since the car clubs made it a point to avoid conflict with gang members in the surrounding areas. All the *cholos* knew what the car clubs were about and didn't go out of their way to start trouble with them.

Lowriders weren't new to our generation. Having a nice *ranfla* has been the dream of every *barrio* teenager back to the fifties where riding low originated with the

Pachucos. I was no exception, but for now, my dreams took shape only in the model cars *Wesos* and I built.

*   *   *

Before I knew it, I was a ninth grader. David and his family had moved away the previous year, and I never saw him again. I didn't think much about David since *Wesos* and I had become such good friends. *Conejo* and the rest of his homeboys were starting their second year in high school, so *Wesos*, Wicked, *Gordo*, Slim, Fish, *Flaco*, and I became the *cholos* of choice at Simons, and the seventh and eighth grade youngsters looked up to us.

We were also old enough to have a healthy interest in *rucas*. My homeboys and I made it a point to walk home from school with a few of the homegirls, particularly Sad Girl, whenever possible. I don't know how she got the name Sad Girl, since she was always a happy jokester. The homeboys seemed to have a knack for either accenting or reversing a character trait when bestowing a *barrio* name. Sad Girl was an eighth grader with a quick temper underlying a shapely exterior. All we noticed was the shape until one day we learned how thinly veiled Sad Girl's temper really was.

"What did you call her?" *Wesos* said, confronting Sad Girl as he, Wicked, Fish, and I strolled leisurely down the center of a *calle* near her *cantón,* along with another homegirl and Sad Girl's best friend, Rosa.

"Never mind what I called her. She deserved it," Sad Girl retorted.

Wesos shrugged and glanced at me.

"It matters," I said, looking her directly in the eyes.

"I called her a *mayate*," Sad Girl confessed.

Fish let loose a small laugh at Sad Girl's unabashed attitude toward blacks.

"*Ay!*" Wicked exclaimed. "Why didn't you tell us sooner?"

"Don't worry about it. I can take care of myself," Sad Girl boasted. She seemed annoyed that we were making such a big deal of what she had said.

Suddenly, a late model four-door sedan swerved around the corner and screeched to a stop, nearly hitting Fish. All of us, caught off guard, jumped back. Two *mayates* hopped out of the front seat along with two girls out of the back. The *mayates* immediately drew large metal Afro combs with the teeth filed to sharp points. We just stood there not knowing what was going to happen. Then one of the *mayates* stepped forward.

"South Side Village Kaaa-rips!"

"Twelfth Street *Los* Sharkies," we countered with a cold stare of our own, trying our best to disguise how nervous we really felt.

"I know. We's don't wants no trouble with y'all ess-says. Your girl," he pointed at Sad Girl, "disrespected her." He shot a glance at the larger of the two *mayate* girls.

"What do you want to do about it?" I said, taking a deep breath and looking him directly in the eye as I held my ground.

"This ain't about us. They needs to take care of their own bizness and we stays out of it."

Before I knew it, Sad Girl was in the girl's *cara*, her fists flying. I watched them a moment, then looked at the driver. He just nodded. My homeboys and I and the two *mayates* from South Side Village Crips just watched as Sad Girl and Rosa mixed it up with the other two girls.

When it was over, the Crips loaded their girls back into the *ranfla* and drove off. It had been a fair fight. Nobody won, nobody lost. The *mayate* girls made their point: there was a price to pay for disrespecting them.

The next day when we told the rest of the homeboys what had happened, they agreed that it was Sad Girl's fault. She should have told us what happened sooner. She had put us all in jeopardy; one of us could have gotten hurt, especially if the *mayates* had been packing. There would have been retaliation, and the *mayates* were severely outnumbered if you counted all of the homeboys from the *barrio*. Things could have easily escalated into a race war. I guess the *mayates* knew this as well as we did. That's why they didn't make it an issue between us. Let the girls handle it. We were able to respect that and keep the conflict at that level.

During the rest of the year, there were other incidents with the *mayates* that were handled in a similar manner. All of us knew how far it could go without erupting into a major war. Clearly, no one wanted that. Still, we continued to hear from homeboys at Fremont Junior High and Garey High School about the increasing violence between the South Side Village Crips, the Pirus (Swahili for blood) on the northeast, Ghost Town on the north, and Sin Town Crips from the northwest. It wasn't our affair, so we stayed out of it. We had enough business defending our *barrio* against the constant threat posed by the *juras*.

*   *   *

In 1974, the winds of violence swept through Pomona. *Pleitos* began occurring with more frequency between the homeboys from Twelfth Street and the *vatos* from Cherrieville, an old *barrio* located northwest of us. Orange Grove Avenue framed Cherrieville on the north, White Avenue on the east, and we shared a common border along Mission Avenue not too far west of the police station.

Bad blood had existed between Twelfth Street and Cherrieville since the fifties when two *veteranos* got into a serious conflict. It was handled in much the same manner as the problem between Sad Girl and the *mayate* girl. There had been a fair fight and everyone went home thinking the problem was resolved. But it wasn't. Ill feelings festered below the surface like an infected wound that from all appearances looked as though it had healed. I found out later that the riots at Sharkie Park had begun when the *juras* interrupted a baseball game intended to promote peace between the *barrios* of Chino, Cherrieville and Twelfth Street. It seemed the *juras* didn't want us to get along. Peace between the *barrios* somehow wasn't on their agenda. In any case, whatever peace there had been between Twelfth Street and Cherrieville quickly deteriorated.

Spring came sooner than usual that year. One Monday after school, all of the homeboys from Simons were kicking back in front of the school "holding up the walls." We stood side-by-side with our backs to the bricks and our heels clicked together so our toes pointed in opposite directions. *Conejo* and three homeboys roared up in his root beer brown '57 Nomad, lowered to the bone. He parked his *ranfla* and strolled up with Big Jerry, *Bala,* and *Lobo.*

"*Órale,* Homies. *Q'vole,*" *Conejo* greeted us. "*Sabes que*? Homeboy Bad Boy got into some blows with them *vatos* from Cherrieville, *ese*."

"Is my *carnal* O.K., Homes?" Wicked asked with a sense of concern.

"*Sí mon, ese, pero* you *vatos* need to be *trucha porque* Cherrieville might hit us. The *veteranos* want everybody to be ready for *pleito*, so stash some bats around," he eyed a row of bushes that ran back from the *calle*, "and have some *fileros, tambíen*. You *vatos* better back each other up, and if anybody runs, I want to know who the *chavala* is." *Conejo* paused. He leaned toward us, his eyes searching each of our *caras* for the slightest sign of weakness before he continued. "*Somos Calle Doce. Los* Sharkies don't run from nobody, *entiendes*?"

"*Sí mon*, Homes. *Somos Calle Doce*," we chanted in unison.

"*Órale*. We'll cruise by *mañana. Al rato*, Homies."

They strolled back to *Conejo's ranfla* and cruised down the *calle*, but *Conejo's* burning stare remained with me. He had given me that same look when David introduced us two years prior. Since then, I had learned to return a look of confidence and resolve any doubts, no matter what I was feeling inside. I had seen *Conejo* get into a *vato's cara* once for showing weakness and disrespecting him with a sideways glance. I didn't want to be the recipient of his wrath, no matter what the reason.

"Forget Cherrieville!"

"They come around here, we'll show them who's bad."

"*Puro chavalas!*"

We all had something to say about Cherrieville as we returned to the schoolyard. *Gordo* led the way. He was ready to go take care of them by himself if necessary. Fish, *Flaco*, and Slim were primed to join him. Only Wicked kept his thoughts to himself. I could never tell exactly what was on his mind.

Wesos and I shared a quick glance as we followed the others. I couldn't help thinking that on the outside we all looked the same as we did yesterday, or any other day for that matter, but inside I knew something was different. I could sense the fear lurking under our tough veneers. *Conejo's* message had changed us somehow. None of us had ever gotten into blows with a rival *barrio* before this, and we didn't know what to expect. I sensed, however, that we all realized the time had come for us to walk the walk.

On Tuesday, we all kept *trucha* and did exactly what *Conejo* told us to do. We hid bats and *fileros* in the bushes near the schoolyard wall where we hung out.

Pomona had two junior highs and one high school on the south side, all within our *barrio*. The young *cholos* at Fremont Junior High followed the same instructions as we, while the older homeboys at the high school were sent on *movidas*.

Conejo and the older homeboys cruised by several times to check up on us. Since they came out of Simons, the *veteranos* wanted them to make sure we held our ground and had backup, if needed.

On Friday we were out holding up the walls in our usual spot in front of the school when *Conejo's ranfla* rolled around the corner and stopped at the curb. He and his homeboys stayed in the *ranfla*. *Conejo* beckoned us with the homeboy nod, a slow upwards tilt of the head.

"*Órale, Homies. Trucha porque* the homeboys just did a *movida* on Cherrieville at Ganesha. They might come by, *ese*, so be extra *trucha*. We got to go *porque los juras* are hot, *Homies. Al rato, gatos.*"

Just as quickly as *Conejo* arrived, he was gone. We returned to our wall echoing the same threats against Cherrieville we had bantered about on Monday. Only now the stakes had been raised. The possibility of something serious happening loomed large before us. None of us wanted to be the *cholo* caught with his Khakis down, so every lowrider that passed brought a temporary halt to our conversation until we were certain it wasn't some *vatos locos* from Cherrieville looking for a little Shark meat.

Early Saturday afternoon, I went over to *Wesos's* pad. He said that Wicked had told him that nobody from Cherrieville had been hit in the *movida* on Friday. Even so, there was enough Shark meat in the water to provoke them.

On Monday after school let out, we were all hanging out at the wall. Someone noticed Wicked wasn't there. In fact, he hadn't been seen at school all day. As we pondered his whereabouts, Bad Boy drove up in his *jefito's ranfla* with Wicked riding shotgun. We all strolled over.

"Cherrieville hit our *cantón* last night!" Wicked blurted out in an uncharacteristic manner.

"What?!"

No one could believe it.

"*Sí* mon. Go check out our *cantón, ese*," Wicked confirmed.

"*Sí mon*. They are going to pay, Homes," threatened Bad Boy.

About a dozen of us headed to Wicked's *cantón* which wasn't too far from school. When we got there, Wicked and Bad Boy were already standing in the front yard.

"*Mira!* What'd I tell you?" Wicked admonished.

All the windows in the front of the *canton* had been shot out and the front walls were peppered with bullet holes. The front door had been blasted by a shotgun blast, leaving two jagged holes the size of fists.

In the garage, Bad Boy's *ranfla*, a cherry apple green '67 Chevy Impala, had had all of its windows smashed and had suffered a few dents on the doors and side panels.

All of us were tripping out because the *vatos* from Cherrieville had the *huevos* to hit Wicked and Bad Boy's pad. Somehow they'd found out where Bad Boy lived and had done their own *movida*. We didn't stay long because Wicked's *familia* was still pretty shaken up, as were the *gavachos* who lived next door. Luckily, neither of Wicked's parents nor his younger brother and three sisters had been hurt when Cherrieville made their hit.

That night I couldn't sleep. I kept seeing the windows of Wicked's *canton* shattering with each Cherrieville *bala*. I knew the *Calle Doce* homeboys weren't about to let this go unchallenged.

* * *

During the week, we heard about some hits the *veteranos* were doing in Cherrieville. On Friday, *Wesos* told me that a *vato* from Cherrieville got shot. He didn't die but it was enough to satisfy our taste for vengeance.

The weekend passed without further event and again, on Monday, Wicked didn't show up at school. After school, *Conejo* and Bad Boy pulled up in *Conejo's ranfla*. Bad Boy was furious.

"My *carnal* and homeboy Fish got stabbed yesterday at Sharkie Park by Cherrieville," exclaimed Bad Boy.

We couldn't believe it!

"*Sí mon, ese*. Fish is still in the hospital," Bad Boy continued. "They stuck him in the stomach. Wicked is at the *canton*. He told me to tell you *vatos* you better go visit him."

"Keep *trucha*," *Conejo* warned. "They're going to pay, *ese*." Then he and Bad Boy sped off.

Wesos, Gordo, Flaco, and I walked to Wicked's pad. As we approached their *cantón,* I noticed a new front door and new plywood covering the windows. Bad Boy's *ranfla* was still in the garage but its windows had been replaced and fresh Bondo covered all of the dents.

Wesos knocked at the front door. Wicked's mom opened the door and paused for a moment before stepping aside to let us enter. Without a word, she went into the kitchen. While she never said much to any of us, I could tell she was less than pleased with what had happened to her *mijo* and *cantón.*

We knew the way to Wicked's room, located at the end of a skinny hallway, and burst in unannounced, surprising Wicked who was lying on his bed with white bandages wrapped around his otherwise bare chest.

"*Qué paso,* Homes?" Gordo asked.

Wicked forced a small smile and spoke in a weakened voice.

"It was messed up, man. They got me good!"

We all laughed but the pain in Wicked's eyes quickly brought us down. Still, he was eager to tell us how it went down.

"We were kicking back at the park all day. Little by little, the homeboys went off in different directions. There must have been about twenty of us left when we seen five *ranflas* turn the corner. *De volada,* we knew it was Cherrieville. They came in fast and hard. By the time we could get it together, they bum-rushed us, Homes. I was throwing blows with two of them, *ese.* Then I felt something like a burning in my right side right under my arm pit. It hurt! I tried to get away but I tripped and started to fall and then I got stuck on my left side."

"Man, Homes!" *Wesos* exclaimed.

"I went down, *ese.* Everything happened so fast. All I remember was seeing homeboy Fish getting beat down then I blacked out, Homes. Next thing I know, I'm in the hospital."

"The homeboys got messed up, eh?" I said.

"*Sí mon.* My *carnal* told me that our homeboys loaded up in five *ranflas* and ram-packed them in Cherrieville," Wicked stated, adding, "Homeboys stuck a couple of them, *tambíen.*"

"Man, Homes. This is getting crazy," added *Wesos*, summing up all of our thoughts with one comment.

Wesos, Gordo, Flaco, and I kicked back with Wicked for a few more minutes then left. Although he seemed glad we had stopped to visit him, he was still very weak from the attack and looked like he was in constant pain. It was a lot for a fourteen-year-old to endure.

During the next few weeks, both Fish and Wicked returned to school. Fish still had his stitches and displayed them proudly like a *barrio* badge of honor. Wicked behaved differently. He wasn't acting tough and strutting around like Fish, and we couldn't understand why. This made him seem weak. We soon learned everything that happened that day at Sharkie Park, except one thing. Wicked neglected to mention the profound effect the attack had had upon him. It caused him to question some of the choices he had made up to this point in his young life and to rethink his "wicked" ways. Gradually, our perception of Wicked started to change.

3

Intimidation

Soon May arrived and I turned fifteen. Other than a place to meet the homeboys, school held no interest for me. I looked forward to summer when we could hangout without worrying about getting caught sneaking out of class.

Basketball season was winding down, too, and Simons Junior High was scheduled to play Fremont which had the reputation for being the roughest school in Pomona. It was half *mayate*, half *Raza* with a few *gavachos* squeezed in between. Homeboys from Twelfth Street and South Side Village Crips ruled the halls.

My older *carnal* who was athletically built and into sports year round attended Fremont from 1968 through 1970. While my *carnal* wasn't down for the *barrio*, the homeboys left him and his jock friends alone because they had a certain respect for their choice to pursue sports, not to mention their size and strength.

Fremont would have been my junior high instead of Simons, if my *familia* hadn't moved to the south side after the Sharkie Park riots. Even though I wasn't very interested in the interschool basketball rivalry, I was excited about attending this game because I hoped my old friends Fat Joe, *Payaso*, Nite Owl, Black Crow, and the twins *Travieso* and J-Bird would be there. I looked forward to seeing all of them.

On game day, the boredom of school was broken only by a pep assembly in the morning and the homeboys talking about showing those *vatos* from Fremont how down we were. Fremont may be located in the heart of the *barrio* and considered hard core, but we were just as down as they were.

After my last class, I headed toward the lunch area across from the gymnasium to meet up with the other homeboys from Simons and wait for the *vatos* from Fremont. Nearly fifteen minutes passed and no one showed. I waited some more. It was almost game time, and I was still the only homeboy there when *cholo*'d down *vatos locos* from Fremont swaggered around the corner and congregated in front of the gymnasium. In all there were about sixty of them.

I thought to myself, *we really showed those* vatos *from Fremont how down we were. Talk is cheap.*

A sense of relief spread over me when my eyes landed upon Fat Joe and Black Crow leaning against the gymnasium wall. As I made my way toward my old friends, I could feel the burning stare of sixty pairs of eyes watching my every move and most of all my expression. I was under the microscope and couldn't show the least amount of fear. One wrong move and they would be all over me and I'd wake up in the hospital, if I was lucky. The weight had fallen on my shoulders, and all I could do was try my best to keep my cool. Luckily, Fat Joe recognized me before I had gone too far.

"*Órale,* it's *Braso!*" he exclaimed in surprise.

His smile broke the tension as he reached out to shake hands. Fat Joe and Black Crow will never know how glad I was to see them and the rest of my old friends who gathered around. As I shook hands with each of them, *mi mente* flashed back to when we were all just eleven years old, riding our bikes up and down the *calles* of the *barrio*. Those days seemed so long ago. So much had changed and yet, so much was the way it had always been.

"*Órale,* Homes. Where have you been, *ese?*" *Travieso* inquired, bringing my thoughts back to the present.

"*Sí mon.* We thought you disappeared, *ese,*" echoed J-Bird.

"*Chale,* Homes. I've been around. I come here now."

"*Órale!*" Nite Owl faked a pained expression. "Where do you live, *ese?*" he asked.

"Down on County Road," I responded.

"*Órale,* Homes," *Payaso* jumped in. "You live in the sticks, *ese!*"

Everyone busted up laughing.

"*Sí mon*," I agreed.

"*Órale, Braso*. How's your arm, *ese*?" Fat Joe inquired jokingly.

"Strong as ever, *ese*," I retorted. "I see you're still fat, Homes."

"Hey! *Trucha*, Homes. I'll have to sit on your arm and break it again, *ese*," he bounced back, prompting another round of laughter.

The reunion felt better than I had expected, and I realized that our gang lifestyle was causing us to grow up faster than our peers. I could see it in everyone's *caras*. Still, we continued kidding around as we filed into the gymnasium where the *vatos* from Fremont took up nearly half of the bleachers on the far side of the gym. Since none of my homeboys had shown their *caras*, I joined Fat Joe and the others.

I was busy talking with *Travieso* when the whistle announced the starting tip-off. I happened to glance over to the entrance and saw *Gordo* and three other homeboys from Simons stroll in and sit on the home team side. Every time I glanced at him, he seemed to be staring at me. I didn't trip on it because I was enjoying myself with my old friends and all the *vatos* from Fremont.

After the final buzzer sounded, we filed outside and hung out for a while. *Travieso* gave me his phone number and said to call him when school was out for the summer.

"*Ay te, wacho*, see you this summer," I offered my friends as we shook hands and headed in different directions. I turned to cross the lunch area to see what was up with *Gordo*. He and the three homeboys who showed up for the game were standing near some benches.

"*Órale*, Homes. I didn't see you before the game started," I said.

Gordo shrugged it off and didn't have much else to say. I didn't think much of it.

After the game, the *vatos* from Fremont gathered outside the gym door. Some of them seemed interested that I was now standing with *Gordo* and the other homeboys from Simons but everything remained cool. They eventually cut their path across Simons with the same authoritative swagger as when they had arrived. Once they were gone, I went home.

At school the next day, *Gordo* gave me the silent treatment, but I didn't trip. I really didn't think much about it even though it continued for several days until I ran into *Wesos* in the hall between classes.

"*Órale*, Homes. What's going on with you and *Gordo*, *ese*?" *Wesos* asked.

"I don't know, *ese*. Why?"

"I heard he thinks you're a *chavala* 'cause you sat with those *vatos* from Fremont at the game," *Wesos* explained.

Suddenly, all the silent treatment made sense.

"He's trippin'!" I blurted. "If he'd had been there from jump street like he said, we'd have all strolled in together. We all claim Twelfth Street, so what's his problem?"

"Don't ask me, *ese*. I'm just delivering the *wila*," *Wesos* shrugged.

"If he wants to make it an issue, you have him come and see me, *ese*!" I said sharply and strolled off leaving my friend *Wesos* bewildered. I didn't care. I was mad that *Gordo* was upset with me. If anyone was a *chavala* it was *Gordo*. He was the one that showed up late, not me. Until he was ready to approach me about this, I saw no need to kiss up to him.

Soon track and field season was upon us and I had forgotten about the incident with *Gordo*. I kept busy with my own affairs and didn't hear any more about whatever problem he seemed to have with me.

With encouragement from my *carnal*, I decided to try out for the track team and to my surprise, I was accepted. I loved running. I loved the rush of adrenaline at the sound of the starting gun, the feeling of fresh air surging through my lungs, and the freedom that I experienced when sprinting down a track as fast as I could go.

After school one day, I was on the field behind the school stretching and warming up for practice, when I saw *Gordo* strolling toward me. At first, I acted as though I didn't see him. As he drew near, I stood up. *Gordo* was short and fat and I didn't want to make an easy target in case he decided to rush me.

"Eh, *Braso*. I need to talk to you," he said in a normal tone of voice.

He didn't seem angry but with *Gordo* you couldn't tell. He could be your best friend one minute and ready to gut you the next.

"Yeah, about what?" I asked casually, trying to remain cool.

"Not here, *ese*. Let's go over there."

Gordo pointed toward the portable classrooms, wooden rectangular structures that lined one side of the track field.

"*Vamanos*," I responded and let him lead the way.

By the time we disappeared between two of the classroom structures, I could feel my palms sweating. All kind of thoughts raced through *mi mente*. I was glad that I had my spiked track shoes. If I had to fight my way out, at least I could use them to inflict some damage on *Gordo*. When we reached the back of the classrooms, to my amazement, we were no longer alone. *Flaco* and a couple of the homeboys stepped out from the edge of the building where they'd been waiting. No one said a word and I knew for sure that I was going to need those spikes to get out of this.

Gordo turned to face me. It was the moment of truth as we stood *cara a cara* only inches from each other. I could smell the chili he'd had for lunch. I dared not blink as I stared into his cold dark eyes.

"What's your problem, *ese*?" *Gordo* broke the silence.

"What problem?" I shot back.

"You know what I'm talking about, *ese*. Why were you with those *vatos* from Fremont and not with us?"

"*Órale, Gordo*. This is stupid. We're all from Twelfth Street."

"Na, *Braso*. I don't think you're one of us, *ese*. I think you're scared."

His expression intensified as his glare searched my eyes for any hint of weakness.

"Scared of what? I was there before any of you," I responded without hesitation. "Man, this is stupid. You were the one talking about how you and the rest of the homeboys were going to be there before the game. *Qué paso?*"

Gordo stood silent for a moment then he moved aside and looked at *Flaco*.

"Kick *Braso's* ass," *Gordo* commanded.

Flaco came toward me.

"*Chale*, Homes. I'm not fighting you, *Flaco*! Isn't Nite Owl your *primo?*"

"*Sí, mon*," *Flaco* answered a bit confused.

"I grew up with your *primo, ese.*"

Flaco stopped. He didn't know what to do or say. *Gordo* tried to push him into me to instigate blows but that wasn't going to happen. *Flaco* knew that if he had any part in messing me up, he would have to deal with his *primo* Nite Owl. *Sangre* may be thicker than *agua,* but right now I was just as much *familia* as he was, and *Flaco* wasn't about to take any chances. I could see in *Flaco's* eyes that he felt the same as I did. All of us knew it was stupid. We should have turned on *Gordo* and beat him down for getting bent out of shape over nothing and showing weakness and not taking me on himself.

"*Sabes que?* I'm leaving," I said and headed back toward the track field.

Gordo continued talking behind me, but I figured if he was going to do something he would have done it by now, so I ignored him and kept walking. When I made it back to the track field, I sat down. My heart was pumping and my body was tingling all over as though I'd just completed a 100-yard dash in record time.

As I sat on the ground, trying to calm myself, I remembered when a group of boys came up to me in sixth grade. One of them wanted to fight me. I told him, "no," and luckily they left me alone. *Gordo's* attempted intimidation was more intense but to my surprise the same response I used in sixth grade worked today. Still, I hated having to deal with attempts at intimidation and all the stuff that went with it. I was furious at *Gordo* for being so messed up. He had his chance at me, but when it came down to it, he tried to make someone else do his dirty work. That day I lost all respect for *Gordo*.

*   *   *

Summer was only a month away. The rest of the year I hung out with *Wesos* and the *vatos* who still liked me. *Gordo* tried continuously to drive a wedge between me and as many homeboys as he could but most of them didn't buy his bull. *Gordo* had an older *carnal* who was down for the *barrio* and he tried hard to emulate his *carnal*. He had a little group of followers and aspired to be a leader, or a "shot caller" as we referred to them, but I knew he didn't have the *cora* or the *huevos*.

Homeboy Wicked recovered from the wounds inflicted upon him by Cherrieville at Sharkie Park, but that *filero* must have cut deeper than any of us had realized at the time because he continued to drift away from us. He stopped dressing like a *cholo* and quit holding up the walls at school with the rest of us homeboys. He even told us to call him by his real name. If it weren't for his older *carnal* Bad Boy, Wicked would have caught it from the homeboys. Regardless of what any of us said or did, his *mente* was made up and he simply dealt with the pressure and intimidation as best he could. I respected him for that.

As the school year wound down, things between the *juras* and our homeboys heated up. One evening, a car load of our homeboys were cruising the *barrio* when the *juras* stopped them. Words were exchanged and an altercation ensued. Four homeboys got beat down pretty bad, so bad that two of them ended up in the hospital. This altercation wasn't taken lightly by the *veteranos*, who decided to send some homeboys out with a *wila* for the *juras*. The *wila* was delivered in the form of a drive-by on the police station at Park Avenue and Mission.

Our homeboys shot out all the windows on the west side of the building. By the time the *juras* could react, the *vatos locos* were gone. As a result, the *juras* tried to come down hard on every *cholo* in the *barrio* but the homeboys had it together. Everybody stayed off the *calles* for a while, but still the *juras* refused to back off, so the homeboys were sent to deliver another *wila*. They simply strolled up to the back of the police station and started shooting into the building. Again, they got away clean.

This time the *wila* came through loud and clear. The *juras* finally figured out that homeboys were willing to go to war with them if they didn't back off. That week a construction crew bricked in all the windows at the police station and installed cameras to monitor the exterior of the building. Apparently, the *juras* didn't want a war with the homeboys because they did back off. Even so, it was only a temporary solution and the tension remained high between the *juras* and the *barrio*.

I was proud to be a *cholo*. Homeboys had a voice and we had the power to make ourselves heard. I knew there was a price attached to this kind of power, but I seldom thought about that and it was never discussed at home. *Mi jefita* always told me to be careful and offered to drive me whenever I went somewhere. She never asked what I was doing or whether I was involved in any of the things she heard about on the news or read in the paper. My *jefito* didn't beat around the bush, but he didn't confront my situation head-on either. He would simply say, "Don't come home crying if you get your butt kicked."

Denial is a dangerous drug in the hands of parents. Even so, it was easily available on every *calle* in the *barrio* and a lot of parents, including mine, were addicted.

For me, it was as simple as enjoying hanging out with the homeboys. I didn't need to wrap myself in denial. My destiny didn't require deep thought or contemplation. The homeboys gave me a sense of self-importance and showed me how to earn respect. That was enough reason for me to embrace influences such as violence and intimidation that, for better or worse, were beginning to shape my life.

4

Calle Doce

I finished finals at Simons Junior High and headed home, glad that school was over. As I entered my *cantón*, I noticed President Nixon's face on the television. It was the summer of 1974, and news of the Watergate scandal was the hot topic, but none of that interested me. I went to my room and hunted up *Travieso's* telephone number, then called him up to let him know that I was coming into the *barrio* on Friday.

The rest of the week dragged. *Mi jefita* had a list of chores she had been saving for me to do once school was out. So I passed the time till Friday helping her clean up around the *cantón* and yard.

Finally, Friday arrived. I awoke early and popped a tape of *Santana* in the eight-track player. *"Oye Como Va"* started playing as I went to the closet and grabbed a pair of Dickies, better known as "Khakis" among the homeboys. I set up the ironing board that I kept in the corner of my room and retrieved the iron and a can of spray starch from the hall closet. I carefully spread my Khakis across the ironing board and soaked the edges of the pant legs with starch so I'd get a sharp crease that would last all day. After ironing my Khakis, I put the iron to my blue bandana that I'd folded into a headband. I grabbed a clean T-shirt from my *cajón* and ironed it with plenty of starch. Then I set about shining my Stacy Adams before I hopped in and out of the shower and carefully got dressed, not wanting to mess up the perfect creases on my Khakis.

I reviewed the results of my efforts in my dresser mirror. I wanted to look my best for the homeboys, since I knew they'd clown me if I didn't look absolutely *bonarood!* My *jefito* didn't mind the *cholo*-style look, but for some reason he wouldn't let me wear the *bandana* in his presence, so I neatly tucked it over the front right side of my belt like soldiers who used to fold their military caps over their belts when they weren't wearing them. I let mine drape proudly at my side and laid my creased out Pendleton over my left arm and went into the kitchen where *mi jefita* was straightening up a small stack of bills.

Travieso and J-Bird used to be my neighbors when we lived on Eleventh Street. Even after *mi familia* moved to Mayfair Street, they still weren't all that far away. Now they lived on Twelfth Street and we lived all the way out on County Road. I wasn't about to ride my bike all the way across town and it was way too far to stroll. Since I knew *mi jefita* was headed into downtown Pomona to pay some bills, I asked her for a ride.

My *jefito* glanced up from his paper as *mi jefita* told him she wouldn't be long. He didn't say anything but I could see his eyes pause momentarily on the *bandana* hanging over my belt.

"Be careful and make sure you get a ride home; it's too dangerous to be walking*,*" *mi jefita* cautioned as she stopped the *ranfla* in front of *Travieso* and J-Bird's *cantón*.

When I used to kick it with *Wesos, mi jefita* didn't seem to worry as much because she trusted the neighborhood. With *Travieso* and J-Bird, it was different. She had known Travieso and J-Bird's *jefita* since we had lived across the *calle* from them when we were young, so she didn't have a problem with me going to visit them either. In fact, she seemed glad that I kept in touch with my old friends. Her caution seemed to be directed toward the increasing violence on the *calles* in the *barrio*. *Travieso* and J-Bird lived in the heart of the *barrio*. I don't know whether she was aware of the current trouble between our homeboys and Cherrieville or whether she was concerned about trouble from the *juras*. I never asked. She always told me to be careful and to get a ride home and I always said, "O.K., Mom."

"Call me if you need a ride," she added as I stepped out of the car. "And, be home by ten."

I leaned in the open passenger window to press for another hour. "Dad said I could stay out till eleven."

"I said ten, and keep out of trouble."

"Man!"

"Don't man me. I'm your mother," she stated firmly. A smile soon broke through her maternal armor and she added, "I love you, *mijo*."

I just nodded and hurried toward *Travieso* and J-Bird's *cantón* before I had to endure additional instructions. I hated that mushy stuff, anyway.

As I knocked on the door, I could hear *mi jefita* drive away. I knew the sound of her driving by heart. She always seemed to take an extra second or two while shifting gears. I expected to hear the gears grind, but just when I thought the teeth were about to be ripped loose, she'd re-engage the clutch and head on down the *calle*.

It was about one o'clock and the sun was high overhead. Only a few clouds blemished an otherwise perfect blue sky. It was a great day to spend with my friends.

Travieso's jefita answered the door, *"Sí?"*

She didn't seem to recognize me. I decided not to remind her and simply responded, "Is *Travieso* and J-Bird here?"

"Sí. Esperate."

She left me at the door alone. In a few moments, J-Bird appeared and led me through the *cantón*, by way of the kitchen where he introduced me to his *jefita*. She admitted that she remembered me but seemed busy cleaning the kitchen cabinets.

I followed J-Bird back to the bedroom he shared with *Travieso* who was ironing his clothes. *Travieso* glanced up as he slid the iron down the edge of his Khakis.

"*Q'vole*, Homes. I was wondering what time you would show up, *ese*."

"Who brought you, *ese*?" J-Bird asked.

"*Mi jefita*, Homes."

"*Órale*."

Travieso lifted the iron from his Khakis. "Eh, Homes, check out the crease," he said as he slid his finger down the edge. "*Como un filero*, Homes."

"*Sí mon, ese*. Check these out," I said proudly showing him my creases.

J-Bird slid his fingers down the crease in my Khakis and jokingly said, "*Trucha, ese.*"

Travieso was sufficiently pleased with his creases and set the iron aside. He grabbed his Khakis from the ironing board and other clothes that had been laid out neatly on the bed.

"*Dispensa*, Homes. I'm going to take a shower."

As *Travieso* left the room, J-Bird yelled after him, "Use the soap this time, *ese*." J-Bird and I enjoyed a laugh. *Travieso* turned and flipped us both off. I knew he couldn't say what he really wanted to say because his *jefita* in the kitchen would hear him. *Travieso* continued to the bathroom.

"Eh, Homes. You want something to eat?" inquired J-Bird.

"*Sí mon*, Homes," I answered. I knew J-Bird's *jefita* could cook as well as mine.

"*Órale*, Homes. There's some forty-fives in the *caja*. Put one on. The record player is over there," he pointed to the corner of the room near the window. "I'll be right back."

While J-Bird went to the kitchen, I fingered through his record collection. He and *Travieso* had a good selection. I finally chose a record by War with the song "Me and Baby Brother" and queued it up on the record player.

As I relaxed on the edge of J-Bird's bed, my eyes wandered around the room, stopping first on a poster with two fists clenched against broken chains and a caption reading "Chicano Power." Next, my eyes traveled to another poster. This one had a picture of an Aztec Indian holding a woman in his arms. Both posters were pinned to the wall with small nails stuck in the corners. My eyes then migrated to a set of shelves standing against the wall opposite the door. A couple of nicely assembled lowrider models drew me to my feet. I was impressed with the quality of construction and paint job.

Just then, J-Bird returned with a plate full of *burritos*. "Here, Homes. Grab a few."

I grabbed one and quickly sunk my teeth into it. Ummmm, it was good and the chili was hot the way I like it, so I immediately reached for another.

J-Bird set the plate on the desk and took a burrito for himself. He sat down on the bed leaned back against the headboard to eat.

"Eh, Homes. So, how was Simons, *ese*?" he asked.

"It was alright but a *vato* named *Gordo* started to give me problems after the Fremont game."

I explained to him the whole messed up story.

"*Órale*, Homes. If that *chavala* ever comes to the *barrio*, I'll take care of him," J-Bird asserted.

Travieso returned from his shower. Already dressed and slicking his hair back, he looked *bonarood*. He spotted the plate of burritos on his desk and immediately helped himself. "Eh, Homes, *te acuerdas* when we used to live on Eleventh Street?"

"*Sí mon*, Homes. Eh, do you remember when you *vatos* set your Christmas tree on fire and almost burned down your *cantón?*" I asked, flashing back on my own memory.

"*Órale, Braso*. Don't remind us, *ese*. I still have my *jefito's* boot print on my butt." J-Bird's comment prompted a round of laughter. "Pick another record," he nodded toward the record player as he tied his shoes.

The War song finished and the needle spun toward the center of the record with a clicking sound. I quickly located my favorite Santana record and placed it on the turntable.

J-Bird took one of the speakers and propped it up in the open window which faced the back yard, then removed the back panel from the speaker and pulled out a shoebox.

"Come on, *ese*. Let's go out back."

Santana's "Evil Ways" played as we strolled out the back door into the back yard and behind an old truck that had been abandoned near the back of the garage. J-Bird set the shoebox on the rusted truck bed and looked around. A brick wall behind the garage blocked the view of any neighbors and the truck provided enough seclusion that we could see someone come out the back door without them seeing what we were doing. J-Bird removed the box lid and looked at me as he said, "Check it out, Homes."

I leaned toward the box for a closer look and saw two black socks, neatly rolled, and an aerosol can of clear spray sealer in the box. I was puzzled.

"What's this for?" I inquired, noticing a patchwork of dried paint and sealer on the cement slab extending between the garage and the brick wall.

J-Bird and *Travieso* both burst out laughing.

I felt stupid.

"*Órale*, Homes. There's always a first time, *ese*," *Travieso* said with a smirk as he handed me the can. "Here, Homes. Shake it up till you hear the little ball rattle."

I shook the aerosol can while J-Bird and *Travieso* each picked up a sock and wiggled it back and forth.

"Got's to loosen the dry paint, Homes," *Travieso* explained with a smile on his face and a look of anticipation in his eyes.

Suddenly, I heard the ping of the little ball hitting the insides of the can. J-Bird and *Travieso* unrolled their socks and laid them out carefully next to each other over the patchwork on the pavement.

J-Bird reached for the spray can and I placed it in his outstretched hand. He kneeled down and began to spray the toe of the sock, carefully working his way to the heel. A sweet cloud of fumes slowly engulfed him. I stepped back slightly as the cloud drifted in my direction. J-Bird repeated the process on *Travieso's* sock then set the spray can on the truck bed and neatly rolled his sock with the saturated foot area inside, leaving the outside of the rolled sock dry to the touch. He held the sock to his mouth and took a deep breath. *Travieso* leaned down, rolled up his sock in the same manner, held it to his mouth, and sucked in a lungful of fumes. He held the sweet vapors in for a moment then slowly exhaled and handed his sock to me.

"Here, Homes. Take a sniff."

I raised the sock to my mouth.

"Take a deep breath, Homes," J-Bird encouraged.

I sucked in a deep breath. For a moment, the sweet smell soothed my throat as it traveled in and down. Then suddenly, it hit my lungs like an explosion of wild fire. It felt like a blow torch burning me from the inside out. I coughed and choked and coughed, hugging the edge of the truck bed for support.

J-Bird and *Travieso* burst into laughter.

"*Órale*, Homes. Take it easy, *ese*," J-Bird reassured me as he patted my back to help restore my breathing.

I put the sock back in *Travieso's* hand and tried to pull myself together as I struggled for a breath of fresh air. I could feel the accelerated rhythm of my pulse pounding as blood carried the airborne elixir through my brain.

J-Bird handed me his sock. "Here, Homes. Take another sniff."

I took the sock and held it to my mouth. This time I didn't breathe so deeply then gave the sock back to J-Bird. A sensation of wooziness overcame me as the fumes fogged my brain. I started getting dizzy and the pounding in my head grew louder turning into a painful throbbing sensation. I didn't like it so I passed on additional offers and watched J-Bird and *Travieso* enjoy the fog until the aerosol can ran dry. They were a trip, arguing over who was going to get the last spray. Finally, they decided to share the last intoxicating breaths.

We returned with the shoebox to their room. J-Bird placed it behind the speaker, turned off the stereo, and we left their *cantón*.

It was about 4:00 p.m. as we strolled east on Twelfth Street toward Park Avenue. It was a nice day. The light covering of clouds had burnt off earlier that afternoon and now the sky was empty. The *barrio* was alive, as some of the *Raza* worked on cars in the driveway while others attended to their lawns. The fragrance of *carne asada* grilling on the barbeque gradually overcame the smell of the aerosol spray in my nostrils. Mexican music floated on the air with a new song tuned in at each different *cantón* as though we were running down the dial on the radio. Every wall or fence with sufficient space bore the *placasos* of our homeboys to let everybody know this was our territory. Each homeboy had a unique way of tagging a wall with his street name. It was a matter of pride, more than aesthetics.

"Where are we going, Homes?" I asked.

"To the Macias' pad," J-Bird answered.

I returned a puzzled look.

"That's where all the homeboys kick back, *ese*," *Travieso* added. "Did you bring some *feria*, Homes?"

"*Sí mon, ese*. Ten *bolas*," I replied. Ten dollars.

"*Órale*, Homes. Save five *bolas* for tonight's meeting and pitch in a *bola* every time the homeboys get *pisto, ese*," J-Bird advised.

"What meeting?" I asked.

"The homeboys get together every Friday night and everyone has to bring five *bolas*, Homes," J-Bird explained. "Don't worry. You'll see, *ese*."

I didn't give it another thought.

In a few minutes, we neared Park Avenue. I could see a bunch of lowriders parked in front of a house on the corner. Most of them lined the street, with a few *ranflas* angled into the front yard. *Man!* There must have been about eighty *vatos* in the yard alone. I had no idea how many more were kicking it in the back.

As we crossed the *calle*, one of the *cholos* leaned into his *ranfla* and turned up "*Viva La Raza*" by Zapata. A few of the *cholos* gave J-Bird and *Travieso* a quick nod of recognition and me a lingering stone-faced glare.

Homeboys had a look reserved for rivals that was called "mad dog." It was more of a piercing stare than a look and was also used on strangers. Homeboys could mad-dog someone or get mad-dogged themselves. Whatever the case, it was considered a challenge and usually led to blows.

I passed off the glares and kept my eyes moving, not looking at anyone for too long. I was excited to be around so many hard-core homeboys.

Most of the *vatos* were in their mid to late thirties. Some were younger than me. They looked to be at most ten or eleven years old. *Conejo*, Bad Boy, Big Jerry, *Bala*, and a lot of *vatos* from Simons had gathered near a large tree. We strolled over to join them. Everyone shook hands.

"*Q'vole*, Braso. It's good to see you in the *barrio*, *ese*," Conejo said as he studied the three of us. "There's some *pisto* in the cooler. Go ahead and get some."

There were four coolers and a keg of beer sitting in a tub of ice in the shade. We each got a *pisto* from a cooler. I rubbed the cold can on my forehead before popping it open and taking a long drink. Man, it felt good as the cool liquid rolled down my throat. I'll take a good, cold *pisto* over sniffing paint any day. That stuff gave me a mean headache.

As we savored the cool *pisto*, J-Bird introduced me to several homeboys that were about my age. Some of them I already knew, like Fat Joe and some of his friends, but there were many that I had never seen before today.

One *vato*, in particular, caught my attention. He was about my height and stood confidently by himself sipping a *pisto*. He had a muscular upper body and a dark complexion with the deep piercing stare of a *matón*, the same look that I had seen in *Conejo*. I could tell that he was well respected by the other homeboys our age. I tried not to stare at him and looked away as soon as he glanced in my direction.

J-Bird decided it was time to meet some more *vatos* and led me directly to the mysterious stranger who interrupted J-Bird's introduction.

"Li'l Capone, *ese*."

"*Órale. Braso*, Homes." I looked squarely into his piercing gaze as he scanned me for any sign of weakness.

"*Órale*."

We shook hands before moving on to another group of homeboys then back to the ice chests for another *pisto* but I couldn't shake the image of Li'l Capone's hard-core, *matón* look. It certainly figured into how he got the name Li'l Capone. He must be one *vato loco*.

All day, homeboys were holding down the *barrio* big time. I felt proud to be with them. The air was filled with unity and a singular frame of mind which was generally relaxed unless a *ranfla* went past and then everyone would tense up. If either the *gente* or the *ranfla* looked familiar then the homeboys relaxed again. If neither did, we all held steady until the *ranfla* passed. Everyone had to be *trucha* because nobody knew when a car load of rival gang members might do a drive-by or the *juras* might show up. I was learning that survival in the *barrio* was a matter of being ready for any kind of threat at any time.

Suddenly, one of the homeboys yelled, *"La Jura!"*

Everyone stopped dead.

The warning quietly echoed through the ranks as about a dozen *veteranos* moved calmly toward the back of the *cantón*. I thought it was because they were wanted by the *juras* until I noticed one of them retrieve a sawed-off shotgun from the scruffy hedge row running alongside the *cantón* and conceal it behind his leg. Then, I realized they were all packing and ready to defend the *barrio*, no matter what.

I watched as the *juras* slowed for the stop sign at the intersection of Park Avenue and Twelfth Street, paused a moment, then slowly cruised in front of the *cantón*. The two *gavacho juras* stared at us from their patrol car as they slowly passed, almost as if in slow motion, while Eric Clapton bellowed "I Shot the Sheriff" from the stereo in a *ranfla* in the front yard. I could see hate beaming from the *juras'* eyes. Their stares reminded me of the *jura* who chased one of the *veteranos* into the bushes during the riots at Sharkie Park and came back empty handed. But this time was different. They didn't intimidate me. This time, I felt confident enough to beam the hate back at the *juras* without feeling scared.

Everybody stood silent and motionless. We held our ground and stared the *juras* down. It was a trip.

Once the *juras* had gone, the shotgun was stashed back in the hedge and the *veteranos* returned to what they were doing before the interruption. Voices once again mixed with the music and everyone relaxed. It was as though someone had slowed a record spinning on a turntable and suddenly released it to return to its normal speed. For a moment I thought of what might have happened if the *juras* had decided to stop. There were only two of them. The odds were not in their favor.

It was 6:00 p.m. when I heard the familiar rumble of some bad-looking bombs equipped with glass packs, so called because of the fiberglass packing in a simplified muffler that removed most of the high and mid-range frequencies from the exhaust but left the base thumping lows. Six car loads of *veteranos* slowed to a stop. Some of the older homeboys strolled up to the first *ranfla* and talked for a moment then one of them turned toward the *cantón* and yelled, *"Vamonos!"*

Everyone moved at once, gathering up *pisto* and *cuetes* and heading for their *ranflas*. The older homeboys rode in front and the youngsters rode in the back with never more than four in back. Don't ask me why, but a lone homeboy in the back seat always rode on the right side.

J-Bird, *Travieso*, Black Crow, and I slid into the back of a deep blue '64 Impala, lowered to the bone. I didn't know the *veterano* behind the wheel or the homeboy riding shotgun in the passenger seat but Black Crow did. We all sat low in the seats so only our heads could be seen from the street.

Once all the *ranflas* were loaded, we drove off slow and low in single file as one long caravan. There must have been nearly twenty *ranflas* with five to six homeboys in each *ranfla* as we cruised down the *calle* at not much over 5 mph to the sound of "Mighty Mighty" by Earth, Wind and Fire.

In Pomona, as with most of the Los Angeles area, the *calles* slope from the center line to the gutters so the water doesn't block traffic during heavy rains. At intersections the slope of the cross street forms a large dip on either side of the intersection.

As the first *ranfla* approached an intersection, it slowed and steered slightly to the right into the dip as if making a right hand turn but then steered slightly back to the left as it crossed the intersection then back to the right into the second dip and finally back into the traffic lane on the other side of the intersection.

We cruised east on Grand Avenue. With darkness descending, the rhythmic left-to-right, up and down, right-to-left motion of the string of tail lights that snaked out in front of us as the *ranflas* crossed each successive intersection mesmerized me. Each bounce seemed perfectly choreographed with the music.

Past Towne Avenue we veered left into Washington Park, followed the loop through the park, which was crowded with *gente*. Everyone in the *barrio* knew that danger lurked nearby when the Sharks were about, so no one dared stare at us. The loop through Washington Park brought us back out onto Grand Avenue where we doubled back, heading west toward Sharkie Park.

At Sharkie Park about thirty or so homegirls, or *cholas* decked out in their starched Khakis and tight blouses, heavy eye shadow with eye liner, and fluffy, feathered hair were kicking back. Everything about them said, *"Yo soy Chicana!"* As we passed, they jumped up and whistled and shouted, *"Q-vo!* Ooh, baby dolls! *Pomona Los Sharkies Rifa!"* We simply nodded our acknowledgement in staid *cholo* style but maintained our cool. There was a certain decorum required when cruising through the *barrio* because we were on display with a show of strength and unity just as if we were soldiers in a military parade.

We cruised down Grand Avenue past Sharkie Park and White Avenue until we reached Hamilton Boulevard where homeboys started parking their *ranflas* near a small stone building that was once the *barrio's* only Catholic church. The memory of *mi jefita* walking up these steps to Sunday Mass when I was a little boy flashed through *mi mente*. Now the building stood abandoned, no longer needed, since a larger church had been built across the *calle*.

Once we parked, J-Bird, *Travieso*, Black Crow, and I climbed out of the back seat and followed the other homeboys into the old structure. A few homeboys stayed outside and kept *trucha*.

"Get your *feria*, Homes," *Travieso* reminded me as we entered a small lobby area already crowded with homeboys.

Two *veteranos* stood at the double doors leading into the chapel. One of them held a box. I dropped my five *bolas* in the box like everyone else as I filed into the chapel which had been stripped of everything, including pulpit, pews, and statues. Light filtering through the stained glass windows mixed with a haze of cigarette smoke to give the chapel an eerie glow.

There had to be close to three hundred or more homeboys squeezed into the chapel. They were everywhere and it was standing room only. The buzz of conversation filled the smoky room. I followed J-Bird, *Travieso*, and Black Crow who crowded in with some other youngsters holding up the walls halfway up the right side of the chapel.

The only chairs were in the front of the chapel at three long tables that were positioned in a horseshoe shape. This is where the *veteranos* sat. They were all *cholo'd* down, some in their late twenties and others nearing forty. I didn't know any of them but did recognize Nite Owl's two older *carnales* and a couple of the other *veteranos* from when we used to ride our bikes before my family moved out of this *barrio*.

The *veterano* who was sitting at the end of the table on the left side stood up and the chapel immediately fell silent. He didn't have to say a word. He was tall and husky. His short black hair was slicked back and a thick *brosha* tapered down around the corners of his mouth. He stood silent for a moment, looking around the room, before speaking.

"*Órale*, homeboys. *Los Sharkies Calle Doce* is now in order!" he said with authority. Then he returned to his seat, and one of the *veteranos* who was collecting *feria* at the door rose.

"We collected one thousand and four hundred *bolas*," he announced and sat back down.

A third *veterano* took to his feet. He also had a thick *brosha* and wore a gangster hat with the brim turned all the way down. The shadow from his hat fell over his eyes.

"All is secure," he announced gruffly and sat down.

"*Q'vole*, homeboys. Do we have *vatos* that want to get jumped into the *barrio*?" asked a thin, dark skinned *veterano* who remained seated. "If we do, you *vatos* need to step into the middle."

J-Bird looks at me, "That's you, *ese!*"

His comment caught me off guard. My eyes darted from J-Bird to *Travieso* and back. Neither of them had mentioned getting jumped into the *barrio*. I was shocked and honored all at the same time, and didn't know what to do. *Travieso* gave me a gentle push that was noticed by homeboys all around us. I had no choice. I felt the eyes of everyone on me as I slowly stepped forward. I was joined by homeboy Slim and five other youngsters from Simons Junior High. All eyes focused on the seven of us as we stood, surrounded by hundreds of *vatos*, in the center of the chapel.

Another *veterano* rose from the tables. This one was short and stocky with a blue *bandana* crossing his forehead. He stepped around the table and strolled directly to me. I didn't know what to think, except, *man, why me first!* If I had to fight this *cholo* my butt was already his. All seven of us youngsters put together couldn't make an impression on this *vato loco*.

I wanted to run but knew that if I showed any fear not even J-Bird and *Travieso* would carry what was left of me out of here. I stood my ground as the *veterano* stared at me from behind the blue *bandana* which covered his eyebrows creating shadows that fell across his eyes. All I could do was stare back into those dark shadows. Finally, he spoke.

"*Órale*, homeboys. Who's going to raise their hand for this *vato*?" he said as he scanned the crowd to see who would raise their hands. I noticed J-Bird, *Travieso*, and a few of the homeboys from Simons raise their hands.

"I see a lot of youngsters. What about you older *vatos*?" he inquired.

Homeboy *Conejo*, Bad Boy, Big Jerry, and *Bala* held up their hands.

"*Órale, vato,*" he said as he gave me a slow nod before moving to the next youngster.

All seven of us went through this then the *veterano* stepped out in front of the entire group.

"*Órale,* youngsters. So you *vatos* want to be from the *barrio*? *Sabes que Calle Doce* don't have no *chavalas*. Take a hard look around you, *porque* homeboys have to prove themselves and *vatos* are no exception. I don't care how you *vatos* do your *movida*. *Sabes que,* when you do, I'll hear about it. You *vatos* got two weeks to take care of business. *Escucha me, carnalitos.*" He paused a moment and stared each one of us directly in the eye before continuing. "If you die for *Calle Doce, Calle Doce* will revenge your death."

Then it was over. The *veterano* returned to his chair. I turned and walked through the other homeboys back to J-Bird and *Travieso* who gave me congratulatory slaps on the shoulder and back. I didn't really notice; my thoughts were elsewhere.

The *veteranos* moved on to a discussion of a street festival on the following Sunday at Sharkie Park but the word *death* kept reverberating through *mi mente*. It was the first time anyone had mentioned the possibility that one of us might die. Homeboy Wicked had been beat down and stabbed by some *vatos* from Cherrieville but he didn't die.

While *mi mente* bounced from one thought to another, the *veteranos* at the table discussed all the things that would be needed for the street festival, then moved on to a discussion of proposed sweatshirt designs. I didn't hear a word of that discussion.

Then one of the homeboys stepped forward and pulled out a dark blue sweatshirt with the picture of a shark and I snapped back to the meeting. It had "SHARKIES" embroidered in an arc above the sleek sea predator and "POMONA" printed below. All of the words appeared in light blue, Old English style lettering. The homeboys cheered. I snapped back into the discussion as it was decided that this would be our official sweatshirt, and dark blue and light blue would be our official colors. Everybody agreed enthusiastically with shouts and whistles.

When the meeting adjourned, everyone filed out of the chapel and back to the *ranflas*. We caravanned to Sharkie Park. J-Bird, *Travieso*, Black Crow, and I rode with the same *veterano* to the park where we all pitched in for more *pisto* and three carloads of homeboys cruised to the liquor store.

It was about 10:00 p.m. and the homeboys were all kicking back. As I sipped a cool *pisto*, I wondered about the *movida* I was supposed to do within the next two weeks. A million questions ricocheted through my brain but there was no one to ask. I had hoped that Black Crow or the *veterano* who drove us, or even J-Bird and *Travieso*, would clue me in as we caravanned from the chapel to Sharkie Park, but none of them breathed a word to help me.

After we arrived at the park, J-Bird and Travieso found a youngster with some spray paint and they busied themselves trying to get high. I couldn't ask any of the other homeboys about my *movida* since that would be considered weak and show that I was nervous. I was nervous all right, close to the point of being scared, but there was no one other than a homeboy that could help me since there were penalties for taking *barrio* business out of the *barrio*. Only the *pisto* helped, so I stole another sip.

"*Q-vo*, Homes."

I turned my head to see Nite Owl and Slim standing behind me. Slim was one of the seven youngsters who were in the same boat with me. I stood up to shake hands.

"*Q-vo*, Homes" I said.

"Check it out, eh," Nite Owl said. *"Ven mañana en la noche* around eight-thirty, Homes, we got some business to take care of, *ese*." Nite Owl's lips broke a smile for a brief moment. "It will get you and Slim into the *barrio*."

"*Órale*, Homes," I said enthusiastically as we shook hands again.

As Nite Owl and Slim strolled away, I noticed the homeboys returning from the liquor store with the *pisto*. I went to get one. I was relieved by Nite Owl's comment and pleased that he had decided to help me out. I relaxed and quit troubling over what I needed to do. This opened the door for thoughts about what Nite Owl had planned. Whatever it was, it had to be done, or I would have to move as far away from Pomona as I could to avoid the wrath of the *Los* Sharkies homeboys.

I enjoyed the rest of the night at the park and got a ride home from one of the homeboys. I was asleep as soon as my head hit the pillow.

5

Movida

Saturday morning, I awoke to the smell of eggs and bacon. I got up and ate breakfast, then helped *mi jefita* with some chores around the house, cleaned my room, took out the trash, and mowed the lawn. When I finished with my work, I showered and started laying out the clothes I wanted to wear. Since I was going to take care of business with Nite Owl and Slim, I selected my black Khakis and a dark sweatshirt.

Mi jefita gave me a ride to J-Bird and *Travieso's cantón* at around two in the afternoon. As soon as I arrived, they pulled out the shoebox and we went out behind the old truck where they unrolled the socks, soaked them with spray paint, and started sniffing. They offered me some but I declined. The last thing I needed before doing my first *movida* was a headache. J-Bird and *Travieso* finished off the paint and immediately started arguing over who should get the last sniff just as they had the previous day. I wasn't all that interested in listening to them argue, so I told them that I was going to do a *movida* later that evening.

"*Órale*, Homes," *Travieso* offered as he reached out to shake hands.

"Be *trucha*, Homes, and don't get busted, but if you do, *ese*, don't be a *rata*," J-Bird cautioned.

"*Sí mon, porque* all *ratas* die, *ese*," added *Travieso*.

"*All* ratas *die*" was the unspoken code of the *barrio*. It didn't need to be said; everyone knew it. While I didn't know anyone who had actually ratted to the *juras*, there were plenty of stories of what happened to those that did. *Ratas* were always dealt with harshly, especially in *la pinta* which to some degree was an extension of the *barrio,* since there were so many homeboys doing time.

J-Bird and *Travieso* finally put the shoebox away and we decided to head over to Sharkie Park. *Travieso* said the homeboys would be out in force since it was a weekend. He was right. When we strolled up, the homeboys were all over the park.

We kicked back the whole afternoon without a care in the world. Conversations drifted from one topic to the next. We relived old times in the *barrio* when J-Bird, *Travieso*, Fat Joe, Black Crow, *Payaso*, David, Nite Owl, and I cruised the *calles* on our bicycles. *Travieso* recalled the time we rode to Sharkie Park and encountered the riot. It seemed so long ago. Now we were hanging out in Sharkie Park, and if the *juras* showed up we'd be the ones fighting them off.

By 8:00 p.m. it was already dark. Nite Owl and Slim drove up with an older homeboy. They parked. I joined them at the edge of the park. We shook hands.

"*Órale*, Homes. You down, *ese?*" Nite Owl asked, his eyes searching for any sign of weakness.

"*Sí mon*, Homes. I'm down, *ese!*" I responded without a moment of hesitation.

"*Órale, pues.* Here's the deal. We're going to hit Cherrieville, so kick back, *ese,* I'll let you know when it's time."

The four of us strolled toward the *pisto* and each grabbed a cold one, then Nite Owl, the older homeboy, and Slim left again. *Mi mente* filled with random thoughts about what was going to happen. I could picture the homeboys from Cherrieville hanging out in their *barrio* drinking their share of *pisto*. I tried not to think about it and took a sip of my *pisto*, but I wanted to keep *mi mente* clear so I drank slowly. Luckily, the time passed quickly and in what seemed like only a few minutes Nite Owl, Slim, and the older *vato* returned.

"*Vamonos*, it's time to take care of business," Nite Owl said.

We climbed into the *vato's ranfla*, the older homeboy behind the wheel and Nite Owl riding shotgun. I climbed in the back first and slid over behind the driver. Slim settled in behind Nite Owl. The engine roared and we headed out on our mission. Homeboy shoved an eight track tape into his player and *"Ballero"* by War surrounded us. We cruised through the *barrio*, past the Catholic church. All of us crossed ourselves as if asking for God's protection and His blessing for the success of our *movida*. The madness of our gestures didn't occur to me as we headed into battle with the enemies of our *barrio*.

"*Órale*, Homes. When we get to Cherrieville, *ese*, homeboy is going to park his *ranfla* and wait for us. We're going to walk up on these *vatos* and blast 'em, Homes," explained Nite Owl as he leaned around to face the back seat.

I simply nodded with no change in my expression but I'm thinking, *we're going to walk up on these* vatos *and blast 'em! Are you* loco? I wanted to see how we were going to do that.

Before long, homeboy killed his lights and music as we pulled into an alley near Hamilton Boulevard on the edge of Cherrieville. It was dark with only the sound of the engine and the ping of rocks kicked up by the tires hitting the metal below our feet. Soon, homeboy stopped near a garage and shut off the engine. Gradually, the sounds of night filled the silence with a slight noise here and there but nothing distinct or recognizable except the far off barking of a dog. Still we waited quietly to scope out the scene making certain that no one was aware of our presence.

Nite Owl nodded quietly, *"Vamonos!"*

We carefully opened the doors and climbed out. Homeboy came around and unlocked the trunk. Nite Owl reached in and threw back a tarp revealing several weapons. He pulled out a rifle and whispered, "This baby is a twenty-two semi-automatic, Homes."

Slim reached in and picked up a large revolver.

"This is a 45, *ese*."

Nite Owl, holding the rifle in one hand, grabs a small chromed pistol and looks at me.

"Can you handle a 38, Homes?"

"*Sí mon*," I replied without hesitation.

"Are you sure?" he questioned. "I don't want any mistakes!"

"My *jefito* showed me how to shoot a *cuete*, ese."

Nite Owl nodded and handed me the *cuete*. It felt cold as ice in the palm of my hand as my fingers squeezed around the handle and gently stroked the trigger guard.

"*Órale pues,* let's do it," Nite Owl whispered proudly.

"*Trucha,*" the older homeboy advised. "Get one for me, *ese,*" he laughed quietly as he carefully pressed the trunk lid down far enough to stay shut while keeping it ready for a fast getaway.

In the dark, we ran across a field, pausing only for a moment to check both ways before hurrying across First Street. My heart was racing a hundred miles an hour as we tripped over some railroad tracks and quickly ducked into a row of bushes where we waited. Everything was quiet. When we were convinced that no one had seen or heard us, we emerged from the bushes and headed east along a wooded fence that must have been about ten feet high and seemed to stretch on forever. Suddenly, Nite Owl stopped. I looked up at the top of the fence and took a deep breath; there was no backing out now.

Slim and I tucked our *cuetes* under our belts, then Nite Owl and I helped Slim up to the top of the fence. Before he dropped over to the other side, he helped pull Nite Owl up while I pushed. I handed Nite Owl the rifle which he passed down to Slim on the other side then Nite Owl leaned down and helped haul me up.

From the top, I took a quick glance behind me then looked for a way to climb down.

"Come on," Nite Owl whispered with a sense of urgency in his voice.

I quickly dropped to the ground and discovered we had landed in the yard behind a Catholic church. All was quiet in the church, so we headed east again and soon encountered a short chain link fence surrounding a trailer park. We easily hopped it and strolled quickly past a row of trailers. I could hear a variety of muffled and distorted voices and sounds that all seemed to mix together: TV news from one trailer, rock music from another, and the discordant voices of a couple arguing. I wondered, *what is their problem?* I didn't have the time to stop and listen.

We kept moving through the trailer park until we came upon another fence. This one was illuminated with a string of lights. Nite Owl nodded silently toward the fence. He didn't have to say a word. I already knew what he meant. Cherrieville was on the other side.

Cautiously, we moved north, unscrewing light bulbs as we went. I figured we must be coming back this same way and if things didn't work as planned, it might be to our favor if these lights were out. My imagination ran wild. All I could do was try and blink the images from *mi mente* as fast as they appeared, but the picture of the *veteranos* fighting hand-to-hand with the *juras* in Sharkie Park kept reappearing as we pushed on along the fence.

Then Slim, who had taken the lead, stopped and pointed at a section of fence. This was where we would enter enemy territory.

We easily scaled the six-foot wooden fence. As my feet hit the ground, I had no doubt we were in their *barrio*. I could see the warning, a big red "C" and "V" painted on the fence behind me. I knew what we would do to them if we caught them in our *barrio*. I could only imagine our fate if we were discovered here. Time slowed and I could feel each breath pass in, dispense its oxygen to my lungs, then pass out as we maneuvered our way deeper into their *barrio*.

Cherrieville *placasos* were everywhere. They marked the fence we had just scaled and the shadowy sides of several small businesses along a *calle* off to our right. We quickly moved to the cover of bushes between two houses and an aged picket fence that ran along a sidewalk. Across the *calle* was one of Cherrieville's main hangouts but it was deserted. There was not a soul in sight. Nothing moved on these *calles*. We sat silently in the bushes for at least thirty excruciatingly long minutes. Still nothing. Not even the quiet stirring of a breeze or the pained moaning of the legendary *La Llorona*.

"Man, Homes! These *vatos* must be in hibernation," Nite Owl whispered with disappointment.

It was Saturday night. Homeboys, even the *vatos* from Cherrieville, wouldn't miss the opportunity to celebrate.

"*Sí mon*, Homes. Maybe they're partying somewhere," I added.

"*Sí mon*, Homes. Let's go, *ese*," suggested Slim, equally disappointed.

Nite Owl took one last look around then relented.

"*Vamonos*," he said.

As we started to get up, I noticed a pair of headlights round a corner down the *calle* and head toward us.

"Wait, Homes!" I whispered. "Here comes a *ranfla!*"

We sunk back into the shelter of the bushes. As the *ranfla* passed under a street light, I could see it was a primered red Impala, a '66 or '67. These *vatos* were low riding hard and slow just like we did as we caravanned from the Macias' pad to the meeting at the old church. The only difference was that these *vatos* were alone.

We took aim with our *cuetes* through the slats in the fence. As they neared our position, I could hear Junior Walker and his All Stars bellowing "Shoot Your Shot" from the *ranfla*.

Slim turned anxiously to Nite Owl. "Is it Cherrieville, Homes?" he asked.

"It has to be them, Homes. They're too relaxed," Nite Owl replied. "As soon as they get in front of us, unload."

The air, heavy with tension, pressed against my body from all sides. My heart was racing. I held my *cuete* in both hands with my right index finger nervously poised on the trigger. I braced myself against the fence. The music slowed, each beat matching the rhythm of my heart and bringing the *ranfla* a few feet closer. As it passed in front of us I could see two *vatos* in front and two in the back.

"*Calle Doce!*" yelled Nite Owl.

BAM! BAM! BAM!

Our *cuetes* exploded like cannons belching deadly fire into the ranks of the enemy. I could hear the *balas* sing through the air and slam into the steel body of the *ranfla*. Glass shattered and the *ranfla* stopped right in front of us. One of the *vatos* in back started waving his hands and yelling at us.

"Cherrieville, Homes! Cherrieville! We're from Cherrieville!"

"We know," snickered Nite Owl as we all continued to unload on them.

They didn't hear Nite Owl's announcement because of the loud music, so they must have thought we were their homeboys, mistaking them for some rival gang. They certainly didn't waste time belaboring the point. The *vato* waving his hands ducked down quickly enough as a *balazo* smashed into metal near his head. The power of each *bala* as it exploded from the *cuete* in my hand gave me a sensation that I had never known before. Complete control. My grip tightened with each pull of the trigger.

In a moment, it was over. The ring of gunfire echoed in my ears. A pungent, acrid cloud of gun smoke hovered over the bushes near the picket fence and we were gone. We didn't wait around to see if anyone had gotten hit. We ran hard and fast, retracing our steps. We scrambled over the first fence, hot footing it through the trailer park. In seconds, we were back to the short chain link fence that butted up against the ten-foot wooden fence. I could see the church. We all hesitated a second, catching our breath.

"Let's get to the other side from here," yelled Nite Owl.

Climbing up the short five-foot fence, we easily reached to top and dropped over to the other side. I went over it like a monkey. With the railroad tracks in sight, we all broke into a run.

Suddenly, Slim hit the ground and Nite Owl pulled me down with him just as a *jura* zoomed into Cherrieville with lights flashing and sirens blaring on nearby Hamilton Street. Back on our feet, we reached the *ranfla*. Homeboy was ready for us. He had the trunk open and engine running.

"*Órale*, Homes. I heard the *balazos* from here. Did you *vatos* get one for me?" he asked as we quickly stowed the *cuetes* in the trunk.

"*Sí mon!*" Nite Owl reported.

We piled into the *ranfla*. Homeboy backed out of the alley and cruised west away from the action. In a moment, we were up on Corona Expressway with the wind blowing freely through the windows.

Homeboy turned to Nite Owl and asked, "Are they down, Homes?"

Nite Owl glanced at Slim and I in the back seat and replied, "*Sí mon, ese.* They're down."

"*Sí mon,* Homes. We're down!" Slim added as he put out his hand to shake. As Slim and I shook hands, homeboy behind the wheel reached up and adjusted the rearview mirror so he could see both of us.

"*Órale*, Homes," Nite Owl said, his eyes locking onto ours through the mirror. "Check it out, *ese. Calle Doce* don't have no *ratas, ese.* When it comes to *movidas* for the *barrio*, you don't discuss them to no one. *Entiendes,* Homes?"

"*Sí mon,*" Slim and I replied in unison.

Headlights from the *ranflas* behind us illuminated homeboy's eyes which stayed on us for several moments, searching for any signs of weakness, before returning to the road.

"Where's your *cantón, Braso*?" homeboy asked.

"Down on County," I replied, my eyes still glued to the mirror.

"*Órale*, Homes. We're going to take you to your *cantón* first. Do you have a place to stash the *cuetes*?" he asked.

I thought for a moment then replied, "*Sí mon*."

I tried to relax and enjoy the fresh air blowing on my face. Oblivious to the other cars around us, I was surprised when we pulled up in front of my *cantón*. I instructed homeboy to park inside the carport behind the apartments and told him to wait while I got the key for the storage compartment. I quickly ran around to the front of the apartment building. I was happy to see that my *jefitos' ranflas* were gone. I hurried inside, grabbed the key for the storage compartment, and quickly returned to the carport.

Nite Owl helped me stash the *cuetes* in the storage compartment where they were out of sight and wouldn't easily be found. I locked up.

"*Órale*, Homes. We'll be by *en la mañana* to pick them up," said Nite Owl.

We all shook hands and they left.

I went inside, took my clothes off, and tossed them in the laundry. I still smelled like gunpowder so I jumped into the shower then climbed into bed. I tried to sleep but every time I closed my eyes, I could see those *balazos* puncturing that *ranfla*. I wondered if we had killed anyone. As hard as I tried to think of something else, anything else, that movie replayed over and over in my head. I don't remember going to sleep that night, but at some point *mi mente* must have had enough and simply shut down.

In the morning, first thing, I checked the newspaper but there was nothing printed about our incursion into Cherrieville. The irresistibly delicious smell of *menudo* penetrated the house. I filled up a large bowl, making certain to pile in plenty of beef tripe and hominy. Everyone else had already eaten, so I enjoyed the meal by myself. After breakfast, I returned to my room and starting laying out my clothes. I planned on going to J-Bird and *Travieso's cantón* to hang out with them and the other homeboys in the park when I heard a knock at my door.

"Your friend is at the door," my little sister shouted through the closed door.

Órale, homeboys are up early today, I thought as I opened the door to my room.

"Your friend is at the door," my sister repeated.

"I heard you the first time," I said as she moved aside and I headed to the front door. When I got there, I found Nite Owl waiting outside.

"*Órale*, homeboy's in back," Nite Owl informed me as we shook hands. There was something different about the handshake. It had all the same motions but it seemed to come with an added element of respect, kind of like when you pass a test and no one even expected you to show up.

I got the key for the storage shed and we strolled to the carport behind the apartment building. Homeboy was leaning against his *ranfla* watching some kids play basketball at the other end of the building.

"Did you hear anything about last night?" I inquired as we quickly transferred the *cuetes* from the storage shed to the trunk of the *ranfla*.

"*Nada*, Homes," Nite Owl responded.

I looked at homeboy and he just shook his head.

"*Sí mon*, Homes. Me neither," I said, adding, "I'm going to the *barrio* later."

"You need a ride, *ese*?" homeboy asked.

"Na, Homes. My *carnal* can drop me off."

We shook hands again and they left. I went back inside and finished getting ready. My *carnal* wasn't leaving till after noon so I hung out in my room and listened to music. At around 2:30 p.m. my *carnal* knocked on my door.

I always liked riding with my *carnal*. He had a 1974 Pinto station wagon lowered to the bone and clean with chromed side pipes. The root beer brown, metal flake paint sparkled in the sunlight. He even had some lights hooked up under the fenders that he would turn on at night which made it look like his *ranfla* was moving down the *calle* in a spotlight and really showed off his rockets and whitewall 5/20s. He dropped me off at J-Bird and *Travieso's cantón* then headed to his *ruca's* pad.

Their older sister let me in. She was always polite but never had much to say to me. She went about her business and I strolled back to J-Bird and *Travieso's* room.

"Did you take care of business, Homes?" J-Bird asked.

Travieso looked at me with the same question in his eyes.

"*Sí mon*," I responded adding no details. I remembered what homeboy told me last night, plus J-Bird and *Travieso* were already hip to the program. Besides, the details weren't important. What mattered was the *movida* was done.

"*Órale*, Homes. You don't have to worry about the meeting this week," *Travieso* said.

"*Sí mon*, Homes. All you need now is a *tac* for the *barrio, ese*," added J-Bird, who went to the closet and pulled out a cigar box. He put the box on the bed and opened the lid. He pulled out a little bottle of India ink, a small sewing needle with a thread wrapped around the tip. "Where do you want it, *ese*?"

"Put it on his right hand, *carnal*," offered *Travieso*.

We sat down on the edge of the bed and I gave him my right hand. J-Bird examined my hand turning it this way and that looking for the perfect location. He finally selected a spot on the back of my hand in the fleshy part between my thumb and first finger. He dipped the tip of the needle into the dark, black ink and started poking my skin. I could feel the sharp sting of the needle each time it punctured my skin but I resisted the urge to pull my hand away. Gradually "XII" appeared amidst the messy mix of blood and ink on the back of my hand.

"*Órale*, homeboy. Check this out, *ese*," J-Bird said as he added the last two pokes and wiped the area clean with a wet towel. "This *tac* shows your loyalty to the homeboys and our *barrio*. That *movida* will start to bring you a reputation, and having a reputation, Homes, brings you respect. Respect to us is love, *ese*." He drew out the word love, giving it special emphasis. *Travieso* nodded in agreement.

Suddenly, it all clicked. This was what it was all about. Love and respect for my homeboys, and my homeboys having love and respect for me. Love and respect was what the *barrio* was all about. Love and respect was what made us homeboys. It all seemed so clear and natural. There were no maybes. No uncertainty. No middle ground. You were either down with the *barrio* or you weren't.

I held my hand in front of me and stared at my first *tac*. I didn't care that my skin still stung from the invasive pin pricks or that the "XII" was uneven. I was proud of what this mark represented. To me it was a badge of courage, a symbol of my triumph over fear. Most of all, I was proud to be a homeboy and proud to be from *Calle Doce*.

"*Órale*, homeboy. You're a baby gangster now, *ese*," J-Bird announced proudly.

"*Sí mon*, Homes," echoed *Travieso*.

J-Bird returned the ink and needle to the cigar box and the cigar box to the closet then he and *Travieso* finished getting dressed. I was anxious to join the other homeboys in the park, but, as I should have expected, J-Bird and *Travieso* had to fill their lungs with some paint fumes before leaving, so out came the shoebox. We went back behind the old truck by the garage where they unrolled their socks and soaked them with a fresh supply of paint, and like always, they argued over the last hit. As J-Bird returned their supplies to the shoebox, he shook a can of black paint, making sure it wasn't empty, and slipped it into his back pocket.

Finally, the three of us strolled down the *calle* toward Sharkie Park. Part way there, J-Bird noticed a brick wall that was free of *placasos*. He pulled out the can of spray paint as he turned to me and said, "*Órale*, Homes. We got to throw our *placasos* on this wall, *ese*. It looks empty." Then, he sprays "*EL BRASO*" with the ease of a master artist, quickly followed by "*TRAVIESO*" and "*J-BIRD*." J-Bird turned away from the wall and glanced at me.

"The name of the homeboy who throws the *placaso* always goes last," J-Bird pointed out.

"That way homeboys know who threw the *placaso, ese*," *Travieso* explained.

It was the first time I'd seen my name on a wall and it looked good. J-Bird and *Travieso* seemed to recognize that this was another first for me and were happy to share in the moment before J-Bird turned back to the wall and finished by spraying "*LOS SHARKIES CALLE DOCE POMONA RIFA!*"

Placasos signified to all in the *barrio* that we were homeboys and proud to be from *Calle Doce*. They served as a warning to outsiders and rivals that this was our territory and that they passed here at their own risk.

When we got to the park, many of the homeboys were already there. Others were pulling up as we arrived. I spotted Nite Owl and Slim. I grabbed a cold *pisto* and strolled up and greeted them, "*Q-vo*, homeboys." As we shook hands, Nite Owl noticed the "XII" on my hand.

"*Órale*, Homes. You got a *tac* for the *barrio*, eh?"

"*Sí mon*, J-Bird put it on," I explained proudly. "Did any of those *vatos* get hit, *ese?*"

"*Chale, ese.* They got lucky, Homes."

"*Órale*, Homes. All those *balazos* and nobody got hit!" I was surprised as we had unloaded everything we had on them.

"*Sí mon, ese.* Next time," chimed Slim.

I spent the rest of the afternoon kicking back with Nite Owl and Slim. It was a nice Sunday afternoon and homeboys were out in numbers. I kept wondering if Cherrieville would try some retaliation but nothing came down and I got a ride home that evening from one of the homeboys.

For the next four days nothing came down. I spent most of the time with Nite Owl, who wasn't into paint fumes like J-Bird and *Travieso*. On Thursday, Nite Owl told me to meet him at his *cantón* on Friday before the homeboys' meeting.

I awoke early on Friday and couldn't wait to go over to Nite Owl's pad. I was also excited knowing that we would join homeboys for the meeting.

Nite Owl lived on 11th Street at Main with six *carnales*. When I arrived at his *cantón* and knocked on the front door, his *jefita* directed me to the back yard where Homeboy and his *jefito* were downing some *pistos* and playing cards with five men in their mid to late forties. The sweet aromatic fragrance of barbeque filled the air. Homeboy offered me a *pisto* and I followed him as he went over to turn the sizzling *carne asada* on the grill.

"Check it out, Homes. See those five men, *ese?*"

"*Sí mon*, Homes," I replied.

"The homeboys call them 'the untouchables.'"

"*Porqué*, Homes?"

"They're the original homeboys from the *barrio*, *ese*. They go back to the early forties, Homes," he explained.

"*Órale*, Homes. *El serio?*"

I watched them for a moment as they sat there throwing cards on the table and making their bets. In *mi mente* they were true heroes. I was impressed.

"*El serio*, Homes. They started *Los* Sharkies," stated Nite Owl. His voice conveyed the respect he felt for these men as he continued. "*Mi jefito* told me the youngsters coming up in his time started to call themselves '*Los Winos, Twelfth Street.*' Then in the fifties they called themselves '*Los Santos de Noche*' but all of them got jumped into *Los* Sharkies when they got older, and it's been *Los* Sharkies ever since, *ese*."

"*Órale*, Homes!"

"*Sí mon*. The Shark has put fear into the hearts of our enemies for many years, *ese!*" he stated proudly. "Once a homeboy, always a homeboy, *ese*."

I was tripping. After all these years, these old men were still hanging out and considered themselves to be homeboys like the rest of us. I couldn't believe it. They were the masters. I was honored to be in their presence and hung on every word they spoke.

Before I knew it, a '67 Caprice, lowered to the bone, pulled up, and a homeboy yelled to us from the *ranfla*, "*Vamanos*, it's time for the meeting!"

Nite Owl and I joined the homeboy in his *ranfla* and cruised to the Macias' pad. By the time we arrived, the other homeboys were lining up for the caravan. Homeboy, driving, cranked the volume on his tape player. "Shot Gun" by Junior Walker and The All Stars exploded from the speakers. We cruised down Grand Avenue to Washington Park, back past Sharkie Park ending up at the old church.

The meeting started off just the same as last week. The tall and husky *veterano* with the thick *brosha* stood up and the chapel immediately fell silent. He surveyed the room and reported, "*Órale*, homeboys. *Los* Sharkies *Calle Doce* is now in order!"

The *veterano* who collected the *feria* at the door rose and reported the amount collected then sat down and the *veterano* with the thick *brosha* and gangster hat announced, "All is secure," and he sat down.

Next, the thin dark-skinned *veterano* who had led the proceedings when I was called out with Slim and the five other youngsters stood up and stepped forward.

"*Órale*, I heard the good news, and I want to be the first to welcome the youngsters into the big *Calle Doce* gang, *Barrio Los* Sharkies," he announced.

All seven of us stepped out with pride and he shook hands with each of us. Other homeboys put out their hands to shake as I made my way back toward J-Bird and

Travieso. It felt really good to be accepted as a homeboy, but still I knew that one *movida* had simply gotten me in the door. I still needed to earn their trust and most of all their respect.

"*Órale*, now for the bad news. We have a youngster in our midst who wants to get jumped out. *Caiga, ese.* You know who you are!" stated the *veterano*.

Reluctantly, the youngster made his way to the middle. Then, the *veterano* called down the homeboys who raised their hands for the youngster. Six of them came down and, in front of everyone, gave that youngster a beating he'll never forget. They beat him down so bad they had to carry him out, but before they did the *veterano* issued a warning as one of the *vatos* who came down on him grabbed him by the hair and raised his head.

"Let this be an example for all of us, *porque* there's only two ways out of *Calle Doce*. Getting jumped out and death," he cautioned sternly.

The *vato* dropped the youngster's head on the floor and the homeboys that had vouched for him dragged him out.

What was he thinking? I couldn't understand why he wanted out, but at the same time I came to the realization that getting out was much harder than getting in.

Nothing else was said about us youngsters during the rest of the meeting. The homeboys discussed the street festival planned for Sunday, and a few other things, and then adjourned to Sharkie Park where we kicked it for the night.

During the next few weeks, I found out that the tall, husky *veterano* with the thick *brosha* who called the meetings to order was the vice president. The *veterano* with the gangster hat was in charge of security during the meetings, and the one with the blue *bandana* hung low over his eyes was the enforcer who made certain we all stayed in line and did our share of *movidas*. The thin, dark-skinned *veterano* who did all the talking was the president.

We were divided into three groups. The *veteranos* were the backbone and held all the leadership positions in *Los* Sharkies. Most of them were in their late twenties and a few even ranged into the mid-forties. Homeboys around high school age or a little older comprised the middle group and the rest of us youngsters were called Junior Sharkies or baby gangsters. The youngest homeboy was only eleven years old but had the beginnings of the same dark, *matón* look that I saw in the eyes of *Conejo* and Li'l Capone. Li'l Capone, I found out, was our enforcer. It seemed to make sense.

The two *veteranos* who collected the *feria* at the door were the treasurers. Each week they collected around $1,400, which financed the street festivals and paid for sweatshirts, *pisto*, and, of ultimate importance, *cuetes*. I guessed that a good share of it helped maintain the flow of heroin and other drugs into the *barrio*. For all I knew, some of it probably paid rent and utilities for some of the *veteranos* or simply lined their pockets. Nevertheless, we all paid our *feria* each week as we entered the old church and no one ever questioned where the money went. I enjoyed the rest of the night at the park and got a ride home from one of the homeboys.

6

Sharkie Park

It was a beautiful Sunday morning. I got ready early and left for the *barrio* to help prepare for the festival in Sharkie Park. When I arrived at the park at around 9:30 a.m., the homeboys were already busy setting up the game booths and food stands. Several *jefitas* carried food to some of the stands that were already complete. It was great how the *barrio* came together to get things ready.

My *jale* was to help set up the boxing ring. There were several boxing exhibitions planned for the day. Of all sports I liked boxing the best, so I didn't mind helping bolt the corner posts in place while other homeboys ran the rope around the ring and stretched the canvas over the plywood flooring.

Veteranos wore armbands that had the colors of the Mexican flag which identified them as security. *Juras* kept their distance and generally patrolled around the perimeter of the park while the *veteranos* maintained order within the park. Some of the *veteranos* had gone down to City Hall to get a permit to hold the festival since they were blocking traffic on Grand Avenue on the entire north side of the park. That meant the *juras* had to be there. I could see they hated the fact that we were having this festival, as it was a symbol of the unity of the *barrio*. I knew they'd just as soon have us hide out in our *cantóns* while they controlled the *calles,* but that wasn't going to happen.

As I continued to tighten the bolts on the boxing ring, I watched while *gente* from the *barrio* set up tables and chairs in front of the bandstand which was framed by two large pyramids. Each one reached about fifteen feet into the sky. I remembered the day when J-Bird, *Travieso*, Black Crow, *Payaso*, Fat Joe, Nite Owl, David, and I all cruised into Sharkie Park on our lowrider bicycles and watched the *veteranos* build the pyramids. We returned almost every day for a week while they meticulously painted the tall narrow structures with multicolored zig-zag lines on the front and a magnificent mosaic of Mexican history, which I knew nothing about at that time, on the back.

By noon, everything was ready. I got a ride home from one of the homeboys. I took a quick shower and got *bonarood*. *Mi jefita* was going to the festival with Mary and some of her friends, so she gave me a ride back to Sharkie Park. Since she was going with Mary, she had "reserved parking" in Mary's driveway. As we neared Mary's *cantón*, I could see the *gente* walking toward the park. *Mi jefita* parked and before I could get out, she said, "*Mijo*, please be careful and stay out of trouble." With that, she moved her head to the side and slightly upward positioning her cheek for a kiss. I quickly complied.

"O.K., I'll see you later," I blurted out, since I was in a hurry to join my homeboys.

Mariachi music filled the air as homeboys and *gente* mixed throughout the park. I spotted J-Bird and *Travieso* and hung out with them for a while in a large open area away from the row of booths. When Nite Owl showed up, the four of us strolled over behind the bandstand where *Payaso* and about a dozen homeboys were kicking back near three kegs of *pisto* chilling in a tub of ice.

The collage on the back of the pyramids suddenly caught my attention. It was an artistically orchestrated composition of men and women from the Mexican revolution, Cesár Chavez, *Chicanos* of the zoot suit era, and, of course, *cholos*. Just standing beside them, looking up into their larger-than-life faces, made me proud to be from the *barrio*. When I was younger, I didn't know who these people were, but now it all made sense to me. I understood why they were honored. I understood why homeboys respected the pyramids and why they were proud to have made the sign that marked the entrance to Sharkie Park in woodshop at Garey High School. It measured about waist high and was nearly ten feet long. Constructed of heavy lumber, it had "SHARKIE PARK" engraved in fancy, green, Old English style letters on a dark brown background. Each end of the sign was supported by a series of three posts, each with the diameter of a telephone pole. It made me realize that there was a lot of talent in the *barrio*.

A youngster who had recently gotten a short haircut strolled up, and *Payaso* immediately tore into him, making fun of the way his ears stood out to the side. The youngster didn't like it and immediately beat a retreat. He must have known that, given another couple of minutes, *Payaso* would have made certain that his *placaso* was Dumbo, like the Disney cartoon elephant known for his big ears.

Payaso had a knack for giving homeboys or homegirls their *placasos*. He could always pinpoint some kind of defect and make us laugh by calling attention to it. He seemed to love the attention it brought him.

All of sudden, our fun was interrupted by a loud POP! Everyone jumped at the sound as homeboys converged on the bandstand. The commotion caught the attention of the *gente* who probably thought there was a shot fired. Whispers raced through the crowd.

We spun toward the sound to see a geyser of *pisto* spraying high into the air from one of the kegs. The homeboy who was keeping the pressure up in the keg must have pumped it up too high. Our surprise quickly turned into a good laugh as we all grabbed our cups and scrambled to try and salvage the *pisto* raining from the sky without getting wet.

The day went by quickly. I spent a good part of it watching the boxing matches. Some of the homeboys like Tony, Tavie, and Albert and his little *carnal* Richie had a good chance of turning pro someday. I would have liked to go a few rounds with them but I didn't want to get my butt kicked in front of such a big crowd, so I just watched.

Later in the afternoon, the tempo of the music quickened as a younger band replaced the older men playing the *Mariachi* music. They picked up the pace with the *Chicano* rock beat of tunes by *Santana*, *El Chicano*, Thee Midnighters, and *Malo*. *Gente* moved to the rhythm on a dance floor set up in front of the bandstand. Everyone was having a great time.

The music and dancing continued throughout the afternoon. By around 6:00 p.m., the older *gente* and children started thinning out. Maybe they could sense danger lurking in the approaching darkness. I looked around for *mi jefita* and was pleased to see her across the *calle* at Mary's *cantón*.

HOMEBOY'S SOUL

Nite Owl and I strolled behind the bandstand to get our share of *pisto*. J-Bird and *Travieso* had gone with some homeboys earlier to get high on paint. Fat Joe and *Payaso* strolled to one of the food stands to grab something to eat.

All of a sudden, a big commotion broke out in front of the bandstand where couples were dancing. Someone yelled, *"Pleito!"* The call echoed from homeboy to homeboy throughout the park like dogs barking a warning when a stranger strays into their territory. Immediately, *gente* cleared away from the bandstand as homeboys converged on the front lines surrounding two older *vatos* who were getting busy with each other. I didn't have to go far to get a good view of the action. Neither of the *vatos* looked familiar to me. All of a sudden, a third *vato* leaped from the crowd and smashed a beer bottle across the forehead of one of the older *vatos*, sending him crumpling to the ground with blood oozing from a gash on his head.

WHAM!

A flying bottle exploded on the head of the third *vato* as three homeboys climbed all over him and the other *vato* who remained standing, kicking their butts good. The confusion started to make sense as I saw our homeboys gathering around the older *vato* who lay bleeding on the ground. Before long, the *veteranos* stopped the action and sent the two *vatos*, glass shards sticking out of in their heads, packing with their tails tucked between their legs.

The crowd quickly thinned out leaving mostly homeboys. The *gente* didn't like getting caught in the Shark's jaws when we slammed down on an enemy. I didn't know who the enemy was until Nite Owl told me that the two *vatos* who had gotten out of line were members of a car club called Traffic. The *veteranos* assumed they would return with reinforcements to retaliate, so the homeboys, nearly four hundred strong, quickly gathered on Grand Avenue across the *calle* from the park. In response a dozen *juras* lined up, opposite us, at the edge of the park.

During the festival, the *juras* had remained outside the park and were, for the most part, invisible, allowing us to celebrate in peace. Now, we were face-to-face and the hate flowed from glances and stares that ping-ponged back and forth across the *calle*.

Suddenly, behind me I heard another commotion. I spun around to see an older *vato* get hit in the *cara*. He fell to the ground and tried to get up.

BAM!

Someone kicked him in the chest. The blow sent him careening backwards, his head bouncing, first, off the front bumper of a *ranfla* then into the curb. The sound of his skull shattering gave me pause. This *vato* wasn't getting up any time soon.

Then homeboys jumped another *vato*, hitting him from all sides. He was getting beat down so hard he couldn't even fall to the ground. The blows, which were coming fast and furiously, kept him up.

Suddenly, a police car skidded to a stop in the *calle*. A *jura* jumped out with billy club in hand. Before he had a chance to move, a barrage of rocks pelted him like a heavy rain. He quickly ducked back into the cruiser and threw it in reverse, squealing out of there just as fast as he had arrived. My guess is that his quick reaction probably saved him from getting messed up like the *vato* that had become our punching bag.

Quickly the attention turned to another *vato* who was running backwards, swinging his belt over his head trying to keep homeboys at bay. From behind, a homeboy gives him a mean body block, sending his head slamming into the pavement. Miraculously, he managed to regain his footing and attempted a quick dash to freedom which failed. In seconds, homeboys were all over him, hammering him into the side of a Volkswagen. The thin metal gave way as his bones and flesh smashed into the side panel sending a decorative strip flying off into the air. It landed in the *calle* some distance away.

All of a sudden, the wind picked up. Dirt and dust filled the air. It was crazy. I didn't know what was happening. Then I heard the roar of an engine and felt the dizzying whir of large blades cutting swiftly through the air. Like some kind of a space ship falling from the heavens, the police helicopter descended low overhead. As I reached down to grab a rock, I had to cover my eyes with my arm to keep from being blinded by the maelstrom of dust that had enveloped me. The homeboy next to me threw a rock at the ominous blur of revolving propeller blades but to no avail. He and several others ended up stumbling off in pain trying to rub the debris from their eyes. I kept my eyes covered and loosened the grip of my fingers on the rock, letting it fall back to the ground.

The helicopter hovered overhead for another five minutes then lifted back up into the sky and circled above the park. The *juras* tactic had worked. The dust storm had stopped the fight and saved the three *vatos*. Who knows how many punches they received, or how many more they could have endured.

While the homeboys were dusting themselves off, some brave *rucas* hustled the three *vatos* out of there. When the dust cleared, I saw the *juras* still lined up in the park. They seemed to be getting a mild laugh out of watching us in such a state of confusion.

"This is the Pomona Police Department! You are ordered to disperse peacefully!" The announcement blared from a police bullhorn.

Disperse? We were primed for a fight and eager to exchange blows with the *juras* if that's what they wanted. I'm sure they could see that and had already called for reinforcements that would be arriving any minute. Besides, they still had the helicopter lurking overhead that could bring back the dust at a moment's notice.

The *veteranos* who ran our meetings huddled for a few minutes with two of the untouchables that I had seen in Nite Owl's back yard with his *jefito*. After a brief discussion, the two untouchables strolled toward the *jura* who looked like he was in charge. In a few moments, they returned and the word was passed down for all the homeboys to start cleaning up. The *juras* calmly returned to their vehicles and slowly left the area. It was over just like that.

Nite Owl and I grabbed a cold *pisto* to calm our nerves and started folding up chairs and leaning them against the bandstand. Other homeboys began picking up trash while others dismantled the booths.

Nite Owl told me that the three *vatos,* beaten down by the homeboys, were *veteranos* from Cherrieville, known as *tecatos* for their addiction to heroin. He ran it down to me how the heroin dealers had to have some kind of truce with the different *barrios* in order to distribute their product to those in need.

I don't know what those *vatos* from Cherrieville were thinking or what kind of connections they thought they had, but once the homeboys messed up the *vatos* from Traffic, they must have known that they would be next.

For the moment, we didn't worry about retaliation from either Cherrieville or Traffic since the *juras* patrolled the *barrio*, in force, during the next couple days.

At our Friday meeting, the enforcer explained that the president of Traffic had approached the leadership of *Los* Sharkies and everything had been straightened out, so there was no need for further conflict with their members. It made sense, since all the *vatos* from Traffic were from our *barrio* and everybody knew each other. Besides, they were still struggling to get the car club going and they certainly didn't need us riding their every move. The matter with Cherrieville remained unresolved. We were told to keep *trucha*.

For the next few weeks, I went into the *barrio* every day and hung out with the homeboys. I started spending less time with J-Bird and *Travieso* since all they wanted to do was suck paint fumes. I couldn't handle that stuff. After a while, just being around it gave me a major headache. I found myself enjoying the company of Nite Owl, Fat Joe, *Payaso*, and Black Crow. They seemed more in tune with the mission of *Los* Sharkies and were also more fun to be around.

Early one evening in late July, Nite Owl pulled up to Sharkie Park in his *jefito's ranfla* and yelled, *"Vamonos!"*

Black Crow, *Payaso*, Fat Joe, and I jumped in immediately. No one asked Nite Owl how he got his *jefito's* car. I don't know whether it was just that no one thought to ask or that none of us really cared. The fact was, we were all too young to have a driver's license anyway, and it didn't seem to matter. In the *barrio*, we didn't really care how something happened. We took things at face value. At that moment, we were just happy to be cruising the *barrio* on our own.

It had been several weeks since the incident at the festival in Sharkie Park with Cherrieville, and nothing had come of it. Everything in the *barrio* was calm as the sun descended over the flat dusty hills that separated us from the ocean. A myriad of brightly colored rays shot into the sky. They reflected in brilliant reds and oranges off the clouds and onto the mountains to the north, giving them the beautiful picturesque look of a mural. I enjoyed the view as we cruised past Sharkie Park.

Nite Owl turned his head, half looking into the back seat but directing his comment to Black Crow riding shotgun. "Let's get high, *ese*."

Not them, too! I leaned forward with a frown and said, "I can't stand that stuff. It gives me a headache, Homes."

Nite Owl smiled and said, "We're not talking about paint, *ese*."

Nite Owl carefully opened the glove compartment and withdrew a sandwich size baggie which he handed to Black Crow.

"You'll like *yesca*, Homes," Nite Owl said as his eyes caught mine in the rear view mirror.

Black Crow rolled a large joint and fired it up. He didn't hold it like a regular cigarette, rather pinching it between his thumb and first finger like holding the wings of a bug. Black Crow took a hit then passed it to Nite Owl who filled his lungs with the sweet smoke. It smelled sweet but not the same kind of sweet as the paint fumes. This was sweet and mellow. I immediately liked the smell. Nite Owl took a quick second hit then handed the joint with a red smoldering glow on the tip over his shoulder to me.

"Try it, *ese*," *Payaso* encouraged.

I took the joint between my thumb and first finger, held it to my lips, and inhaled. The warm smoke swept over my tongue and down my throat into my lungs. All of a sudden, a tickle deep inside my chest prompted me to expel the smoke in an uncontrollable burst of coughing and choking. My eyes watered as some of the smoke found its way out through my nose.

The homeboys all laughed.

"Take it easy, *ese*. A little bit at a time," counseled Nite Owl.

As the coughing calmed and I could see again, I passed the joint to Fat Joe. He took a hit then passed the joint to *Payaso* who inhaled a slow stream of smoke as the red glow on the end of the joint burned brightly then dimmed as he moved it away from his mouth. He held the smoke in for a few seconds then gently exhaled.

"Try it again, *ese*," *Payaso* said as he handed the joint back to me.

This time I inhaled slower letting the smoke gradually filter into my lungs. I was surprised that I didn't choke or cough. The smoke felt good.

The joint made several rounds before it had burned down too far to hold. Black Crow grabbed a small clip with alligator-like jaws and transferred the joint from his fingers to the clip. We passed it several more times before the joint was completely gone.

All the while, Nite Owl guided the *ranfla* slowly through *calles* of the *barrio*. Gradually, I felt the *yesca* soaking into every cell in my body. Everything looked smaller. My vision seemed distorted as though I was looking out of a small rectangular hole in an army tank. The world was more colorful than I'd ever seen it and everything was moving past us in slow motion. Even the music of William DeVaugh's "Be Thankful for What You've Got" coincided with the slow even drum rhythm of my heartbeat. I thought to myself, *I'm high!*

After my first high, the next one and every other high became easier and seemed as natural as opening up a *pisto*.

Previously, I had known drugs were prevalent in the *barrio,* but I had no idea how easy they were to get. Most of us youngsters were into *yesca*, or reds, or sniffing paint. We needed something to help pass the time. For me, it was *yesca*. A lot of the *veteranos* were into heroin. They tried to discourage us youngsters from getting caught up, like so many already had, in heroin's deadly web, but the easy money from sales of the drug and the lure of its high was too enticing and overcame the fatherly advice offered up by the *veteranos*.

*   *   *

When I arrived at Dopey's pad, Nite Owl and *Payaso* were already there with Dopey and another homeboy playing poker in the garage. The garage door was open, letting a steady trickle of cigarette smoke escape into the early evening air. I didn't know Dopey that well but I had seen him at the Friday meetings and around the *barrio*. Homeboys called him Dopey because he always had a freshly rolled sock full of paint to inhale.

Homeboys invited me to join the game, so I sat in on the next hand. We usually played nickel ante, straight poker unless *Payaso* was there. He always liked playing with a whole laundry list of wild cards. It was *Payaso's* turn to deal, so naturally Jacks and Jokers were wild. While *Payaso* dealt the hand, my thoughts drifted to the radio sitting on a stubby old wooden dresser in the corner. "The Huggy Boy Show" with Dick Hugg was on and Dick was taking dedications, mostly romantic stuff that you knew no one would ever say face-to-face.

I looked at my cards and realized there was no way I could win this hand unless I got an incredibly lucky return on four discards. No such luck. *Payaso* gave me an equally worthless hand with the next set of cards, so I folded. As I pushed my cards toward *Payaso*, two *veteranos* strolled into the garage. One of them turned and lowered the garage door. I thought it was somewhat coincidental that just as Huggy Boy spun War's "Slipping into Darkness" on his turntable, the closing garage door tuned out the sunlight. I squinted a couple times to force my eyes to adjust.

Homeboy Dopey reached up to pull a string dangling from the light fixture above the card table. The light popped on and, without a word, he stepped outside through a side door.

The two *veteranos* went straight for the old dresser in the corner. One of them shoved the radio aside, reached behind the dresser, and pulled out a neatly rolled blue *bandana*. He set it carefully on top of the dresser and unrolled it revealing a tarnished spoon and what looked like a homemade hypodermic needle. He dug down into the pocket of his Khakis and pulled out a book of matches, along with a rolled up balloon the size of a marble. I was seated facing the dresser, so I could see what he was doing without seeming to be overly curious.

Dopey returned through the same side door with a glass of water in one hand and his ever-present sock saturated with paint fumes in the other hand. He set the glass of water on the dresser for the *veterano* then returned to his chair, glanced at his hand of cards, and, just as though he had never left, tossed a ten cent bet into the kitty.

The *veterano* at the dresser unrolled his balloon and tipped a bit of a brownish colored powder into the bowl of the spoon. He sucked up some water from the glass with the syringe and gently squeezed the water into the spoon letting it mix with the brown powder. I wasn't certain what the brown powder was, but from the care and attention the *veterano* devoted to it, I figured it was heroin. I had never seen any of the homeboys shoot heroin before. Even so, it didn't make me nervous, and I was happy to see that the *veteranos* felt comfortable shooting it around me.

As Nite Owl dealt the next hand, I divided my attention between the cards and the *veterano* who bent one match around and struck it on the outside of the book without breaking it loose. As the match ignited, he carefully turned the book so the entire collection of matches lit up. With his free hand, he gently lifted the spoon over the flame and brought the brown liquid to a boil, then tossed the burning matchbook on the floor and stomped it out with his shoe. He placed a small piece of cotton into the hot liquid and returned the spoon to the dresser top, turning his attention briefly to the hypodermic needle. A quick squirt expelled the excess water, then the *veterano* placed the tip of the needle into the cotton ball saturated with the brown substance. He drew the liquid into the syringe, wrapped the bandana around his upper right arm, and held it tight before letting the sharp point of the needle submerge into a bulging vein in his forearm. Slowly, he pulled back on the handle of the syringe and the brown liquid in the syringe churned with bright red blood before being pushed back into the vein.

Even before all the liquid had disappeared into the *veterano's* vein, I could see the tension in his *cara* suddenly melt. The effect was immediate. He struggled to focus on removing the needle from his arm, then let it drop clumsily on the dresser and leaned back against the wall letting the heroin take control as the other *veterano* repeated the process.

I'll never forget the vacant expression in his eyes. I could see him looking at me but I knew he couldn't see me. It was as though he had stepped through a curtain into another world where nothing of this world mattered.

When the second *veterano* finished, he pushed open the garage door and the two *veteranos* silently departed. Not a word had been spoken the whole time they were there.

I was relieved to have the garage door open again. The sunlight and fresh air felt good. I couldn't imagine why a person had to stick a needle into his body to feel good. It left me somewhat bewildered. I could understand smoking *yesca,* but the idea of shooting heroin scared me. There was something blasphemous about purposely forcing a foreign substance into your veins. I couldn't help thinking that these same *veteranos* would have fought to the death to keep the *juras* from blindfolding them and handcuffing them to a wall, yet a needle full of heroin had done just that. Whoever planted that deadly seed in the *barrio* had some devastatingly destructive intentions and had no compulsions against gambling with a homeboy's soul. I didn't let such thoughts hover in my brain for long. I knew immediately heroin was something that I wanted to avoid at all costs.

Vatos Locos

I couldn't believe the summer of 1974 was fading so quickly. I had become accustomed to my daily trips into the *barrio* to hang out with the homeboys. To me there was summer and then there was the rest of the year. Summer meant freedom to do what I wanted, whenever I wanted, without having to worry about skipping school. I liked summer and easily realized that what I learned in the *barrio* with the homeboys during the summer had far more importance in my life than any education I received sitting behind a desk in a classroom.

The City of Chino, located southeast of Pomona, had a big *barrio* similar to ours that also dated back to the forties. Their *Chicano* youth were just as deep as we were and called themselves *Los* Chino Sinners D Street.

For the sake of pride, both *barrios* were about to go to war.

Ready or not!

Late Sunday afternoon of the first week in August, a car load of homeboys decided to do a *movida* on the *vatos* from D Street. What they and the rest of the homeboys at Sharkie Park didn't know, was that the Chino Sinners were planning a *movida* on us. The homeboys were on their way to Chino and the D Street *vatos* were headed to Pomona.

I was kicking back with about twenty homeboys enjoying some *pisto* at Sharkie Park when we noticed a caravan of six lowriders slowly cruising west on Grand Avenue. *De volada*, we knew these *ranflas* weren't from our *barrio*. Nite Owl glanced at me.

"It's time to walk the walk!" he said, adding, "Stay with me, and stay on your feet!" The two of us ran with the rest of the homeboys to the parked *ranflas* and grabbed crowbars and anything that could help inflict bodily damage, then we waited as the *vatos* from D Street sped toward us. Screeching to a stop in the middle of the *calle*, the Sinners piled out of their *ranflas* with a barrage of verbal insults and profanity. For a brief moment, we faced off like raging bulls before the charge.

In seconds, they were all over us. I didn't have time to think. Nite Owl and I were exchanging blows with a stocky *vato*. He was strong and stubborn, with tattoos covering both arms, and I could feel every crunching blow blast through my defenses. Nite Owl was more effective at blocking this *vato's* blows and delivering some of his own. Next thing I know, a shot from somewhere else slams into the back of my head, and I'm eating dirt. Nite Owl's advice "stay on your feet" echoed through *mi mente* after the ringing stopped. Thinking it was one thing; doing it seemed to be what challenged me at the moment. For a split second, Wicked getting stabbed flashed before me and provided enough motivation for me to get back on my feet.

We were badly outnumbered and it was simply a matter of time. It was blatantly clear that none of us were getting out of there without a severe beating.

BAM!

A shot rang out. Everyone suddenly stopped fighting and looked up. My vision was blurry from a blow to my right eye but I was still able to see homeboy Camel grab his chest where the *bala* penetrated his body but failed to bring him down. I couldn't believe it. He'd been shot, yet he seemed more worried about his *ranfla*. D Street *vatos* were tearing it up pretty bad with their crowbars and chains. Somehow, Camel climbed in the driver's seat and tried to start his *ranfla*.

WHAM!

A crowbar hit his shoulder and glanced off his head. The *vatos* dragged him out onto the pavement where one of them stood staring down at him.

BAM! BAM! BAM!

Three more *balas* pierced his body.

De volada, all of the *vatos* from D Street ran back to their *ranflas* and hightailed it out of our *barrio*. A few moments later, our reinforcements arrived but it was too late.

The beating was our reality. I had learned the hard way that *there's always someone tougher and meaner.*

As I dusted myself off, some homeboys loaded Camel into his *ranfla* and sped up Garey Avenue toward the hospital. I found out later that on the way, they passed a *jura* who did a quick U-turn, hit his red lights, and ordered them to stop. Homeboy driving pulled to the curb and ran back to tell the *jura* that his friend had been shot and he needed to get him to the hospital as fast as possible. The *jura*, who happened to be one of the few Mexican officers on the Pomona force, took one look at Camel and immediately dragged him out on the sidewalk. In a couple minutes, an ambulance arrived and transported Camel to the hospital.

Camel owes his life to that *jura* who gave him CPR on the spot after noticing that, in addition to all the blood he had lost, he had also stopped breathing. It was a strange twist for me, since I had never seen a *jura* willing to help a homeboy. All the ones that I knew were more than willing to beat us down. I wondered if it had anything to do with the fact that the *jura* was Mexican.

While Camel took a trip to the hospital, the homeboys who did the *movida* on Chino were headed back to Pomona empty-handed. The Chino Sinners had been well prepared for their *movida* and had their homeboys laying low in their *barrio*.

As the Chino Sinners raced back to their *barrio*, they zoomed past our homeboys returning from Chino. The Sinners were too wrapped up in their success to notice, but the Sharks noticed them and immediately pulled a U-turn and quietly tailed their six *ranflas* back into their *barrio*.

Our homeboys hung back as the Sinners' caravan pulled onto D Street then turned the corner and stopped in front of a small *cantón*. About thirty *vatos* piled out of the six *ranflas* and were jubilantly greeted by several homeboys who had been laying low in the *cantón*. They all looked like they were ready to celebrate big time with some cold *pisto*.

They didn't know what hit them when our homeboys suddenly rained about a dozen rounds of buckshot on their party leaving five of their homeboys bleeding in the dirt.

When our homeboys returned with the good news, the *veteranos* called an emergency meeting where we were all told what had happened and that homeboy Camel was expected to live. All four of the small caliber *balas* missed his heart. The *veteranos* didn't mention it at the meeting, but I couldn't help thinking how Camel owed his life to that *jura* who pulled him back from death's door.

Camel, who was seventeen, got his name as a result of a car accident when he was younger. His leg was so badly mangled that it had to be amputated just above the knee. Camel learned to walk again on a wooden leg that added a limp to his stroll. Too bad his wooden leg didn't catch the *balas*.

At the meeting, the *veteranos* also passed down the word that the five Sinners who were put down by our homeboys lived as well. During the meeting, the enforcer stood up and called for more *movidas* on the Chino Sinners.

"*Calle Doce Los* Sharkies was disrespected! We need to teach them *vatos* that the Shark has a deadly bite!" he stated.

While I stood there leaning against the wall listening to the enforcer turn up the heat on the Chino Sinners, my eyes moved from one *veterano* to the next. Several of them had shaved their heads. I couldn't believe it, but the more I studied them the more I liked how a clean shaven head gave them a serious *matón* look. I glanced at Nite Owl for his reaction but he was caught up in the fever of the moment. Off to one side, I happened to see *Conejo*. He slowly rubbed his hand through his hair, while he listened to the enforcer, as though he was already planning its removal.

For the next several weeks, homeboys made regular visits to the Macias' pad where those who knew how to cut hair were shaving us down to the scalp. I admired the look and liked the way it felt, not to mention that you could dry your hair after a shower with the single wipe of a towel. It wasn't long before several of the homeboys discovered this new open territory as a fertile ground for tattoos. *Conejo* was the first to put the *Calle Doce* mark "XII" high on his neck behind his right ear. Soon afterwards, a number of others followed suit but added their own twist by tacking the picture of a shark in the same location.

In addition to shaving our heads, *Los* Sharkies were also making regular visits to Chino and the Sinners were retaliating with equal regularity. It was like a pinball machine bouncing *balas* from Pomona to Chino and back. Needless to say, the *calles* were a dangerous place for *cholos* to stroll. Even cruising wasn't that safe.

On one of our *movidas*, Big Jerry, Bad Boy, *Bala, Lobo,* and *Conejo* headed to Chino with bad intentions. As they cruised into enemy territory, they spied a group of Sinners kicking back by some *ranflas* parked in front of an old *cantón* that hadn't seen a new coat of paint in at least a decade. At almost the same time, the Chino Sinners noticed the school of Sharks swiftly swimming toward them. Our homeboys picked up speed and the *vatos* from D Street picked up *cuetes*.

Shots rang out.

Balazos were flying in both directions with several of them slamming into *Conejo's ranfla* as he swerved around the Chino *ranflas*. Several of the Sinners jumped into their *ranflas*. Everyone could smell blood and the chase was on.

Conejo and our homeboys raced away wildly looking for the way out of Chino. One wrong turn soon led to another as two, then three, and four Chino *ranflas* took up the chase.

Before long, homeboys were hopelessly lost in a maze of short *calles* that led nowhere. Feverishly trying to stay one step ahead of their pursuers, *Conejo* swerved down the *calles* blowing through stop signs and stop lights. His lowrider slammed into the pavement, scraping bottom in the dips at each intersection. Sparks flew from the undercarriage as our homeboys hung out the window, clinging to the roof while firing at the oncoming *ranflas*. The Sinners simply fired back and kept coming. Before long, our homeboys ran out of *balas*.

Conejo, wet with sweat and stressed about the seriousness of the situation, slid into a high speed turn onto a small *calle*. Dust flew up from the road as the rear tires squealed around the corner and the rear quarter panel smacked into a sign post knocking it to the ground. The caravan of Chino Sinners took the corner in hot pursuit of our homeboys. Too bad *Conejo* didn't have the chance to read the sign which barely showed above the weeds now because it sealed the fate of our homeboys with the words "Dead End."

In front of the *cantóns* that lined the dead end *calle*, more D Street *vatos* were kicking back. Facing nothing but scraggly trees and wild brush at the end of the *calle*,

Conejo suddenly realized his mistake. He skidded to a stop and tried to back out but the Chino *ranflas* blocked any escape. Our homeboys only chance, now, was to run for it or try to box their way out.

Sadly outnumbered, our homeboys didn't get far. They got a beating that day that they will never forget. Lucky for them the Sinners had also exhausted their supply of *balas* during the chase. Otherwise, the *juras* would have had five homicides to investigate when they arrived ten minutes later. It had to have been the first time these homeboys were glad to see the *juras*. Their joy didn't last long as the Chino *juras* beat them down for extra measure, giving them an additional reason to regret getting caught in Chino.

Conejo and the four homeboys spent three days in jail. When they got out, I ran into them at the Macias' pad. Their faces and bodies were still badly bruised from the barrage of blows they endured. As I looked at them, I couldn't help but think of the song "Right Place, Wrong Time" by Dr. John. The simple fact was that *Conejo* and the others were lucky to be alive and able to tell their story, which they were definitely more than happy to share.

"You're not a *Calle Doce* homeboy," *Conejo* boasted, "until you've received a horse beating and lived to talk about it."

He said it in a joking manner but I could see that deep down he meant every word. *Conejo* was a *vato loco* all the way through. I knew that when death finally caught up with him, he was the kind of *vato* that would smile as he asked the grim reaper, *what took you so long?*

Sangre

By September of 1974, Nixon had already gotten caught with his pants down below his Watergate. Our troops were on their way home from Vietnam, and Camel was out of the hospital, hanging out with the rest of us as if nothing had happened. Except now he had his "war wounds" which he wore like a badge of honor. Camel could have easily bragged about his wounds with all rights due, but he knew the scars spoke for themselves, so he didn't have to boast. The homeboys respected Camel for that and the way he carried himself. So did I. I saw him as more mature from that point forward.

Conejo, Bad Boy, Big Jerry, *Bala*, and *Lobo* recovered from the beating they received from the Chino Sinners but got caught up in trying to even the score. Their attention focused on taking down as many Sinners as possible. They were so obsessed with payback on the Chino Sinners that the homeboys nicknamed them the "Magilla Gorilla Crew" after the popular cartoon series created by William Hanna and Joseph Barbera.

The fall afternoons were still hot, but the cold overcast sky in the morning let you know winter was on its way. Homeboys were letting their hair grow back and in the process, we used a woman's nylon stocking to train our hair to comb neatly back. This let us easily cover it with a blue bandana, low over the eyebrows, barely revealing any earlobes, and with the knot tied low in the back. Those who had gangster hats wore them over the bandanas. Some homeboys had a flair for being different. They wore a rectangular Russian hat made from black fur. Others pierced their right earlobe and sported an earring. I liked the simplicity of a black beanie over my bandana. I didn't need a hat and I certainly wasn't going to wear an earring.

Homeboys Ricky and Tudy, who were both seventeen and best friends from Garey High School, enlisted in the Marines and shipped out to Camp Pendleton in San Diego for Boot Camp. Tudy was third from youngest of six brothers that lived next door to our primary hangout. Eddy, Rudy, and Big Joe were the oldest and were hard core. They were well-respected within our ranks. Tommie and Louie were the youngest. Tudy was in between.

I liked Tudy. Even though his older *carnales* were hard core, Tudy wasn't into the gangbanging. Usually that was enough for me not to have anything to do with someone, but Tudy was different. Something about him told me he had potential and if afforded the opportunity he could make something of himself. I wondered if the Marines might provide Tudy that opportunity.

It wasn't often that I allowed these kinds of thoughts to surface and I certainly didn't speak about them to anyone else. I knew from experience that this line of thinking was a sure path to trouble, so I quietly thought about Tudy with equal parts of respect and envy. I suspected that I wasn't the only one who viewed Tudy in this light.

In October, my *carnal* enlisted in the Marines. For some of the homeboys, the Marines had the only jobs they could get. The pay was good and the picture of a homeboy in his crisp dress blues hanging on the wall in the living room brought a lot of respect to the *casa* as well as the *barrio*.

Marine life was nothing new for homeboys. We were natural soldiers. We had our own version of basic training in the *barrio*. Fighting was second nature and we certainly were not afraid to pull the trigger. The Marines simply taught us to do it better. Throw a rifle in our hands, put a uniform on our backs, dish up three squares, and give us a ticket to see the world; who wouldn't join the Marines?

Soon Christmas was just a few weeks away and celebration was already in the air when Ricky and Tudy came home after graduating from boot camp. Their *familia* and all the homeboys had prepared a big welcome-home party for them.

I went to Nite Owl's *cantón* around noon the day of the party and from there the two of us strolled to Tudy's pad a few blocks away. When we arrived, the delicious aroma of *carne asada* filled the air. Several homeboys attended the grills while others were busy setting up kegs of *pisto* out back. Nite Owl and I filled our cups from a freshly tapped keg.

Ricky and Tudy weren't there yet. Tudy's *familia* drove down to San Diego for the graduation. They were expected back at any minute.

I turned around at the sound of a horn honking repeatedly and saw their *ranfla* pulling into the driveway. Everyone gathered out front to meet them. Ricky, tall and slim and crisply decked out in his Marine uniform, stepped out first and was immediately deluged with kisses and hugs from homegirls and homeboys alike. When Tudy, a stocky figure and also in uniform, climbed out a moment later, he was greeted with a similar flood of affection. Ricky and Tudy looked as happy to see us as we were to see them. After a while, everyone filled their plates and cups then settled down for a relaxing afternoon of *comida* and *pisto*.

Homeboys were still coming and going from Tudy's pad as evening rolled in and darkness overtook our *barrio*. The *pisto* continued to flow and the fragrant smell of *yesca* filled the air. Homeboys were in a relaxed state of mind and buzzing from *pisto* or *yesca* or both. Ricky and Tudy had shed their Marine uniforms and, except for their military haircuts, looked like homeboys again in their khaki's and Pendletons.

Glad to be home and eager to take a cruise around the *barrio*, Ricky joined Tudy's *carnal* Rudy and two homegirls, Rose and Sonia, for a quick run to the liquor store to restock our waning supply of *pisto*. As they pulled away from the curb, suddenly the car jerked to a stop and Ricky leaned out the window and yelled for Tudy, who had just stepped out of the *cantón*, to join them. Tudy hopped in the *ranfla* and they were off.

Towne Shoppe Liquors, known by the homeboys, as the Twelfth Street Liquor Store because of its location at the corner of Twelfth and Garey, had a large wall exposed to Twelfth Street. It was understood that this wall was off-limits to *placasos,* since the liquor store was operated by *gente* from the *barrio* and we were some of their best customers.

Tudy, and everyone else in the *ranfla* for that matter, were pretty wasted, so they didn't notice a carload of Chino Sinners scoping them out as they entered the small parking lot in front of the liquor store. Meanwhile, the Chino Sinners maneuvered themselves into the dark alley behind the store where they could watch as both Ricky and Tudy got out of the ranfla. While Ricky strolled inside to buy more *pisto*, Tudy stumbled around the corner into the darkness of the alley to take a leak.

De volada, opportunity fell into the hands of the Sinners. Quietly, but with stealth and purpose in mind, they approached with crowbars and easily surrounded Tudy as he leaned forward against the brick wall to take a leak.

"De dónde *eres?"* the Sinners queried rhetorically. They knew the answer but were simply adhering to protocol for the sake of honor.

"United States Marines Corps, oohraaa!" Tudy responded in traditional Marine fashion.

The Chino Sinners didn't pursue further discussion.

WHAM!

The first blow hit Tudy on the back of his head and dropped him to his knees. He tried to shield himself from the blows that followed but his arms snapped like twigs against the relentless onslaught of heavy metal and Tudy went down.

Luckily, several homegirls passing the alley on the sidewalk noticed someone getting beat down in the shadows. They ran to report it to Ricky who was loading the *pisto* in the *ranfla*. He set the *pisto* down and decided to check it out, but because of the *pisto* fogging his thinking, he didn't really snap to what was going down. As Ricky made his way to the alley, Rudy tried to climb out of the back seat but Sonia and Rose convinced him that he was too wasted and wisely kept him in place.

As Ricky stepped into the alley, the Sinners were ready for him, too.

WHAM!

A crowbar smashed him across the *cara* and down he went. Two *vatos* lifted him to his knees and shoved the barrel of a *cuete* against the side of his nose and forced him to watch as they continued beating Tudy.

"Sabes que?" growled the *vato* holding Ricky. "Take a good look, *ese, porque* this is what we are going to do to all of you. *Somos* Chino Sinners, the Big D Street Gang. *Y-que?"*

"Sí mon! Give this wila to all your homeboys," exclaimed another Sinner.

Then the other *vato* hammered Ricky with the butt of the *cuete* sending him to the ground. The Sinners from D Street scurried back to their *ranfla*. Sonia and Rose watched with puzzled expressions from the front seat of Ricky's *ranfla*, as a mysterious *ranfla* sped past down the dark alley.

Ricky, still in the alley, faded in and out of consciousness. Blood dripping down his *cara* obscured his vision and pain overwhelmed his every move as he struggled to crawl closer to Tudy. As Ricky touched Tudy's mangled head and felt the pool of blood surrounding his lifeless body, he suddenly realized the gravity of the situation. Mustering all the strength he had left, Ricky rose to his feet and stumbled along the brick wall to the sidewalk.

"Tudy's dead!" he cried to his friends in the *ranfla*, his voice barely audible but sufficient to rally Rose, Sonia, Tudy's *carnal,* and the three homegirls to his aid. Ricky collapsed in Sonia's arms as the others rushed to Tudy's side.

"My God! Tudy! No! Please, no! My God! Don't let Tudy die!" Rose cried as she crumbled by his side, cradling his head in her lap, but the black angel of death hovering overhead blocked her trembling plea from reaching Heaven.

Rudy tried futilely to pick his *carnal* up, but the fog in his head and Tudy's dead weight were too much for him. Ricky was too severely injured to help, and the homegirls, frozen with shock in the midst of the darkness, could only watch in horror.

Suddenly, Rose jumped to her feet and started running fast and hard up the alley and down the *calle*. She ran like she had never run before. She ran till her lungs screamed for air. She covered three blocks down 12th Street, and all the way back to Tudy's pad where the party was still going strong, as fast as her feet would carry her.

Homeboys were kicking back everywhere. I was relaxing on Tudy's front porch with Nite Owl, Fat Joe, some of the *veteranos,* and *Payaso* who was joking about all the scars on one homeboy's head. "Somebody Please" by The Vanguards was playing on the radio in one of the *ranflas*, when I heard a girl's voice screaming but I couldn't make out what she was saying. I didn't know it was Rose.

All of a sudden, the homeboys in the front yard started running toward the screams. Then like the waves building before a tidal flood, homeboys poured out from everywhere, all running in the same direction. All of us on the porch followed suit. If there was a fight, we didn't want to be the last ones there. Halfway down the *calle*, I saw Rose. Tears streamed down her *cara* as she struggled for breath.

"I think he's dead," she cried, her voice trembling with fear.

Then behind me, I heard it again.

"Tudy's dead!"

The words traveled like fire across dry brush in an abandoned field. The idea that Tudy could be dead struck me dumb. *Tudy was a Marine. He went to get some pisto. How could he be dead?* I didn't want to believe it. No one did. Even so, we kept running, running without knowing where we were going.

A *ranfla* raced past as we ran down the *calle*.

Then someone screamed, "The Chino Sinners killed Tudy!"

As I neared the liquor store, I saw five *ranflas* loaded with *veteranos* speed out of the *barrio*. I didn't have to ask to know where they were headed and what they had in mind. Homeboys were everywhere and there was a general state of confusion. Sonia, lost in tears, tried to comfort Ricky who was barely clinging to consciousness. I followed the trail of homeboy's blood that led back into the darkness of the alley. Suddenly, I saw for myself. It was true. Tudy was dead!

I couldn't believe what I saw. Tudy's beaten and battered body lay in a mangled motionless mess on the cold pavement surrounded by a glistening pool of crimson liquid. *Mi mente* swelled with rage as I wandered in circles of disbelief.

Homeboys, who were just arriving, pushed their way into the alley. Others attempted to clear the area but it was impossible. Everybody wanted to see what the Chino Sinners had done. Still others tried to help Ricky but no one really knew what to do.

In moments, Rose returned with Tudy's parents. The mass of bodies parted as Tudy's *jefitos* hurried to their son's side.

"Ah, nooooo! Mi hijo! Porqué mi hijo!" the anguished cries of a heart-broken *jefita* rose above the tumultuous gathering. The sound of approaching sirens intervened. For the first time ever, they seemed like a welcomed source of solace.

The crowd stepped back as a police cruiser screeched to a stop at the entrance to the alley. Other sirens followed, bringing more *juras* and an ambulance. One of the *juras* tried to secure the crime scene but his efforts seemed fruitless. Another *jura* quickly checked Tudy and directed the medics from the ambulance to help Ricky. They immediately carted Ricky off to the Pomona Valley Community Hospital.

Later that night as I listened to the radio alone in my room, Timmy Thomas's tune "Why Can't We Live Together" broke through the confusion that shrouded my brain. I knew that this was a day I would never forget. What had started out as a joyous day, ended in tragedy and sorrow.

Tudy's body was so mangled that his casket, draped with an American flag and topped by his Marine Corps photo, remained closed during his wake attended by hundreds of *gente*. The next day was equally sad as we buried our beloved homeboy while the United States Marine Corps honored him with a twenty-one gun salute followed by the mournful sound of "Taps" blown by a lone bugler.

After most of the *gente* had departed, the homeboys, all wearing *Los Sharkies Calle Doce* sweatshirts, each paid their last respects to Tudy. His oldest *carnal* removed his sweatshirt and placed it on the casket so the Shark would be the last thing we saw as Tudy descended into the ground and our hearts sunk to the bottom of the sea.

Tudy's loss hit the *barrio* hard. Although he wasn't an official member of *Los Sharkies*, he was one of ours just the same, and the Chino Sinners would have to pay dearly for this offense.

Unfortunately, the five *ranflas* full of *veteranos* that went to Chino the night Tudy was killed came home empty handed. The Sinners had their act together and were ready for our retaliation, so they were laying low.

News that surfaced in the days after Tudy's death revealed that a few of our homeboys did a *movida* on D Street and shot one of the Sinners a few hours before Tudy was killed. In their excitement, they left the rest of us hanging out by not informing everyone of what had happened, and Tudy paid the price.

Now it was the Sinners' turn to pay. Full scale war was declared on the D Street *vatos*. The enforcer announced that every one of us had "a mission of death on D Street." Homeboys quit meeting in the old church and developed a strategy for war under a cloak of secrecy at Big Speedy's *cantón*. Big Speedy, one of the older *veteranos*, was hard core and looked the part with long black hair tied in back and tattoos that were older than me.

I had heard that he had connections to *La Qlica*, which is the Chicano version of the Mafia.

La Qlica, the ultimate gang, resided within the walls of *las pintas* throughout the state and recruited *soldados* from the thousands of *sureños* that populated the *Chicano* gangs of Southern *Califas*. They were tough and didn't let anyone disrespect them. The more homeboys the *juras* packed in prison, the stronger *La Qlica* became.

Only *vatos* who had earned the trust of the *veteranos* were invited to attend the secret meetings. That left most of us youngsters out. We were filled in as word was passed down. Even so, we were never privy to any discussions when it came to murder. Nite Owl had told me one time that before we could appear on the invitation list we had to earn the trust of the *veteranos* by showing that we understood when to keep our mouths shut. I knew that this was one of those times.

The *veteranos* circulated a warning that we needed to let everyone know when a *movida* was coming down so we could be extra *trucha*. They were obviously upset that the youngsters who hit Chino kept quiet about it and a homeboy was killed, but there wasn't much they could do now.

One decision that was handed down, which we eagerly welcomed, was the adoption of the James Brown tune "The Payback" as our battle anthem. Along with it came the decree that it was now open season on the Sinners, and our homeboys should begin hitting them as frequently as possible.

The *juras* quickly figured out that Pomona and Chino were at war, but they weren't in much of a position to intervene. I'm not sure they wanted to do anything about it anyway. Casualties mounted on both sides and the *juras* were making lots of arrests. From their point of view, business was good. One less *cholo* was one less *cholo* they had to deal with. In any case, detectives, attorneys, judges, politicians, and others affiliated with the prison industry were all scoring points because of our war; *why should they stop it?*

*   *   *

Three months later on a cool weekday evening in the spring of 1975, four of our homeboys loaded their revenge into an old pickup truck and headed for Chino. There had been a brief lull in the violence and both sides had relaxed a bit.

Homeboys kept a low profile as they cruised into enemy territory. Before long, they spied four *vatos* in a lowrider cruising the *calle*. Surprise was critical to the success of their mission, so the two homeboys in the truck bed slumped down with their shotguns ready to sing, while the homeboy on the passenger side slid down in his seat, his *cuete* poised just below the window. In the rearview mirror of the Sinners' lowrider, the truck must have appeared quite benign with only the driver visible.

The Sharks cautiously closed the distance to their prey as they approached an intersection. Suddenly, the signal changed and the lowrider paused for a red light. Opportunity was at hand and the Sharks could smell blood.

Homeboy driving the pickup truck quickly pulled into position beside and slightly ahead of the lowrider. He glanced down at the Sinner behind the wheel who slowly turned his head. As if in slow motion, the driver's eyes drifted up to meet the stare of our homeboy and, for a moment, their eyes locked. The Sinner watched as a sinister smile moved into place on our homeboy's *cara* and the Sinner turned in shock to warn the others but by then it was too late. When he and the others in the lowrider turned back around, they gazed directly into the steely jaws of the Shark.

The two homeboys in the truck bed popped up and yelled, "*Calle Doce!*" then blasted D Street Sinners repeatedly with both shotguns.

Buckshot splintered the driver's *cara* and penetrated the two *vatos* in the back seat. One was hit in the chest and the other in the stomach. Then, adding death to injury, the homeboy riding shotgun hung out the window and unloaded his *cuete* into the windshield.

In seconds, the deed was done. Our homeboys cruised calmly back to Pomona where they stashed the *cuetes* and hid the truck in a homeboy's garage.

The next day, headlines splashed across the front page of Pomona's Progress Bulletin reported, "Street Shooting in Valley Leaves One Dead, Two Injured."

Pride surged through our ranks when we received word that a Sinner was dead as a result of the *movida*. His *carnal*, one of the two *vatos* in the back seat, had been severely wounded. All in all, the homeboys of *Calle Doce* had paid back the Chino Sinners big time.

During the funeral service for the D Street *vato* that had been kissed in the *cara* by the Shark, some of our homeboys took another outing. They did a drive-by, catching a crowd of *vatos* outside Our Lady of Guadalupe Church at Third and D Street in Chino. They left a *chica* and one of the homeboys wounded in their wake, adding fuel to the hatred that raged between the Sinners and *Calle Doce*.

The Holy Cross Cemetery, where the *vato* was being laid to rest, was situated in Pomona, just East of Garey Avenue on Lexington, a couple blocks from Garey High School. Word was out for homeboys to be extra *trucha*, since the *vato's familia* and homeboys from Chino would be in the area and might try to pull a *movida* on us at school. Rumors also floated that the *veteranos* might do a *movida* at the funeral.

Before lunch, J-Bird, *Travieso, Payaso,* Fat Joe, and I skipped out of class and strolled toward the cemetery with a mixture of curiosity and the idea that we'd add our own touch of intimidation. As we strolled down Lexington and neared the ten-foot chain-link fence that surrounded the cemetery, we boasted to ourselves, "*Sí mon,* Homes. We'll show them who's bad!"

There must have been nearly five hundred *gente* standing around the gravesite. I couldn't count the number of *ranflas* lining the *calles*.

Suddenly, Fat Joe yelled, "*Calle Doce, y-que!*"

Then *Payaso*, J-Bird, and *Travieso* followed with "Big Twelfth Street Gang!"

Moreover, without thinking, I heard myself shout, "*Sí mon.* We did it! *Calle Doce!* We did it!"

J-Bird, *Travieso, Payaso,* and Fat Joe all spun their heads around and looked at me as though I was crazy. Then, everyone at the funeral turned and looked at us. For a moment, there was complete silence then the crowd started moving—slowly at first, then picking up speed. I couldn't believe it! Every last one of them, men, children, old ladies, were all running toward us, and they didn't look too happy.

All at once, we took flight like roaches shocked by the kitchen light. I could hear Credence Clear Water Revival's "Run Through the Jungle" as adrenaline suddenly surged through my veins and my feet pounded a quick retreat. In that moment, I understood what J.C. Fogerty meant with those lyrics. We ran and didn't look back. We didn't need to. We could hear the shouts and screams of the angry mob hot on our tails.

Luckily, the chain-link fence gave us a little head start.

We scurried for the cover of some *cantóns* across Towne Avenue. Fat Joe, puffing for air, was falling behind.

"Run, Homes! If we die because you can't run fast enough, *ese*, I'm going to kill you!" *Payaso* yelled jokingly to help motivate Fat Joe.

"I'm running," Fat Joe managed in between gasps for air, "as fast as I can, Homes!"

I ran behind Fat Joe and tried to push him along as I shouted, "Run, Homes! Run! They're coming!"

I was dead serious. A quick glance over my shoulder revealed that several of them had already scaled the fence and were charging toward their *ranflas*.

"I'm too young to die!" *Payaso* yelled, continuing his levity as he raced ahead running backwards as if to taunt Fat Joe who was soaked in sweat and nearly exhausted. The smile broke from *Payaso's cara* and his expression suddenly sank as he saw a *ranfla* spin around the corner at the end of the block. Just in time, we quickly ducked behind a row of bushes between two *cantóns*. As we huddled there, only the sound of the *ranfla* whizzing past interrupted our panting for breath. Tires screeched at the other end of the block and for a moment, the coast was clear.

"Come on. That garage door is open," *Payaso* whispered as he pointed behind the adjacent *cantón*.

We hurried through an open gate in the fence and made it safely to the small one-car garage. I pushed the rickety door closed after Fat Joe tripped across the threshold. He picked himself up and leaned into some rusty tools stacked against the wall, sucking air like a vacuum cleaner as he relished the opportunity to rest.

After catching my breath, I noticed that the sound of tires squealing had faded and it had grown quiet outside.

"Stay here, I'm going out to the front to see if it's clear," I told *Payaso*, J-Bird, and *Travieso*.

Fat Joe was still sucking air. I couldn't tell if he heard me or not. I, for one, couldn't believe how this thing had mushroomed way out of our control.

I eased the door open and crawled across the backyard on my belly till I reached the gate that led to the front then cautiously stepped out toward the *calle* to see what I could see. I about soiled my pants when *Payaso* bumped my arm.

"What are you doing?" I whispered. "I thought I told you to stay put!"

"*Chale, ese.* I don't wanna die in some old garage, Homes!" *Payaso* retorted.

Just then, we heard tires screech at the corner. There was no time to make it back to the garage. I shoved *Payaso* in the bushes and dove in after him. We both hugged the dirt like a friendly *ruca*. My heart felt like it was pumping at about a thousand beats per second.

ZOOM! ZOOM! ZOOM! ZOOM! ZOOM! ZOOM!

I counted six *ranflas*. As soon as they passed, *Payaso* and I hightailed it back to the safety of the garage. Fat Joe, breathing easier and comfortably seated on a small wooden crate, looked up.

"They're everywhere, man!" I blurted out.

My words were interrupted by more tires skidding and screeching. Then, shots rang out. Sirens quickly followed the gunfire. We didn't know what was going on out there, but it sounded like everything had broken loose.

When things finally quieted down again, we glanced silently at each other then at the door. *Payaso* and I shared a sigh of resignation as we found something to sit on.

Fat Joe pops out, "Whose stupid idea was this?"

"Shut up, *ese*. Nobody told you to yell '*Calle Doce!*'" *Payaso* quipped.

"You yelled out, too!" Fat Joe shot back then looked at me. "'We did it!' Are you crazy?" His voice was full of serious concern.

"Forget them *vatos*, Homes," I said. "They're lucky I didn't have a *cuete*."

"They're lucky! Fat Joe's the lucky one. If I had a *cuete* I would've shot him for slowing us down," J-Bird added, making us all laugh, except Fat Joe who didn't see the humor in it and just shook his head back and forth as if we were all nuts.

It was early evening when we emerged from the garage and cautiously navigated through alleyways back toward the school. With ears tuned to every sound and eyes open wide for suspicious *ranflas*, we then made our way to the Macias' pad where a bunch of the homeboys had gathered.

Nite Owl pulled up while we were downing some *pisto* to settle our still frazzled nerves. He grabbed a *pisto* and reported that one of our homeboys got busted by the *juras* for shooting at a Chino *ranfla*. The *juras*, who were already in the area because of the funeral, witnessed the shooting and busted the homeboy on the spot, carting him off to Juvenile Hall. We simply listened with interest and otherwise kept quiet about our involvement in the events of the day. We brushed it off when Nite Owl asked about the scratches on our arms.

The next morning a news article in the Progress Bulletin reported that our homeboy's pistol jammed after firing three shots at the *ranfla* on its way back to Chino. That's probably the only reason the *juras* got him. The *vatos* from Chino were lucky. If not for their good fortune, they might have had to schedule another funeral.

Inside I was relieved that we had survived with only a few scratches and couldn't help laughing to myself about how fast Fat Joe had run. *It's amazing what you can do when your life depends on it.*

The *vatos* who killed Tudy were never caught, but neither was our homeboy that did the drive-by outside the church. However, soon after the death of the Chino Sinner, the *juras* located the pickup truck. They were able to lift prints and found enough evidence to file charges. They arrested and convicted two of our homeboys.

All four homeboys who piled into the pickup truck that afternoon to avenge Tudy found respect from *Los* Sharkies. Even though two of them now faced life in *la pinta*, it was as though they were prisoners of war doing hard time for the *barrio*. Just as Tudy's Marine photo now hung in a sacred place on the wall of his parent's living room, draped by the same American flag that covered his coffin, these *vatos* had earned a place of honor in our hearts.

9

Rucas

My first year at Garey High School closely resembled my first year at Simons Junior High, except now, as a tenth grader, I had plenty of friends. While a number of the homeboys who were ninth graders when I was in seventh grade had dropped out of school last year, those that remained were now in the twelfth grade. Homeboys *Conejo*, Big Jerry, and some of the others that I admired were trying to stick it out long enough to graduate. Bad Boy, one of the ones that had dropped out, had joined the Marines and was in boot camp. My *carnal,* having graduated from boot camp, was now stationed at an American base in Okinawa, Japan.

The year was 1975 and the Pomona Unified School District merged ninth grade into the high schools causing Fremont and Simons to feed a couple of hundred fourteen to sixteen year old *vatos*, all claiming gang affiliation, into Garey High School. We were hard to ignore. There were just too many of us, and one way or the other everyone had to decide on which side of the line they wanted to stroll.

To me it was like a bulls-eye. There was the outer ring of those who liked the *cholo* look, the inner ring of wannabe *vatos*, and the bulls-eye of true *vatos locos*. I wanted to be in the bulls-eye. That meant that the wedge between myself and homeboys like *Wesos* and Wicked, who had involved themselves in programs such as MEChA rather than joining a gang, was growing larger. We both wanted respect but I wasn't willing to waste time marching and protesting until somebody decided to give it to us.

Gordo, the *vato* that had seemed to enjoy making trouble for me in the ninth grade, kept his distance from me and the other homeboys who were into gang-banging. He quit faking his walk and stopped trying to act tough, so I left him alone. Somehow, he had figured out where he stood. He settled into the outer ring and simply dealt with the pressure from some of the other homeboys who couldn't stand him and wanted to make sure he knew it.

Garey High School was constructed in the new campus style, similar to most universities, with several buildings connected by a maze of sidewalks. In the central area, there was a section of sidewalk that we called "the rail," since it had a metal railing that served us in the same manner as "the wall" we had marked out for ourselves at Simons Junior High. It was just the right height to lean against and a brick wall covered our backs. Everyone passed by it moving from one class to another during breaks. Our homeboys had staked out this territory in the sixties, and everyone knew that this spot belonged exclusively to Twelfth Street. No exceptions. Period.

A lot of *mayates* attended Garey, but only a handful of them were Crips and they knew well enough to leave us alone. The *gavachos* did their own thing and stayed out of our way as well. We didn't tolerate disrespect from anyone, not even from the principal, a rough dude who always had a Pomona police officer escort as he moved around the campus.

While promotion to Garey brought together many of the homeboys from Twelfth Street, as luck would have it, it also brought a *vato* named Robert and his two *carnales* from Cherrieville into our territory. Although Robert tried his best to deny his roots, it didn't matter to us. His *jefito* bought a *cantón* located right behind Garey High. Whether driven by fear or wisdom, Robert's two *carnales* kept a low profile and mostly stayed in Cherrieville. That was definitely a good move on their part since the homeboys wanted to see them dead.

Homeboys had nothing on Robert other than the fact that he was from Cherrieville, but in those days that was enough. During the first few days of school, Robert tried his best to avoid confrontations, but that proved increasingly more difficult as there were just too many homeboys strolling the campus. By the end of the first week, he was getting his butt kicked every day. For a few days he stayed away from school, and we thought we'd seen the last of him but we were wrong; he came back for more. Robert had a pair of *huevos*. Even though homeboys respected his persistence, we weren't about to leave him alone. The blood between Twelfth Street and Cherrieville had run bad for too long.

One day, several homeboys caught Robert in the hallway before fifth period and beat him down so hard that the school sent him home. Later that night, a few of the homeboys rounded up some *cuetes* and hit Robert's *cantón*, catching his *familia* in the back yard. The timing was perfect since his two *carnales* happened to be there and they both got shot. A few days later in an effort to reinforce our *wila*, some homeboys shot up the *cantón* again and continued to hit it every chance they got. While Robert and his *jefito* held out as long as they could, eventually the *movidas* took their toll. Finally, Robert's *jefito* sold the *cantón* and moved to a safer location.

It may seem that homeboys took extreme measures to communicate their dissatisfaction with Robert's *familia*. The fact was that most of our after-school hangouts were in close proximity to Garey High School. All Robert and his *carnales* would have had to do was pick up the phone and let the *vatos* in Cherrieville know where we were, and we would be ripe for the picking. That was entirely unacceptable, so homeboys simply took care of the situation.

Life at Garey wasn't that different from Simons, except that once again we were the youngsters. But I did find the classes more interesting. I really enjoyed woodshop, art, drafting, and history, especially when someone mentioned *Chicanos*, which wasn't that often, but made my ears perk up. I loved hearing about Pancho Villa, Emiliano Zapata, Antonio Lopez de Santa Ana, and Cesár Chavez who was still alive and busy organizing the migrant farm workers.

The *Chicano* movement and stories of the American Indians intrigued me, while discussions of the American Revolution and the European influence on the American culture didn't seem to relate to me at all, not to mention the fact that the history books didn't exactly give us the truth. When it came to who discovered America, it sure wasn't the *gavachos*. The whole idea of discovering land already inhabited by an entire race of people seemed comical at best. How many people know that the Taino Indians inhabited many of the Caribbean islands when Christopher Columbus washed up on a beach in the

New World? And to top it off, *Califas* was once part of Mexico. The Mexicans never crossed the border. *The gavachos moved the line!* I wasn't at all interested in the white man's version of history which was all twisted up with lies.

For the most part, school was a place for homeboys to hang out between parties and kicking back in the *barrio*. Sometimes *rucas* from surrounding *barrios* would cruise by to party with us.

One day, I was kicking back in front of the school with about thirty homeboys during lunch period when two lowriders packed with *rucas* caravanned to a stop in front of us. Several of us strolled up to check them out.

"*De* dónde *eres?*" inquired Li'l Capone.

"*Onta Sur,*" the driver responded.

"Let's party," suggested a choice *ruca* beaming a coy smile from the back seat.

They mentioned that they had a keg at a homegirl's *cantón* in neutral territory. That's all we needed to hear. We had no beef with South Ontario. *De volada*, we packed into four *ranflas* and caravanned to their *cantón*.

As we strolled into the *cantón*, I knew we had made a good choice as we were greeted by the sounds of Redbone's "Come and Get Your Love," and immediately surrounded by some fine-looking *rucas*. This merely confirmed my belief that *Chicanas* are definitely the finest women on God's green earth.

The sweet smell of perfume, blended with the aroma of cold *pisto,* produced an intoxicating effect. Homeboy Black Crow stepped out in the middle of the living room where he started doing his own original dance and offered a *grito* with some original lyrics, "Shaa-ah, the big Twelfth Street Gang, *rifamous!*"

The *rucas* were mesmerized. That was all it took. We each hooked up with a *ruca* and formed two lines, homeboys on one side and *rucas* on the other; then we danced in pairs through the gauntlet. My *ruca* de jour had warm, hypnotic eyes and beautiful, shoulder-length hair. We danced and drank and danced for hours.

Time had stopped and Heaven was at hand when all of a sudden, the front door opened and ten *vatos* strolled in. They were all *cholo'd* down and appeared to be our age. *De volada*, we knew these *vatos* were gang-bangers, *tambien*, and *pleito* was inevitable. It was just a matter of time. Several *rucas* rushed up to them and tried to convince them to leave, but these *vatos* weren't going anywhere. We knew it and they knew it. The *vatos* all settled in near the door which made us uncomfortable since we didn't know if they were packing. Should anything come down, they were the ones that could easily escape out the front door.

We continued dancing for a while but our hearts weren't into it. I overheard Li'l Capone whisper to Nite Owl that we should go stand by the door so we can box them in if they started anything.

"*Vamonos,*" Nite Owl said.

Li'l Capone took the lead. Nite Owl, me, and Fat Joe followed. Adrenaline surged through my veins. Even so, I tried to maintain my cool as we passed in front of them on our way to the door. Li'l Capone mad-dogged one of the *vatos* and got an immediate mad dog in return.

"*Pomona Calle Doce Los* Sharkies, *y-que!*" barks Li'l Capone.

The whole bunch of them jumped to their feet. One of the *vatos* barked back, "*Onta Los* Earth Angels *Sur, y-que!*"

That was it! Li'l Capone was all over that *vato*.

"My pad, you guys! My pad!" a *ruca* shouted.

Another *ruca* screamed then all the wheels came off. I started exchanging blows with a *vato* that was about my size. He had a powerful right hook but couldn't block at all, allowing me to connect with some good combinations.

Behind me, I heard one of the *rucas* crying, "Dammit! I knew it, man! I knew they were going to start something!"

Li'l Capone was holding his own until one of their *vatos* slammed into Black Crow, knocking him into Li'l Capone and sending both Li'l Capone and the mouthy *vato* through the large plate glass window into the front yard. Several of their *vatos* jumped through the broken window to help.

I must admit *Los* Earth Angels were standing their ground, but they were sadly outnumbered and it wasn't long before they realized they were getting a royal butt-kicking.

The *rucas* tried to help them. One *ruca* ran out the door and yelled, "The *juras!* Someone called the *juras*, they're on their way!"

Just as quickly as it all started, the *pleito* stopped. The *rucas* helped their homeboys escape, and at that point, any thought of a love connection with these *rucas* was out of the question, so we piled back into our *ranflas* and headed back to our *barrio*, tripping the entire way on how Li'l Capone had crashed through the window. Homeboy still had shards of glass embedded in his head and arms. The rest of us brandished bruised knuckles, swollen eyes, and busted lips. All in all, it was a good party.

*   *   *

Once again the school year revolved around to summer, my favorite time. Homeboys shaved their heads again and the *veteranos* called a meeting at Sharkie Park to plan another Sunday festival. Homeboys turned out in numbers, but the *juras* and the heroin had taken their toll and the numbers weren't as large as years past. Our president was doing time in *la pinta,* so the vice president was now calling the shots. We gathered behind the pyramids in Sharkie Park and talked over all the plans for the festival, which came off without a hitch. Again, I watched the boxing matches, and everyone had a great time without any *pleito*.

Lobo, one of the older homeboys, had a younger brother everyone called Li'l *Lobo*. He and a few homeboys journeyed over to the Jack in the Box on Garey and Holt Avenues for a bite after the festival. As they were ordering, a *vato* and a *ruca* strolled through the door. Li'l *Lobo* immediately recognized the smell of a juicy red cherry from Cherrieville and mad-dogged the *vato* but got no response. Not one to be ignored, Li'l *Lobo* confronted the *vato*.

"*De* dónde *eres?"* he commanded.

Li'l *Lobo* wanted to see if the *vato* had the *huevos* to back up his *barrio* or whether he would rank out. Sure enough, the *vato* ranked out. Trying to ignore the homeboys, the *vato* stepped up to the counter and placed his order.

Li'l *Lobo* decided to let the issue drop for the moment but caught up with the spineless *vato* outside as he and the *ruca* returned to their *ranfla*. The *vato* noticed Li'l *Lobo's* hand moving toward the handle of his *cuete* hanging over the edge of his Khakis. Without hesitation, the *vato* reached behind his back and drew his own *cuete* and fired. Li'l *Lobo*, a look of surprise on his *cara*, grabbed his stomach and collapsed face first to the pavement where homeboy's soul quietly departed.

Homeboys stayed with Li'l *Lobo's* lifeless body as long as they could before the *juras* arrived then hurried back to Sharkie Park to report the tragedy. After a few days, things cooled down. Several homeboys loaded into two *ranflas* and headed into Cherrieville where they shot two of their homeboys. A third *vato* tried to run but homeboys caught up with him and beat him down, then stabbed him with their *fileros* several times before leaving his bloody body squirming in the *calle*. To top it off, they hurried back to their *ranflas* and each one, in turn, ran over the *vato* before returning to the *barrio*.

The next day, the newspapers confirmed our first "road kill" and reported that the *vato* who shot Li'l *Lobo* got busted along with the *ruca* within a mile of the scene the same night Li'l *Lobo* died. While we were pleased that we had avenged Li'l *Lobo*, it still meant that we had to drape another casket with a Sharkie sweat shirt. Li'l *Lobo's* death simply fueled the anger I felt for the *vatos* from Cherrieville. I itched for a chance to extract my own pound of flesh, but that would have to wait.

As a result of the continuing violence, the Pomona Police Department started putting more Mexican-American officers in our *barrio*. While most of them took their jobs seriously and acted professionally, a few were guided by the desire to impress their *gavacho* peers by being overly physical with us. We had a name for them, "coconuts." Their skin was brown but their heart was as *gavacho* as the creamy white milk hiding inside a coconut's hard brown shell. Homeboys quickly tired of their disrespect.

This was especially true one warm afternoon when homeboys were kicking back at Fish's *cantón* on Grand Avenue. Homeboys had been coming and going all day, and by early evening, it was time for another run to Twelfth Street Liquors for some more *pisto*. Nite Owl made the rounds collecting *feria*. Rudy, Snoopy, and three other homeboys decided to make the run in Snoopy's white '67 Impala.

Usually it took only about twenty minutes to cruise to the liquor store, load up, and return, but it was going on a half-hour and some of the homeboys were wondering what was going on, so Nite Owl, Black Crow, and I decide to step out front. As we strolled out to the edge of the sidewalk, we couldn't see anything so we continued into the *calle*. In the distance, we could see Snoopy's *ranfla* hitting the dips on Park Avenue as it cruised low and slow toward us. As they drew closer, I could even hear the rhythm of "Fencewalk" by Mandrill blasting through the speakers in Snoopy's *ranfla*. Then out of nowhere, a *jura* with red lights flashing swooped in behind him. Snoopy pulled to the curb and stopped as about twenty of us watched the situation unfold.

Two *juras*, a *gavacho* and his coconut sidekick who tried to look tough with his hand resting on his *cuete*, got out of their patrol car and strutted slowly toward Snoopy's *ranfla*. One-by-one the homeboys, hands raised to the sky, crawled out and the *juras* shoved them spread-eagled against the vehicle and searched them for weapons. Luckily, none of the homeboys was packing, but I think that just made the coconut even madder since he seemed to be looking for a reason to bust somebody.

Just then, one of the homeboys in the front yard yelled, "Why don't you leave us alone?"

Someone else yelled, "Is this what you call protect and serve?"

Until then, the *juras* hadn't noticed us gathered in front of Fish's *cantón*. Rudy turned around to see who had yelled at the *juras*, but that just made the situation worse as the coconut slammed him back against the cruiser and jabbed his nightstick into Rudy's back.

At that point we all started yelling. There weren't enough of us to cause them concern, so the coconut, thinking it was funny, jabbed Rudy again. I could see Rudy recoil in pain but that just seemed to heighten the coconut's enjoyment and amused his *gavacho* partner.

Word of what was happening worked its way to the homeboys who were kicking back behind Fish's *cantón* as well as those inside. Suddenly, homeboys flooded into the front yard.

The coconut, determined to hurt Rudy, threw his nightstick around Rudy's neck clamping him into the chokehold for which the *juras* were well-known and swung him around to face us in an effort to fan the flames. Bad move!

De volada, we all poured out onto the *calle* and surrounded the *juras* smothering their laughter like the rushing waters of a tidal wave. A sudden look of panic rolled into their eyes as they were now face-to-face with about a hundred homeboys.

The coconut that had Rudy now tightened his grip on the nightstick. I could see the strain in Rudy's face. His skin was flushed as he struggled to breathe. Bottles thrown by homeboys in the back, smashed into the police cruiser. Still the coconut pressed the nightstick into Rudy's throat trying to use Rudy as a hostage to keep us from rushing him. The *gavacho* struggled to push his way around to the driver's door of the police cruiser but we wouldn't budge. We kept squeezing in tighter.

"Let him go!" echoed through our ranks.

The *juras* were in trouble and they knew it.

Suddenly, the *gavacho* drew his *cuete* and we slowly backed off giving the *juras* a narrow path to the rear passenger door of the police cruiser. The *gavacho* managed to get the rear door open and both *juras* scrambled into the back seat with Rudy's limp body. He looked like dead weight as the *juras* dragged him into the backseat with the nightstick still under his chin. I couldn't tell if his eyes were open, or if he was still breathing.

Beer bottles rained down on the cruiser as the *gavacho* quickly scrambled into the front seat. Seconds later, the cruiser sped away with the siren blaring, leaving all of us standing in the *calle* not knowing if Rudy was alive or dead!

Some of the older homeboys hurried over to Rudy's *cantón* to tell his parents what had happened. *De volada*, his *jefitos* headed to the Pomona Police Station to check on their son, but the *juras* blew them off and wouldn't let them see him.

Word of what had happened to Rudy spread like tear gas through the *barrio*. The *veteranos* called a meeting. They seemed to have a bad feeling that homeboy's soul had departed but no one wanted to believe the worst.

It wasn't until midnight that the *juras* told Rudy's *jefitos* that Rudy was dead. This came as a double blow for his *familia*. Rudy and Tudy were *carnales* and it hadn't been that long since Tudy had died at the hands of the Chino Sinners.

The *veteranos* didn't want any reprisals on the *juras* due to the fact that the *familia* had evidence implicating the coconut who, it seemed obvious to us, had killed Rudy. While the Pomona Police Department had ordered an internal investigation, no one in the *barrio* trusted the outcome of such an investigation, particularly Rudy's *familia*, so they retained an *abogado* to file a lawsuit on their behalf. For once, it seemed the courts might offer us an ounce of justice.

The Pomona Bulletin reported that the *juras* said that they had gone to the scene of a large party where cars were illegally double parked. It was at this location that they had stopped a car and Rudy was arrested. They reported that he had become "combative" and had to be subdued at the time of his arrest and, after arriving at the station, Rudy had collapsed.

We knew better. Rudy had died in the back seat of the police cruiser. Homeboy's soul was long gone by the time the *juras* pulled up at the police station. They knew this all the time and still didn't have the decency to tell his *familia* when they arrived at the station.

Hatred for the *juras* burned the brightest and hottest it ever had since the *juras* hit the pregnant woman during the Sharkie Park riots nearly five years earlier. Homeboys wanted the coconut's *huevos* on a silver platter, but since we couldn't make a *movida* against the *juras* until the lawsuit played out in the courts, we were instructed to start doing robberies at gun shops in preparation for a future war with the *juras*.

Once again, the angel of death hovered over the *barrio* as we buried Rudy, his coffin draped with our sweatshirt. After the funeral, most of the homeboys migrated to *Oso's cantón* to kick back for a while, but no one was in the mood to party. By evening, the few of us who remained were tossing around ideas of our future payback on the *juras* and listening to the Isley Brothers. "Fight the Power" blared through speakers positioned in the front windows of *Oso's cantón* while a warm, balmy breeze blew through our *barrio*.

"We should hit the station like the *veteranos* did," Nite Owl suggested.

Just then, someone yelled, *"Trucha!"*

All eyes turned toward the *calle*.

Oso's cantón was right on Grand Avenue and the yard was small, so homeboy's *ranflas* were positioned to provide us some cover, just in case.

"Trucha!" quietly echoed from homeboy to homeboy as the conversations stopped and homeboys moved for cover behind the *ranflas*.

All eyes fixed on a black '66 Impala lowrider cruising slowly toward us. All we could see were two figures in the front seat as the unfamiliar *ranfla* swerved through the dip at the intersection. Homeboys were ready with six or so *cuetes* aimed at the intruders as they drew closer.

"It's *rucas*, Homes!" yelled *Solo* who immediately stood up for a better look.

The two *rucas* stopped their *ranfla* on the opposite side of the *calle*, leaving three lanes between us and them.

"Where's the party?" the driver shouted.

"*Q'vole*, the party's here!" several of us answered at once.

Solo, not one to wait for anybody else, stepped out between our *ranflas* and into the *calle*. Homeboys with the *cuetes* eased up and took their aim off the *ranfla,* and two other homeboys followed *Solo* toward the *rucas*. It started looking like this might turn into a party after all.

De volada, a dark figure popped up in the back seat like a jack-in-the-box.

"*Trucha!*" homeboys yelled but it was too late.

BAM!

The bright flash of a *cuete* spitting lead lit up the inside of the *ranfla*.

BAM! Another shot rang out!

As I ducked back behind a *ranfla,* I saw *Solo* and the two homeboys in the *calle* trying to run for cover.

BAM! BAM! BAM!

"Chino Sinners, *y-que!*"

Tires screeched as the *ruca* behind the wheel punched the gas and the black *ranfla* raced away down Grand Avenue. My heart was pumping a hundred miles per hour. Homeboy *Solo*, blood oozing from his back, lay motionless on his side. The other two homeboys clawed at the pavement in a struggle to crawl out of the *calle*.

Homeboys raced into the *calle,* but it was too late for those packing to get off a good shot, so they piled into three *ranflas*. The door was still open on the second *ranfla* and an older homeboy on the passenger side glanced at Nite Owl and me and gave a slight nod with his head. Without hesitation, I piled in the back right behind Nite Owl and we flew off in vengeful pursuit of our tarnished honor.

"*Vamos a matar los* Chino Sinners!*"* cried the homeboy riding shotgun as he waved his *cuete* in an angry gesture.

"*Sí mon, las rucas, tambien!*" added the driver, his anger apparent from the way he bounced through a dozen or more stop signs in an effort to catch the black Impala.

Unfortunately, they had too much of a lead.

"*Trucha!*" cautioned the homeboy riding shotgun as a police cruiser pulled out in front of us.

Homeboy behind the wheel slowed without being noticed by the *jura,* and from that point, we silently cruised toward *Chino.*

Things had happened so fast that only now, as we slowed to cruising speed, did I have time to think. This was my second *movida* since climbing the fences behind the Catholic Church in Cherrieville and blasting those *vatos* with Nite Owl and Slim. But this one was different. I didn't have to jump into the *ranfla*. No one would have called me out in front of the *veteranos* at our next meeting if I had stayed behind to help *Solo* or the other two *vatos* put down by the Chino Sinners. I was here because this is where I wanted to be. Even so, I knew that the two older *vatos* had deadly vengeance in their hearts. If we found those *rucas* or any *vato* from Chino, somebody was going to die. While I wasn't sure that I was ready for murder, I was certain that I should keep these thoughts to myself.

Before long we entered enemy territory, having lost the other two carloads of homeboys in the chase. Sinner's *placasos* appeared everywhere, on the walls of buildings, fences, and stop signs. Time slowed. Our senses were tuned to every sound, but it was eerily quiet as we slowly cruised their *calles* looking for the black Impala or any sign of *cholos* kicking back.

We all sat low, only our eyes peering out, so the body of the *ranfla* would provide maximum protection from incoming *balas*. Homeboy riding shotgun and the homeboy behind him held their *cuetes* just below the level of the window. Homeboy driving had his *cuete* resting on his lap. We were ready as we slowly cruised up one *calle* and down the next.

"Where are they?" the homeboy sitting shotgun questioned.

Seconds ticked by like minutes but no *cholos* were out.

"These *chavalas* are hiding out!" the homeboy driving shrugged as he swung back onto Central Avenue and headed north.

Upon returning to our *barrio*, we stashed the *cuetes* at one of the homeboy's *cantóns*. We had to avoid *Oso's cantón* because the *juras* were swarming around it trying to find out what had happened, so we cruised by the Macias' pad where we found out that *Solo* was the only one who had actually gotten hit and he was already undergoing surgery at the Pomona Valley Community Hospital to remove the *balas*.

Homeboys dropped me off at my pad and I went straight to my room, put on some music, and kicked back on my bed, glad to be home. As I lay there thinking, a mixture of thoughts darted through *mi mente*. I wondered how badly *Solo* was hurt. He was sixteen, same age as me. Also, I was upset that we didn't catch the Impala but, at the same time, relieved. I had learned something from this ordeal, *don't jump into the ranfla unless you're willing to go all the way!* The conflict of such thinking tired me, and I eventually drifted off to sleep.

The next day, all the homeboys gathered at Sharkie Park. The good news was that homeboy *Solo* was going to live. The bad news was that one of the *balas* had shattered his spine and he was permanently paralyzed from the waist down.

This *movida* had distracted us from our beef with the *juras* and focused our attention completely on the *vatos* from D Street. For the next couple weeks, our homeboys hit Chino, causing casualties on their side.

In one *movida*, homeboys were on their way to inflict damage on the Chino Sinners when a *cuete* accidentally discharged and struck homeboy *Bala* in the foot. *De volada*, homeboys pulled a U-turn and dropped *Bala* off at the hospital. I never heard how he explained the bullet in his foot, but knowing *Bala*, I'm sure it got a good laugh from the emergency room staff. As a result of the shooting, *Bala* cruised around wearing only one shoe until his foot healed. His *placaso* was now well-supported with a good story.

* * *

As we moved into July of 1975, tension between Chino and Twelfth Street stayed high and we remained extra *trucha*. Rudy's *familia* was in the midst of their lawsuit against the *juras*. The coconut and *gavacho* that killed Rudy stayed shy of our *barrio* and didn't show their *caras de cobardes*. They must have been reassigned elsewhere and instructed to keep a low profile. The *juras* who did patrol our *calles* were extra cautious not to stir up trouble and didn't stay in the *barrio* any longer than necessary.

Homeboys did their best to intimidate the *juras,* but the *juras* had some methods of their own. They made it known that they would retaliate with force if one of theirs was killed. They passed their *wila* to homeboys as they were booked into the Pomona Jail or anytime they got a homeboy in the back of a cruiser. All this talk didn't scare us. Homeboys were down for a payback.

Still waiting for the green light to move on the *juras*, homeboys continued breaking into gun and pawn shops. Other homeboys scoped out and broke into *cantóns* in more affluent areas, *tambíen*, racking up a good supply of weapons and ammunition which we hid at various *cantóns* throughout the *barrio*.

Homeboy *Solo* was out of the hospital and had recovered from his wounds but was confined to a wheelchair. Since he couldn't get around like before, it was easy for homeboys to forget about him. Sadly, his *placaso* seemed to fit him now more than ever, but that was his destiny and no one could change it now.

On any given Friday afternoon in the summer, a dozen or more homeboys could be found kicking back at Sharkie Park. One particular Friday, about fifteen or so of us homeboys rounded up some baseball equipment and started a pickup game with the homegirls. Surprisingly, the game stayed fairly even throughout several innings, probably since none of us were jocks and didn't have much first-hand experience with the game. Besides, we weren't playing to win. We were just having fun. Toward the end of the game, several of the younger homeboys who were keeping *trucha* for us noticed a large caravan of lowriders approaching the park eastbound on Grand Avenue.

Not wanting to take any chances, we stopped the game to check them out. As they came closer, we recognized them as part of the car club Traffic. Their theme song "Lowrider" by War accented their fine *ranflas*, some outfitted with chromed pipes and museum quality paint jobs. Posters taped to the car doors announced a dance they were hosting at Pomona Fair Grounds that evening.

After the caravan passed, we took a break from the game and rested on the grass in the shade of some trees near the *calle*. We hadn't been there long before the sound of War returned and the caravan circled back past the park.

Homeboy Spooky, known for his hot temper, grabbed a couple empty beer bottles lying on the ground next to him and stood up, one in each hand. He had grown up in the *barrio* with all of the older homeboys and had proven himself worthy of our love and respect. While he was white as a blank sheet of paper, his heart was stoned *Chicano*, a real *vato loco* and the only *gavacho* in Twelfth Street.

As the caravan slowly cruised past, Spooky strolled into the *calle*, hands at his side, like he was headed for the other side of the *calle*, but then paused to let a couple of the *ranflas* pass. His eyes seemed to focus in on a dark green *ranfla*, then without warning . . .

WHAM!

Homeboy Spooky unloaded one of the bottles on the driver, smashing him square on the right side of his head. It was *gacho* as shards of glass embedded themselves in his *cara* and blood gushed out from the wound. Without hesitation, the driver punched it and tires squealed as Spooky hurled the second bottle into the side of the *ranfla*.

ZOOM! ZOOM! ZOOM!

All the other *ranflas* in the caravan sped away down Grand Avenue then suddenly stopped just out of range.

As they piled out of their *ranflas*, Spooky and the rest of us homeboys grabbed bats. We were severely outnumbered and knew it. Even the homegirls stayed and were ready to get busy, except for two of them that ran off to round up help. No one knew why Spooky had thrown the bottles but if Traffic wanted *pleito* that was alright with us.

As Traffic assembled beside their *ranflas*, we waited. A minute passed, then five minutes, until a black *ranfla* slowly pulled away from the pack and circled back toward us. I knew they weren't coming back for *pleito* with one *ranfla* but I certainly wasn't ready to let my guard down until I knew what they wanted. The black *ranfla* approached cautiously and stopped close to where the second bottle had smashed into the side of the green *ranfla* less than ten minutes before. When I saw the president of Traffic step out of the black *ranfla* accompanied by four *vatos*, I breathed a sigh of relief. We all strolled up to them.

Their president did all the talking.

"*Qué paso*, Spooky?"

"*Sabes que*, you *vatos* know better than to bring that *vato* from Cherrieville into our *barrio, ese!*" Spooky responded.

"Look man, he's not gang-banging anymore!"

"I don't care, *ese*. I don't want that *vato* in our *barrio!*" Spooky shot back.

A moment of silence followed as the president of Traffic pondered Spooky's demand, then looked Spooky straight in the eye as he said, "*Dispensa*, Spooky. We'll take care of it."

"*Órale,*" Spooky acknowledged as the two shook hands. "*Te acuerdas, ese.* Next time I see him in our *barrio*, I won't be so nice!"

The president, followed by the four *vatos,* returned to their *ranfla*, pulled another U-turn, and led the rest of the caravan away down Grand Avenue. I watched as they rolled out of sight. Just then, I saw the bushes move across the *calle* and six homeboys, each armed and ready, popped up. I couldn't believe it. All this time, they had us covered big time. The two homegirls who ran for reinforcements had brought back the cavalry. Homeboy Spooky seemed to know they were there all along and strolled over to talk with them as the rest of us gathered up the bats and called it quits.

On the way home I thought about what had happened, and the more I thought about it the more I realized Spooky was right. Traffic should have known better than to parade an ex-Cherrieville *vato* through our *barrio*. It was like bringing a spy into the fort. It wasn't going to happen. Period. Spooky made certain of that.

It was late afternoon when I got home, and dinner wasn't ready yet, so I grabbed some leftovers from the refrigerator and took a quick shower before climbing into a pair of pleated Khakis and my *Calle Doce Los* Sharkies sweatshirt. My *jefito* was sitting out back laughing over some *pisto* with his friends from work, and *mi jefita* had left some warm *tortillas* unattended on the stove. I picked up a couple *tortillas* and hurried back to Sharkie Park.

When I arrived, just about everyone was there already. Most of the homeboys were sporting *Los* Sharkies sweatshirts, and even many of the homegirls had on their version which had "Sharketts" in Old English letters curved over a picture of a shark with "Pomona" underneath.

HOMEBOY'S SOUL

The plan was to meet at the park so we could caravan to the Traffic dance at the fairgrounds. The conflicts of the afternoon behind us, we were ready to have a good time and that's what we had. Twenty-five *ranflas* loaded with *vatos locos y locas* from the big Twelfth Street gang arrived at the fairgrounds.

A new band called *Tierra* that was coming up from East *Los* provided the music, featuring the Salas brothers, Steve and Rudy, on a hit "*Baila, Simón*" from their second album. I danced till my feet were sore, then we all loaded into the *ranflas* and headed back into the *barrio* where we continued the party at the Macias' *cantón*.

James Brown's "Papa Don't Take No Mess" jammed from one of the *ranflas*, and homeboy Big Joe started shaking to the rhythm and bending his knees and nodding his head in time. Then, he made a fist with both hands and crossed his arms across his chest like a big letter X. A few more bounces and his arms were upright with his forearms parallel and his fists at his shoulders. Now each arm formed the letter I.

At first, no one could figure out what he was doing.

"Check it out!" Big Joe exclaimed.

Then a couple of the homeboys caught on and they started following the same motions in rhythm to the music. First, with their arms crossed then with their forearms straight up in front of their shoulders. Suddenly, it hit me, XII. Roman numerals for twelve. Twelfth Street.

"The Twelfth Street Hop!" explained Big Joe as he demonstrated the X and the II motions for everyone.

Within minutes, there must have been nearly seventy homeboys and homegirls all doing the Twelfth Street Hop out under the stars in front of the *cantón*. It was crazy. Then, all of a sudden, two beams of light panned across us. All eyes followed the beams back to the spotlights on two police cruisers that had stopped in front of the *cantón*, but no one seemed surprised. Everyone kept dancing the Twelfth Street Hop as we quietly chanted to ourselves, "If the *juras* try to break us up, we're going to have to mess them up!"

All of us were down for *pleito* with the *juras,* and the feeling of sheer power and strength of numbers was compounded by the unity we felt doing our new dance. As the beams of light moved slowly back and forth, the chant quickly turned to *"Calle Doce! Calle Doce!"* which grew louder with each repetition.

While most of us continued doing the Twelfth Street Hop, some of the homeboys started waving at the *juras* and gesturing for them to "Come on!" Wisely, the *juras* remained in their cruisers and didn't overstay their welcome.

That night we were all in the mood for confrontation, and no one was about to tolerate any disrespect. Had they tried to stop us they may have very well had a full scale riot on their hands. Homeboys were ready and willing to march headlong into battle with those *juras*. All we needed was an excuse. As it was, they left us alone and we danced into the wee hours of the night. Then I marched home and went to bed.

* * *

A few weeks later, Li'l Capone, *Payaso*, Dopey, Fat Joe, Black Crow, and I were kicking back in the front yard at Nite Owl's *cantón* where the *pisto* flowed and the smell of *yesca* floated on the air. Talk centered on returning to school in September and plans for the L.A. County Fair.

"Who's jammin', Homes?" Li'l Capone asked before taking a long toke on a joint and passing it to *Payaso*.

A few of us shrugged, but no one other then Li'l Capone and Black Crow seemed concerned, as we were too busy getting high to worry about somebody's music.

"Sounds like 'Cisco Kid!'" Black Crow commented as the sound grew louder.

Admittedly, there was something strange about it since we hadn't heard or seen a *ranfla*. Bested by his curiosity, Li'l Capone strolled out to the *calle* for a look. An expression of concern quickly changed to surprise then a smile.

"It's *Solo*," he yelled.

We couldn't believe it. All of us hurried to the *calle*. Sure enough, *Solo*, all *cholo'd* down with a *bandana* covering his forehead, pushed toward us, the sounds of War's "Cisco Kid" blaring from his wheelchair.

"*Q'vole!*" we all exclaimed. "What did you do to your wheelchair, Homes?"

"Check it out, *ese*," *Solo* replied proudly then boasted, "I got better sound than homeboys' *ranflas!*"

We all laughed but were also interested to see how masterfully he had wired an eight-track tape player to a car battery, with speakers tucked up under the seat of his chair. Most of all we were tripping to see *Solo* back on the *calles*. He looked and sounded good, although there was a glimmer of pain in his eyes that he was trying his best to conceal.

"*Órale*, Homes. You better be *trucha* strolling the *calles* in that thing, *ese*," Nite Owl warned.

To our astonishment, *Solo* smoothly reaches into a pack slung over the back of his chair and swings out a big *cuete*.

"*Chale*, Homes. You know anybody wants to mess with a 45 magnum, *ese?*" *Solo* asked.

"*Trucha*, Homes!" we said in near unison before breaking into laughs.

"*Sí* mon. Nobody's going to mess with me again!" he stated confidently.

"*Órale*, Homes. I hope you don't shoot yourself in the *huevos, ese!*" *Payaso* laughed, which busted us all up, even *Solo*.

"*Órale, vamonos al parque.* Homeboys aren't going to believe this, *ese*," Nite Owl said, gesturing to *Solo's* mobile sound machine.

"*Órale, vamonos!*" *Solo* added.

Solo popped in another eight-track, and "City Life" by the Blackbyrds burst through his speakers as we all grabbed our *pistos* and passed the joints around, heading to the park. I was amazed as I took a hit of *yesca* and glanced back at *Solo*. What a dramatic change *Solo* had undergone. Last time I saw him, he was lying lifeless in the *calle*, bleeding and paralyzed. Now he was up and moving around, ready to hang out with the homeboys just like before, except for the wheelchair which, because of the music, was absolutely amazing. He was even packing big time, just in case. Even so, I couldn't help feeling sorry for *Solo*. I couldn't begin to imagine what he had gone through to regain this much of his life, so I exhaled those thoughts and let them float away with the wisps of smoke from the *yesca*.

10

Fun Zone

September 12 marked the opening of the Los Angeles County Fair. Located along White Avenue, north of I-10 and well on the other side of Cherrieville, the fair served as a rite of passage, offering the youngsters an opportunity to make a name for themselves. *Vatos* could talk the talk, but when the L.A. County Fair came around, it was time to walk the walk.

It all happened in the "Fun Zone." Lined with rides and game booths arranged in a large circle, the "Fun Zone" offered a mixture of flashing lights, loud music, and barkers proclaiming the ease of winning a stuffed toy or some other cheap prize.

The "Fun Zone" also provided a perfect way to ensure that *vatos* from rival *barrios* would clash somewhere along the circle. The *juras* didn't seem to mind the occasional *pleito,* because it gave them the opportunity to bust some heads and kick some butt without having to worry about allegations of "police brutality!" It all seemed designed with a little something in it for everyone.

During school on the first Friday of the fair, homeboys formulated plans to meet at Sharkie Park around seven in the evening and caravan to the fairgrounds. Everyone agreed to wear our *Calle Doce Los* Sharkies sweatshirts.

This was my first trip to the fair with the homeboys and I was excited. After school I hurried home, did a few chores around the house, and laid out my clothes. We had dinner early. Even though I wasn't that hungry, I ate everything and started to excuse myself when *mi jefita* announced that my *carnal* had written to say that he was enjoying his tour of duty in Japan and doing fine. She said he thought he would be able to come home for Christmas. I was happy for my *carnal,* but at that moment I had other things on *mi mente.* As I began to slide my chair back for the second time, *mi jefita* looked at me.

"Where are you going tonight?" she inquired.

"I'm going to the fair with my friends."

"*Mijo,* I don't want you hanging out with those *cholos.*"

My *jefito* glanced up, but luckily he stayed out of it. He knew there was no need to repeat his warning to me about coming home crying if I got my butt kicked.

"Mom, I don't . . ."

"Don't 'Mom' me," she quickly retorted.

"They're my friends, besides we watch out for each other."

"*Sí, pero* your friends can't stop bullets!"

"Don't worry about me so much. I'll be alright," I said, trying to console her, but she didn't buy it.

"That's probably what Tudy told his mom," she said with a sad look of frustration in her eyes. "And he was a Marine."

I was losing ground fast, so I decided it was better to keep my mouth shut. Nothing I said as this point would help anyway. Unfortunately, *mi jefita's* comment caught the attention of my *jefito* who stopped, laid his *tortilla* back on his plate and washed his mouth out with a sip of *pisto.*

"You keep hanging around those lazy, good-for-nothing *cholos* and you'll end up in jail." He paused for another swig of *pisto* before continuing. "Don't think I'm going to bail you out!"

Oh no, here we go.

"Remember, if you go looking for trouble, trouble is what you'll get!"

Once he got started, I had no choice but to sit there and act as though I was listening.

"You think you have friends? Your friends won't pay your bills, and they can't get you a job. And, when your butt is sitting in jail, you think your friends are going to take up a collection to bail you out?"

I stood there silently.

When I didn't answer, he pointed at me and said with a mad rage in his eyes, "If you don't want your ass kicked right now, you better answer me."

"No," I responded quickly.

"You think your *cholo* friends are bad, you ain't seen nothing if you mess with me! I better not ever hear that you are stealing or selling drugs for your money, because the day I do, you're going to get an ass-kicking you'll never forget; then you'll pack your stuff up and get out of my house!" He paused a moment to let his boiling blood settle to a simmer. "Do you understand?"

"Yes, sir," I muttered.

What else could I say? When I was a little boy and I did something really bad, my *jefito* would take his belt and tan my hide. Believe me, a few welts on my skinny butt were enough to bring me back to the straight and narrow. Over the years, I learned that I could avoid the belt by not arguing with him. So as I stood there enduring another lecture, I knew enough to know that this was a good time to keep quiet and let his words swim in one ear and out the other.

However, not all of his advice escaped me. He communicated his passionate distaste for laziness through example, unconsciously motivating me to cut lawns in the summer. I even accompanied him to his part-time job where I earned a few extra bucks.

My *jefito* hated *cholos*, primarily because he thought of them as lazy. That's where we differed in our opinion. Of course, some of the *cholos* I knew were lazy and sold drugs or stole for fast money, but most of the homeboys, particularly the ones with nice *ranflas*, worked for their *feria*. But none of that mattered much, it was my life and I liked the excitement and sense of power that came with being a *cholo*. Nothing my *jefito*, or *jefita* said would have made a difference.

Once he finished his lecture, an awkward silence hung over the kitchen. This time, the silence was broken by the sound of a car horn out front. I quietly pushed my chair up to the table, hoping not to inspire any additional comments.

"I'll be back later tonight, Mom," I said in a subdued voice as I planted a kiss on her cheek, then with an added, "I love you," I was gone.

Outside, I climbed into a brown '72 Monte Carlo, lowered to the bone, and shook hands with Henry who greeted me with, "*Órale*, Homes." Then he asked eagerly, "You down for tonight?"

"*Sí mon,* Homes. You know I'm down."

Most of the homeboys were already kicking back at Sharkie Park when we arrived. Henry parked his *ranfla,* and we immediately strolled to the *pisto,* each of us grabbing a cold one. After a few more homeboys rolled in, *Conejo* called everybody together.

"*Sabes que*, Homeboys. Check it out. We got fifteen *ranflas,* so when we cruise to the fair, we caravan by fives and meet in the parking lot. All the homeboys with *ranflas* leave your *llaves* next to the battery just in case you get busted, so homeboys don't have to walk back. The *ranfla* you go in is the *ranfla* you come back in, *entiendes?"* He glanced around at everyone to make certain before continuing.

"*Órale,* once inside there is a little park next to the grandstands. We'll all meet there, first."

Conejo squatted down and picked up a stick lying next to him. Everyone moved in for a better view as he dragged the tip of the stick through the dirt to form a large circle.

"This is the 'Fun Zone' and this is the entrance," he said as he added a straight line at the bottom of the circle. "We go in by tens. As you get to the entrance, the *juras* will see you coming, so be ready for them. They're going to take you *vatos* to the back and pat you down for weapons, so stash all your *fileros y cuetes* in the *ranflas* before you go in. This is all about boxing, so I don't want anyone packing."

I could tell from the way his eyes scanned each homeboy for any sign of disagreement that he was deadly serious about this.

"After the *juras* pat you down, they'll let you go in. Once the first group gets through, the next group can go in. Ten at a time."

He pointed the stick to the right side of the circle.

"Once inside the 'Fun Zone,' I want the first ten homeboys to stroll to the right and kick back. Then, the next ten will go to the left. By the time we're all in, we'll have forty homeboys on each side. Don't bunch up. Stay in groups of ten and leave enough room in between that you can still see each other."

Conejo dropped the stick and stood up.

"This is about pride for your *barrio*. We don't take nothing off nobody. Once the first group gets into blows, the next group will rush in like a wave *y el otro, tambien.* I want everybody to keep *trucha* and back each other up. *Calle Doce* don't run from nobody, *entiendes?"*

"Sí mon!" everyone replied in unison.

Then, we all headed to the *ranflas*. Nite Owl, Fat Joe, *Payaso*, and I all jumped in with Big Jerry. Dopey rode shotgun. *Conejo* lead the caravan, with Big Jerry following slow and low, west on Grand Avenue to the beat of "Soul Power" by James Brown. At White Street, we turned north and cruised past the eastern edge of Cherrieville, then under Interstate-10 and across McKinley Avenue to the entrance of the fairgrounds.

The thrill of anticipation pounded in my chest as we pulled into the parking area. Big Jerry left his *llaves* under the hood next to the battery and we all headed for the entrance to the fair. The smell of food blended with a myriad of noises filling the warm night air. The first two groups of homeboys headed for the entrance. Nite Owl, J-Bird, *Travieso*, Fat Joe, Black Crow, *Payaso*, Slim, Big Jerry, *Conejo*, and I were next, so we strolled with stone faces slowly toward the gate. The fair was packed with *gente* who would quickly glance in our direction as we approached then wisely turn away. As we passed into the fairgrounds, a couple *juras* eyed us but didn't approach, so we quickly made our way to the little park where we kicked it until the rest of the homeboys were in.

"*Trucha,* it's time for *Calle Doce* to get busy!" *Conejo* announced.

I glanced to my left. The first group was on the move, headed for the "Fun Zone." Then, the next and it was our turn. As we moved out, I could see homeboys in front and behind. I could feel the tension in the air as we moved through the crowds of *gente* which made way for us like the Red Sea parting for Moses. I could also feel the burning stare of some fine *rucas* checking us out, but business came first.

I watched as the first group of homeboys reached a painted arch with flashing lights inviting all to enter the "Fun Zone." *De volada*, the *juras* swooped in and ushered our homeboys aside out of sight. In a few moments they re-appeared and passed through the painted archway and strolled off to the right. The next ten homeboys strolled toward the entrance and received the same welcome from the *juras*. When they re-appeared, they entered through the arch and strolled off to the left. Everything was going as planned.

Now it was our turn. As soon as we neared the archway, *de volada*, six *juras* in riot helmets swooped in on us.

"O.K., fellas. Let's go for a little walk!" one of the *juras* said in a stern, deep voice. My muscles tightened. I tried to keep my cool and followed Nite Owl as the *juras* corralled us into a narrow alley-like space, strewn with trash, between a canvas-covered chain link fence and the backside of some game booths. It was dark enough that the *juras* could do some serious damage if they wanted.

"Alright. Everybody up against the fence and spread 'em!" they commanded.

We all turned and complied by stretching our hands out above our shoulders, grasping the thin metal links of the fence between our fingers, and spreading our legs out as we leaned forward. One by one, two *juras* patted us down for weapons as a sergeant stood watching.

"You guys from Twelfth Street, uh?" he asked.

We all nodded "yes" and a couple homeboys replied, *"Sí mon!"*

"Didn't we just get some Twelfth Streeters?" he asked turning to the *jura* next to him.

"Sure did," the *jura* replied.

"What is this, Twelfth Street Night?" he quipped.

The other *juras* joined him in a quick laugh.

"Alright, everyone turn around!" one of the *juras* ordered.

We all put our hands down and turned back from the wall, straightening the pleats on our Khakis.

The sergeant pulled a short pencil and small spiral note pad from his breast pocket.

"Listen up! I want your names first, then your a.k.a.'s, and don't lie to me or I'll you'll regret it!" he said as he walked up to *Conejo*.

The sergeant studied *Conejo* a moment and then said, "Tricks are for kids, so you can't fool me you silly rabbit!"

All of us started to laugh as *Conejo* simply offered his real name. The sergeant scribbled on his little pad, then made his way down the line one-by-one until he got to *Payaso*.

Payaso gave the *jura* his real name, but being the clown that he was, he looked the sergeant directly in the eyes and gave his a.k.a. as "Gazoo!"

We were all laughing inside but had to hold it so as not to give up homeboy's game.

"Gazoo!" the sergeant repeated as he turned to the other *juras*. "Isn't that . . ." he paused a moment. "Isn't that the, uh, cartoon character that comes out on the Flintstones?"

"The Jetsons, Sergeant," one of the *juras* corrected. "He's the one with the big head!"

We couldn't hold it any longer. Almost in unison, we bent over with laughter. The *juras* thought we were laughing because he said "big head," but we were laughing at how Payaso had these *juras* going. Whatever the reason, they thought it was funny, too.

As the *juras* escorted us out of their make-shift holding cell, the sergeant asked another *jura*, "Hey, don't we have Cherrieville and the Black Angels here as well?"

"Yeah, I think they're holding hands!" came the response.

I knew "holding hands" meant that the two *barrios* had aligned for the fair since they knew we'd be out in force. It didn't matter to me, the more the merrier.

"I got my money on Twelfth Street," the sergeant added with the sly smile of an astute gambler.

"I don't know, Sarge. Looks to me like these boys got their hands full," commented one of the *juras*.

"Forget it! We'll still kick their asses!" blurted *Conejo*.

"You guys better. I got my money riding on you boys," the sergeant laughed before letting his expression turn serious again. "I'll kick your asses if you make me lose!"

"How much did you bet?" Nite Owl inquired of the *jura* standing next to him.

"Thirty bucks!"

"You might as well give it up right now," Nite Owl advised, "because Cherrieville and whoever else they got to help them are nothing but a bunch of *chavalas!*"

"*Sí mon. Puro chavalas!*" we echoed.

"We'll see who's left for us to drag out of here!" the sergeant said as we strolled on into the "Fun Zone."

All the banter helped me relax for a moment, but as soon as we entered the "Fun Zone," the noisy crowds brought back the tension. We moved off to the right and waited while Fish and Slim spread the word about Cherrieville and the Black Angels to the rest of the homeboys.

Once everyone was past the *juras*, homeboys started strolling through the "Fun Zone" looking for a *cholo*, *gavacho* or *mayate*—it didn't matter, as long as they wanted *pleito* with us.

My eyes searched every face for a challenge, but most everyone looked away or avoided my gaze entirely. Then, up ahead I saw a group of about twenty Sharketts who had stopped to talk briefly with the first group of homeboys before drifting our way.

"*Trucha!* The *vatos* from Cherrieville and *Onta* are kicking it by the funhouse," warned Sad Girl.

"*Órale*, pass it on. Make sure the homeboys on the other side know what's up," *Conejo* replied to Sad Girl who moved on with her homegirls to pass the word; then he turned to us and said, "Be *trucha*, Homes. It's time to get busy, *ese. Calle Doce, rifamous!*"

That was all it took. Adrenaline shot into my system and blood surged through my veins. As we strolled toward the funhouse, my sweaty palms clenched into fists at my side. I was already throwing blows in *mi mente* with each one landing dead center on target. I wondered, *how many* vatos *do they have? How good are they? Whatever happens,* I thought to myself, *I have to stay on my feet.*

We continued toward the funhouse. I could see the two-story structure rise above the heads in front of us, but I couldn't see the *vatos* from Cherrieville and *Onta*. Then suddenly the crowd parted and there they were. They were there in force, forty maybe fifty of them. I couldn't tell for sure. They all wore matching sweatshirts with their *barrio* colors and Cherrieville or Black Angels on the back. Cherrieville's sweatshirts were solid black with Cherrieville across the back in cherry-red letters, three cherries with short green stems, and Pomona underneath. The Black Angels wore black sweatshirts with their name in white letters across the top, a picture of the grim reaper in the middle, and *Onta Sur* on the bottom.

They were in two separate groups but close enough to each other that it was obvious they were "holding hands." All of them were kicking back in a little area off to the right of the funhouse and away from the crowd.

De volada, their feathers perked up as they saw us. They were too focused on us to notice the second wave of Sharks closing in on their left flank.

The first and second waves dove in like kamikazes. I followed *Conejo,* who showed his *cora* and headed straight for them without any hesitation. Tonight, there would be no courting ritual with these *vatos* like the ones that interrupted our party with the *rucas* from the Earth Angels. Everyone knew we had come here to dance, so let the music begin.

"*Calle Doce!*" we yelled as we plowed headlong into their ranks.

Fists were flying in all directions. I felt the soft flesh of some *vato's cara* give way as I cut loose. Suddenly, I felt the stunning impact of a fist knock my head back. I could see flashes of light and hear a ringing sound in my ears as several other blows glanced off the side of my head, but I was numbed to any sensation of pain. Time slowed and my vision narrowed as I focused in on my target, anyone in a black sweatshirt.

I don't know if it was fifteen seconds or fifteen minutes later, all I know is the *pleito* was vicious and the *juras* were letting it run its course. Then out of nowhere, a big *jura* grabbed me. All I could see was the blur of his club headed for my *cara*, with the force that could deliver a homerun. Somehow, I managed to slip loose and felt only the rush of air sweep past my nose. Suddenly, my field of view widened out enough to see that the punches we had been exchanging with Cherrieville and *Onta* were polite greetings compared to the hurt the *juras* were trying to inflict upon us.

I put some quick distance between the *jura* with the club and my head, but in doing so I bumped into a *vato* from Cherrieville. We both slipped and fell to the ground. *De volada,* I scrambled to my feet and gave him a hard kick in the *cara* for my trouble.

Suddenly, I was flying through the air, landing hard against a trash barrel. As I quickly scrambled to my feet, I saw the offending *jura* waving his arms.

"Break it up!" he yelled as he turned toward two *vatos* who hadn't noticed him and were still exchanging blows. Without warning, his club sent a *vato* to the ground. As the *vato* crumbled, I noticed a cluster of red cherries on this back. *Órale, hit that* vato *again,* I thought to myself, but the *jura* went for another *vato* in a black sweatshirt and skillfully beat him with his nightstick.

When things settled down, the *juras* had about thirty *vatos,* including some of our homeboys, on their knees with their hands on top of their heads. I knew they were on their way to jail for the night. Everyone else was standing around in a group, each guarded by several *juras. Vatos* with black sweatshirts were lined up against a row of trash barrels, cherries on the left and grim reapers on the right. The Sharks were lined up against the front of the funhouse. Somehow, the *juras* had separated homeboys from the different *barrios* and were escorting us out of the fairgrounds first.

"Don't try to come back in or your butts will go to jail!" the sergeant warned as he and some of his men ushered us into the parking lot.

We gathered around *Conejo's ranfla,* laughing off the *juras* warning and checking out each other's battle wounds. No one was seriously hurt, and only about a dozen homeboys got arrested and were only charged with disturbing the peace. *No problem,* I thought. *They'll be out en la mañana.*

In the morning as I rolled out of bed, my whole body ached. I couldn't believe it. I hurt in places I didn't even know existed. And of all days, today, I had to mow lawns. But it didn't matter; I had all week to recover.

On the last weekend of the three-week fair, things got equally crazy. Friday night the older homeboys exchanged blows with some *vatos* from a *barrio* in East *Los.* There were a few arrests but no serious injuries. When Saturday came, homeboys and homegirls were out in force again. No one wanted to miss it. I caravanned to the fairgrounds with *Bala*, Nite Owl, Black Crow, Big Jerry, and Li'l Capone. Big Jerry rode shotgun in *Bala's* white '72 Caprice. It was a beautiful machine that *Bala* had lowered to the bone and trimmed with chrome all around. The eight-track blasted "Get Down Tonight" by K.C. and the Sunshine Band.

At the fairgrounds, *Bala* parked and stashed his *llaves* next to the battery. Li'l Capone put his arm around my neck and looked into my eyes with his deep piercing stare.

"You down, *ese?*" he asked.

"*Sí mon,* Homes. You know I'm down!"

What else could I say? To me it seemed like a stupid question but Li'l Capone draped his arm across Nite Owl's shoulders and asked him the same thing. Nite Owl gave the same response.

"*Órale,* you *vatos* stroll with me tonight," Li'l Capone stated.

Suddenly, I felt honored that Li'l Capone wanted us with him. The *veteranos* were grooming him to be a future shot caller and he had a lot of respect from the homeboys. His invitation was definitely an honor and put us on the front line as we entered the "Fun Zone."

We had about sixty homeboys on each side, in groups of ten, with several homegirls packed in between the groups. It didn't take long till we spotted some *vatos* from Chino strolling past a pinball arcade. They were out in force, too, wearing their black trench coats with Chino in white Old English letters above a skull with a tilted crown and pierced by a dagger underlined by the word Sinners. Most of them wore either a gangster hat or a *bandana* and all of them looked *loco*, even their homegirls.

As soon as we saw each other, the dance began. Our homegirls went toe-to-toe with their homegirls while we exchanged some mean blows with the *vatos*. As the *juras* swooped in to break it up and kick a few butts, I became separated from Li'l Capone and Nite Owl. Somehow, I was able to avoid the confrontation with the *juras* and strolled with several homeboys toward the entrance to the "Fun Zone." We planned to regroup there, then find some more Chino Sinners and get busy with them.

As we kicked back near the entrance, several *juras* ran past us toward the left side of the circle. This could only mean one thing; a group of homeboys had found some Sinners. We hurried toward the action to get some for ourselves.

Through the crowd I saw Li'l Capone and Nite Owl coming toward us. Just as they passed the bumper cars, ten Black Angels bum-rushed them from out of nowhere. Li'l Capone shot a quick glance at me then got busy and dispatched one of the Black

Angels to the ground. *De volada,* he downed two more but the black sweatshirts kept coming. Li'l Capone shot another glance in my direction that seemed to say, "C'mon, help us out here!" But it was no use. As hard as I pushed against the crowd, the rush of *gente* trying to get away held me back.

Within seconds, the *juras* had our homeboys and the whole group of Black Angels on their knees, hands resting on their heads. They were going to jail and there was nothing I could do. I could feel the anger boiling in Li'l Capone's eyes, burning into the back of my skull, as the *juras* rounded us up and pushed us toward the exit. I didn't realize at the time that this incident would prompt a dramatic change in my relationship with Li'l Capone.

Back in school the week after the fair closed, I marked my time until the weekend when I could kick back with the homeboys in the park. On Saturday, I got dressed and strolled to Sharkie Park. It was early afternoon and Nite Owl, Black Crow, and many of the *veteranos* were already kicking back by the time I arrived.

I hadn't been there long when a light blue '69 Riviera cruised up and parked. Three *veteranos* strolled over to speak with the three "border brothers" inside the *ranfla*. They talked for several minutes then all of a sudden, one of the *veteranos* opened the driver's door, dragged the *vato* out, and started beating him down. The other two *vatos* in the *ranfla* piled out and within seconds, fists were flying in all directions. A dozen or so *veteranos* who were watching the events unfold, rushed over and beat those *vatos* down like rabid dogs then threw them back into the *ranfla*.

"Next time you try to burn us, you're dead!" warned one of the shot callers before he spit on the driver and walked away from the *ranfla*.

The driver, who was obviously feeling a lot of pain, managed to start the *ranfla* and drive away. *These* vatos *are lucky,* I thought to myself as I grabbed a fresh *pisto* and nodded my head to the beat of "Who's That Lady" by the Isley Brothers oozing through the speakers.

I was kicking back with about six homeboys near the restrooms, where the *pisto* lay on ice, when I saw Li'l Capone and a group of five homeboys strolling my way. Li'l Capone stopped to talk with the *veteranos* for a minute then strolled up, claimed a can of *pisto*, and popped it open. As our eyes met, he nodded his head up as if to say "*Q-vo*" then turned and said something to one of the homeboys standing next to Nite Owl.

"Let's roll up some joints," suggested Nite Owl.

We all strolled into the restroom. Li'l Capone stepped into one of the stalls to take a leak while a couple of the homeboys rolled up some *yesca* on the sinks. When Li'l Capone finished, he came up to me and laid his right arm around my neck, then grabbed his right fist with his left hand. As he squeezed harder on the headlock, he leaned his head forward to focus his piercing stare into my eyes.

"*Órale*, Homes. You down, *ese?*" he asked as he tightened his grip even more.

"*Sí mon*, Homes. You know I'm down, *ese!*" My *cara* was flushed with blood and my voice sounded funny as his arm squeezed my neck.

Luckily, one of the homeboys fired up a joint and handed it to Li'l Capone who released his left hand to take several deep tokes before releasing his right arm and handing me the joint. I took a few quick hits and passed it on hoping that was the end of it, but Li'l Capone wasn't through with me yet. As I exhaled, he started bouncing lightly, shadow punching me in the arm and chest, so I went along with it and started punching back. The other homeboys loved it and began cheering us on. Suddenly, Li'l Capone let loose a quick, hard right jab into my chest.

"You down, *ese?*" he demanded.

"*Sí mon*, Homes!"

I couldn't figure out what he wanted and I certainly didn't like the direction this was going but I didn't know what else to do. Suddenly, he drew back for another punch.

BAM! BAM! BAM!

Gunshots echoed through the restroom like a cannon.

BAM! BAM!

We all rushed to the doorway where one of the *veteranos* was on his knee pumping round after round into the light blue Riviera as it cruised in front of us on Grand Avenue moving in slow motion toward Garey Avenue. *De volada*, the other *veteranos* leveled their *cuetes* and fired into the *ranfla*.

BAM! BAM! BAM! BAM! BAM!

I could hear the *balas* tear into the metal. The windows exploded, showering fragments of shattered glass on the occupants for what seemed like an eternity. Then, one of the *veteranos*, ran into the middle of Grand Avenue and fired several rounds from a high-powered rifle into the trunk and rear window of the *ranfla*.

It sounded and smelled like a war zone. Then, just as quickly as it started, everything turned silent. A gray haze of gunpowder floated like a fog over Sharkie Park. Remarkably, the Riviera continued rolling slowly down the *calle*. Homeboys grabbed the *pisto* and hustled off in *ranflas*. Nite Owl and I ran toward Dopey's garage which wasn't too far away. As I crossed the *calle*, I heard sirens in the distance and saw the Riviera bounce slowly over the curb and come to rest against the stop sign at the corner of Grand Avenue.

I didn't see which direction Li'l Capone ran. For the moment, I wasn't concerned about what was going on with him. My present concern centered on not being around when the *juras* arrived, and they arrived in force, with sirens blaring from their police cruisers, seconds after Nite Owl and I slammed Dopey's garage door shut behind us. We spent the rest of the afternoon in Dopey's garage sipping a six-pack of *pisto* that Nite Owl had wisely grabbed as we'd made our escape from the park. The *juras* ran around picking up shell casings and digging *balas* out of the Riviera which they eventually towed off. Then they all cleared out just before dark and I split for home as the sun set on another Saturday in the park.

Thin Line

In November 1975, our *veteranos* got together with the *veteranos* from Cherrieville and decided to call a temporary truce in the warfare between our two *barrios*. The word was that this one-day truce would allow homeboys from both *barrios* to spend some time getting to know each other, since the opportunity for meaningful dialogue rarely presented itself during a drive-by shooting. The real reason was to provide our homeboys the opportunity to pulverize the *vatos* from Cherrieville in a football game on Thanksgiving Day in Sharkie Park.

While such a truce wasn't exactly unheard of, it was certainly rare. It had been five years since a baseball game between our two *barrios* resulted in a riot with the *juras*. Such a truce wouldn't have been possible a year or even two years ago due to the elevated tension between our *barrios*. But since then things had cooled a bit.

The idea of a football game seemed like an excellent way to promote *barrio* pride while alleviating some of the conflict and hard feelings that had developed over the years between our two *barrios*. Some of the *Calle Doce veteranos* grew up with the *veteranos* from Cherrieville. Many of our homeboys had relatives among the Cherrieville homeboys but the hatred between our *barrios* had grown to such a level that bloodlines no longer mattered.

When I lived on Eleventh Street across from J-Bird and *Travieso*, we all attended Hamilton Elementary School which bordered both *barrios*. A couple of *vatos* from Cherrieville were friends of ours. Back then, we didn't know or care about *barrio* pride, but in the intervening years, all that had changed.

On the day of the game, I left the house early and went directly to Sharkie Park for a meeting where our shot caller laid down two basic rules for the game. First, none of us youngsters were allowed to pack a *cuete*. The *veteranos* would handle security. Second, if any *pleito* broke out, it was to be one-on-one. With the protocol out of the way, we selected our offensive and defensive teams.

It was a great day for a game. The weather was perfect, clear and sunny. Homeboys were relaxed and calm. I was kicking it with Nite Owl, J-Bird, *Travieso*, Slim, and some of the other homeboys at Sharkie Park when the call went up.

"*Trucha* Cherrieville!"

In the wink of an eye, the atmosphere changed from relaxed to tense. Nite Owl, Slim, and I looked at each other as our eyes landed upon the red '66 Impala with its left side patched and primed. It cruised up Grand Avenue with a caravan of at least fifteen other *ranflas* and pulled up on the opposite side of the park. As Cherrieville *vatos* piled out of their *ranflas*, I could see the same stone expressions that we wore reflected in their *caras* as well as a prevailing sense of doubt that we had actually come together to play football rather than throw blows or *balas*.

But the reality of the game hit after the *veteranos* met in the middle of the field and tossed a coin. Cherrieville won the toss and decided to receive. One of our *veteranos* kicked off and the game had begun.

Both sides held their ground and didn't allow any points to be scored during the first quarter. *Vatos* on both sides were big and the tackles hard but fair. Luckily for me and the other youngsters, we were sidelined. The older homeboys were taking care of business for both sides and I didn't mind at all. I could see my skinny butt getting ground up and spit out the minute I stepped on the field. During the second quarter, Cherrieville managed a few key plays and squeaked by with a touchdown. We countered with one of our own. The pattern quickly repeated and the score remained even at two touchdowns all going into the half.

During halftime, both sides sent runners to the liquor store for *pisto* while planning their strategy for the second half.

Going into the third quarter, we maintained our focus on a ground game. It didn't take long for us to realize that this wasn't going to work. As many times as our offense gained control of the ball, the Cherrieville defense shut down our efforts to win a first down. We had to go to the air if we were to have any chance of winning. Just as time ran out on the third quarter, a long bomb caught Cherrieville off guard and scored but failed to achieve the extra point.

With the minutes ticking by in the fourth quarter and the score holding at 20 to 14, the cheap shots started flying. It wasn't long until tempers flared and the fists began flying. No sooner did the *veteranos* break up one *pleito,* then another two *vatos* were going at it. It quickly escalated to the point where the game had to be stopped to let everyone cool down, but as soon as the game resumed, so did the blows.

Everyone knew that *barrio* pride was riding on the outcome of this game and neither side was about to accept defeat, so the truce was rapidly crumbling. Finally, the situation got so bad that the game had to be stopped completely as the *veteranos* from both sides struggled to regain control long enough for Cherrieville to return to their *ranflas*.

As the *vatos* from Cherrieville piled back into their *ranflas*, a clicking sound that resembled the rhythmic chirping of crickets filled the air on both sides of the park. I glanced around to see one of our *veteranos* clicking the hammer of his *cuete*. From the sound of all the clicks, there must have been hundreds of *cuetes* ready to cut loose in both directions with only the slightest provocation. As it was, everyone went home early with some fat lips and black eyes but otherwise no serious damage. Bottom line: no one got shot. All in all, it was a good Thanksgiving Day and I had time to join my family for one of *mi jefita's* wonderful turkey dinners.

Later that evening I thought back to the game with Cherrieville, though not so much about the game itself. Rather, my thoughts centered on how our *barrios*, homeboys, and struggles as Chicanos were the same.

*   *   *

Soon after Thanksgiving, Christmas decorations started showing up in store windows. Personally, I wasn't into the whole idea of Christmas. While I liked receiving gifts, I didn't like the idea of having to go out and buy a bunch of presents. Basically, I couldn't afford Christmas, as my summer mowing jobs were non-existent during this part of the year. Whatever *feria* I got my hands on went to clothes or *pisto*.

For me, Christmas meant another one of *mi jefita's* wonderful dinners and another vacation from school. That's where my thoughts were as I strolled through the halls of Garey High School on a cool December morning. Those thoughts were interrupted the moment I saw a beautiful brown-eyed *ruca* with full voluptuous lips coming my way. I found everything about her attractive. The way she walked. The way her dark hair framed her face, a face that was the vision of beauty itself. As our eyes met, she gave me a smile that will live in my memory until the day I die. I wanted to run up to her and sing the lyrics to "Tell Her She's Lovely" by El Chicano, but all I could do was smile back as she walked past.

Sitting in class the rest of the morning was a lesson in futility. I couldn't get her off *mi mente*. As I moved between classes, she seemed to be everywhere. I couldn't tell if she was following me or I was following her or whether I had skipped school and was really still at home in bed dreaming.

By lunchtime, I couldn't stand it any longer. I saw her talking with a couple girlfriends outside the cafeteria and I decided it was time to make my move. I tried to be cool as I strolled up behind her but I could see one of her friends telling her that I was there. Even so, she maintained her cool and didn't turn around. As I drew nearer, the smell of her perfume overcame me and my thoughts started to scatter. I had to act fast before I lost it completely.

"Q-vo?"

She turned.

"Hi!" she said with a smile echoing in her warm inviting eyes. As if that weren't enough to melt my stone cold heart, her soft melodic voice cut straight to my soul. I knew right then that she could drive my *ranfla* any time she wanted, if I had one that is.

"What's your name?" I said, struggling to keep cool as *mi mente* raced ahead, wanting to know everything about her.

"Sandra. What's yours?"

"*Braso.*"

I don't remember her two friends leaving but suddenly, it seemed that we were the only two people left on earth. I do know that we talked the rest of lunch period but don't ask what we talked about. Simply being in the presence of such beauty was enough for me.

The bell, marking the end of lunch period, brought a rude ending to our conversation. I walked her to her locker, taking it extra slow, knowing the homeboys would notice as we strolled past the rail.

"Can I walk you home?" I asked.

She nodded then reluctantly we parted and I headed for my next class with a big old smile on *mi cara*.

While my grades may not have reflected a renewed interest in my classes, meeting Sandra marked the beginning of nearly perfect attendance. I walked Sandra home after school every day for the next two weeks. On the last day of school before Christmas break, we stopped in front of her house as usual but the look in her eyes was different. I knew she had something on her mind, but I couldn't guess what it might be until she took my hands and looked into my eyes.

"I want you to meet my parents," she said in her warm, soothing style.

I was petrified but how could I refuse.

*   *   *

Her *jefito* was a big man with a rough voice. I knew he could snap me over his knee like a twig if he so desired. He didn't waste any time in setting down the ground rules for seeing Sandra.

"You are more than welcome in my house as long as you are dating my daughter. The two of you will sit in the living room with the rest of the family whenever you are in the house. Do you understand me?"

"Yes, sir!" I responded quickly, knowing that this was not the time to ask for clarification.

Even though I hadn't thought about it before, I liked the sound of the word dating. It didn't really dawn on me until her *jefito* mentioned it that we were, in fact, dating. To me, Sandra and I clicked from the first moment we laid eyes on each other, and it just seemed natural that we would spend time together.

Sandra had two older *hermanas*, three younger *hermanas*, and an *hermano*. I had seen her *hermano* in his blue '64 Impala earlier that year but didn't really know him. He was a couple years older than I. Sandra said that he had recently joined the Marines and was in boot camp, training at Camp Pendleton in San Diego.

Sandra's *jefita* was a pleasant lady. Looking at her, you could easily see the roots of Sandra's beauty. Both of her parents were very nice to me and treated me with respect whenever I visited.

After the Christmas break, Sandra and I continued to spend as much time together as possible. But dating Sandra caused a problem. Now that I spent most of my time with her, some of the homeboys became suspicious of my commitment to *Calle Doce*, even though I still went to all the meetings and hung out with the homeboys whenever I could. They noticed that I wasn't around as much as in the past, and to some this became a point of contention.

I knew that whenever one of the younger homeboys had suddenly changed his pattern of hanging with us on a regular basis, we looked upon it as a sign of weakness. That was the case with Wicked after he recovered from getting stabbed by the *vatos* from Cherrieville in Sharkie Park. He quit hanging out with us and quit using the name Wicked. Even though he had been through a lot, the homeboys lost all respect for him.

Li'l Capone was the most bothered by the way I had decided to redirect my attention. I received word through Nite Owl that Li'l Capone was disappointed with me, and as far as he was concerned, this was my second strike, the first being when I didn't come to his aid in the Fun Zone at the fair. But what could I do? I enjoyed spending time with Sandra, and if Li'l Capone had a problem with that, he'd just have to deal with it. There was nothing I could do about it or for that matter, nothing that I wanted to do about it.

In the early months of 1976, homeboys J-Bird, *Travieso*, Black Crow, and a few others my age moved on from sniffing paint fumes to heroin. That may be why J-Bird and Black Crow "allowed" themselves to get busted while breaking into a local gun shop to steal some *cuetes* for the war against the *juras* which was still on hold, pending the outcome of the wrongful death case filed by Rudy's *familia*. They both were sent to Juvenile Hall, or "juvi," as we called it, for burglary.

Meanwhile, homeboys planned a big party at the Macias's pad for Saturday night. Homeboys and homegirls came out in force. Since Sandra's *jefitos* would not allow us to go out on an actual date, I went to the party solo.

It wasn't long before I started wishing that Sandra was there with me. I suddenly realized how much time we had been spending together in the few months we had known each other. So much so, that spending time apart seemed unnatural. In any case, I never liked dwelling on what I didn't have. Besides, the *pisto* was flowing and, even without Sandra, I was determined to get my share and have a good time.

While grabbing a cold *pisto*, my eyes fell upon *Gata*, named by the homegirls for her beautiful green eyes. Given the weakness of my soul, my fate was sealed. I knew *Gata* had a crush on me, but since I had been with Sandra, I didn't trip on the idea. But tonight was different. Sandra was nowhere around and *Gata* could see that I was in the mood to party. She strolled over and asked me to dance. That's all it took. One thing led to another and before I knew it, we were locked in each other's arms in the back of a homeboy's *ranfla* getting busy to *"Se Me Paro"* by Johnny Chingas. I don't know if this was her first time but it was definitely mine.

Later that night thoughts of what had happened floated into *mi mente* along with a confused mixture of feelings. I'm not saying the experience with *Gata* wasn't great. It was. But for some reason I now felt guilty. As hard as I tried to force the guilt down, the harder it fought to reach the surface. Once I realized that sleep was out of the question, I tried to justify my actions with the idea that I now had bragging rights with the homeboys but that didn't work either. Suddenly, a face appeared on the problem that seemed to be troubling me. I could picture a baby staring up at me from *Gata's* arms. The thought that she might now be pregnant with my child made me sick to my stomach. I wasn't ready to raise a baby, especially with someone I didn't love. And as if that weren't bad enough, I realized that as a result of our physical encounter I had lost any respect I had ever for *Gata*.

Gata knew I was seeing Sandra and I was worried that she would trip but she stayed cool about the whole situation. A week went by and I got wind through another homegirl that Li'l Capone was hot for *Gata*. I didn't want to step on homeboy's toes. Besides, I still liked Sandra and I already had enough problems with Li'l Capone, not to mention that if Li'l Capone found out, Sandra would certainly catch wind of my dalliance with *Gata*. To complicate matters Sandra's older *hermana* was good friends with *Gata's* older *hermana*. I was receiving a fast education on how love was a road fraught with danger. I quickly decided that I had better slow this *ranfla* down before it was too late.

The following week passed without incident and on Saturday, I returned to Sharkie Park to kick back with the homeboys. That evening Li'l Capone and a homeboy, known as Pirate, for his unsuccessful efforts to mimic a pirate's laugh, strolled up. Li'l Capone immediately shined on me but nothing happened. About half an hour later, Li'l Capone and Pirate came up to me.

"Let's go to the back," Li'l Capone suggested.

"*Órale*," I answered, thinking we were going behind the pyramids to smoke some *yesca* but I quickly found out that Li'l Capone had other ideas. As soon as we got behind the pyramids, Li'l Capone blurts out, "Throw some blows with Pirate!"

At first, I thought he was joking but his eyes told a different story.

"Throw blows with Pirate or I'm going to kick your ass!" he commanded in an unmistakably serious tone.

When I didn't move, he shoved me toward Pirate. I'm thinking *what did I do?* I couldn't figure out his game.

"I'm not fighting Pirate!" I asserted.

"You're throwing blows with one of us. Take your pick, *ese!*" he reiterated.

I could tell Li'l Capone wanted an excuse, any excuse to lay into me. A quick glance at Pirate told me that he really wasn't into this bull any more than I was. Give me a *vato* from Cherrieville or a Chino Sinner, and I'd do my best to beat them down, but I couldn't see any reason to hurt my own homeboy. Li'l Capone had some misconception with me, even so I didn't harbor any ill feelings toward him. In fact, I backed off of *Gata* because of my love and respect for Li'l Capone, but he wouldn't let go of whatever was eating at him. This time he pushed Pirate into me.

"Throw blows with *Braso* or I'll kick your ass!" he told Pirate who didn't want any trouble with Li'l Capone so Pirate started throwing a few punches at me but nothing hard. I just stood there waiting to see where all this would lead.

Then out of nowhere … WHAM!

A hard punch smashed into my jaw and snapped my head back. Pirate was as stunned as I was, when I noticed Li'l Capone standing there ready to hit me again.

"Fight!" he said with fire in his eyes.

Pirate immediately responded with a hard punch to *mi cara. Forget this*, I thought. I wasn't about to just stand there as some kind of a punching bag, so I started to throw serious blows with Pirate. We exchanged blows for several minutes then Pirate slipped on the grass. As he fell, I managed to grab him and get in a quick punch to the *cara*. I was about to deliver a second when I felt a crunching pain in my side. This time I knew the source. I let Pirate drop to the ground and quickly spun around to face Li'l Capone so he wouldn't hit me again.

"That's messed up, Li'l Capone. Why don't you leave homeboy *Braso* alone?"

All of us turned to see Marty, Nite Owl's thirteen year old *carnal*, addressing Li'l Capone. "*Órale,* Li'l Capone. What's your trip?" he continued.

"This isn't your business, *ese!*" Li'l Capone responded but Marty didn't back off.

"*Chale*, Li'l Capone. Leave *Braso* alone!"

The youngster had a lot of *huevos* to stand up to Li'l Capone that way. Li'l Capone wasn't swayed by his comments and told Pirate and me to keep fighting. Pirate's right hand was bleeding pretty badly at the knuckles from a close encounter with my teeth. I could tell he didn't want to continue the fight.

"*Caiga, Braso.* Let's go," Marty said.

"If you go," Li'l Capone threatened, "I'll get you later, *ese!*"

All I could see was that Marty had provided a way out of this mess with Li'l Capone.

"*Órale, Braso!* I'll get you later, *ese!*" Li'l Capone yelled as I strolled off with Marty.

"I'm telling Nite Owl!" Marty yelled back.

"Tell your *carnal, ese!* I'll kick his ass, too!" Li'l Capone retorted.

Marty and I strolled around to the front of the pyramids then headed toward his *cantón*.

"*Órale,* Homes. What did you do to Li'l Capone?" Marty inquired.

"*Nada,* Homes. I don't know what his trip is."

When we got to Marty's *cantón,* Nite Owl wasn't home, so I washed the blood off my *cara* and headed home. As I strolled through the dark, quiet *calles,* I kept wondering what had just happened with Li'l Capone. *What was he trying to prove? What was I supposed to prove?* I couldn't figure it out. When I got home, I dropped the reflective thinking and went directly to bed.

On Sunday, I didn't return to Sharkie Park. Instead, I stayed home to recuperate. Then Monday came and I was hesitant to go to school but decided to go anyway since I'd have the chance to see Sandra.

Homeboys were manning the rail, as usual, but Li'l Capone was nowhere in sight. He was usually there strutting about like a peacock with its feathers out, letting everyone know he was in charge. Homeboy Pirate was there with a clean white bandage on his right hand. He just stared at me as I strolled past him on my way to class.

At lunchtime, I still hadn't run into Li'l Capone, so I figured he didn't make it to school. I saw Sandra and she told me that she had to go home after fifth period to help her *jefita,* and for me to come over after school.

When the last bell rang, I hurried out of the building. I had to pass by Pirate's pad, which was right across from the school, on the way to Sandra's *cantón.* Pirate and four other homeboys were already kicking back in his front yard.

"I'm going to get you, *Braso,* for messing up my hand!" yelled Pirate as I strolled past.

I could tell by the tone of his voice that the show was for the other homeboys, so I didn't stop and didn't reply. I wasn't on the prowl for trouble. I was anxious to spend some time with Sandra and wasn't about to be deterred by the opportunity to mix it up with Pirate or any of the other homeboys who were hanging out with him.

By the time I got to Sandra's *cantón,* she had finished the chores for her *jefita.* She invited me to stay for dinner and we watched television with her *familia* until it was time for me to head home. I didn't tell her about the trouble I was having with Li'l Capone, because I didn't want to dig up any possibility of her finding out about *Gata.*

During the next few days, I saw Li'l Capone here and there around school. He would shine me on but never said anything. His silence was almost worse than his punches since I didn't know what he might be planning or when he might strike.

On Saturday, a *veterano* that lived nearby hosted a party at his apartment. When I got there, a lot of homeboys were kicking back with a *pisto* while others were dancing with some of the homegirls to "Night Owl" by Tony Allen. Li'l Capone was nowhere to be found. *Good*, I thought to myself.

As another *rola*, "Thin Line Between Love and Hate" by the Persuaders, came on, homeboy *Malo* strolled up to me and suggested that we go out back. As the two of us strolled around behind the apartment complex, I was hoping we were going back there to smoke some *yesca*, but I'd been wrong in that line of thinking before so I kept *trucha*. When we got to the carports, a lot of homeboys were hanging out in the darkness so I felt better. Just then, *Malo* stopped and all the homeboys formed a circle around the two of us. It suddenly became obvious to me that we weren't there to smoke a peace pipe.

"Let's go at it, *ese!*" blurted *Malo*.

Not again, I thought.

"*Órale, Malo*. I'm not fighting you, Homes," I stated but it didn't matter what I said. *Malo* immediately started firing punches into me like a boxer working a punching bag. I tried my best to block the blows without firing back but wasn't having much success and soon found myself on the ground.

"*Órale, Malo. Ya estuvo*, Homes! You kicked his ass!" exclaimed *Conejo*.

Malo suddenly stopped hitting me.

"*Órale*, Homes. Let's get a *pisto*," *Conejo* said as he helped me up from the ground.

I dusted my clothes off and combed my hair as we strolled back to the party where I quickly downed a *pisto*. *Conejo* didn't ask and I wasn't in the mood to explain the situation with Li'l Capone and how it seemed to be escalating. I got a fresh *pisto*, slipped out with the sounds of "The World Is A Ghetto" by War echoing through the dark alley, and I headed back to my *cantón*.

On the way home, I passed a pack of stray dogs walking side-by-side with the top dog out in front leading the pack. One of the dogs saw me and stepped ahead of the others, placing himself between me and the pack. What the top dog saw was someone challenging his position and he turned his head and growled. That was all it took to encourage the errant dog to fall back into place.

I thought about the homeboys and *Los* Sharkies *Calle Doce* as I continued through the darkness. I knew some of the homeboys, like Li'l Capone, wanted to be top dogs. I just wanted to be one of the pack and enjoy the respect and love of the other dogs. Unfortunately, what I was finding out was that my love and respect for them was making me look weak. Once a homeboy appears weak, everybody puts pressure on him to bring him back into line or drive him away. I suspected that the pressure on me was going to continue and would probably get worse. I wasn't about to become a punching bag for my own homeboys but at that moment, I had no idea what to do about it.

I skipped school for the next few days, so I wouldn't have to deal with any of the homeboys, particularly Li'l Capone. But the days quickly stretched into weeks. It didn't take long for *mi jefita* to notice that I wasn't going to school and to start questioning me. What was I going to say, *my own friends are beating on me!* I didn't even tell Sandra but *mi jefita* figured it out. She put the bruises on my *cara* together with not wanting to go to school and came up with what was really going on.

When my *jefito* found out, I thought it was going to hit the fan but it didn't. All he said was, "You're the one that has to live with your own decisions."

A month passed and I still hadn't ventured into the *barrio* and wasn't ready to face the music at Garey High School. *Mi jefita* suggested that I try another school to finish out my education. So, I enrolled at Pomona High School on the north side of the city.

Mostly *mayates* attended Pomona High with only about a third *Chicanos*. I soon found out there were about twenty *cholos* who claimed to be members of North Side Pomona but these *vatos* hadn't been in any hard-core banging. Homeboys from *Calle Doce* didn't even recognize North Side Pomona as legitimate. These *vatos* knew full well that I was from *Calle Doce* so they left me alone. I suspected it was because of the reputation *Los* Sharkies had for hard-core banging. When I dropped out of Pomona High three weeks later, it wasn't because of any *pleito* with the *cholos* from North Side Pomona. It was more that I had lost my two reasons for going to school.

At Garey, I liked hanging out with the homeboys and enjoyed seeing Sandra. The homeboys and Sandra provided me enough reason to tolerate attending classes often enough not to get kicked out of school.

I didn't know anyone at Pomona and the idea of just getting an education didn't register very strongly with me. My heart, which was still in the *barrio* of *Calle Doce,* had been shattered by the very homeboys that I loved and respected the most. I felt lost and on my own.

One day my *carnal,* who was stationed at *El Toro,* came home for the weekend. *El Toro* was a small Marine base located about 35 miles south of Pomona near San Juan Capistrano, the famous home of the swallows. Seeing him looking good in his green fatigues, I couldn't help but wonder what the Marines would be like. Slowly, the thought of joining the Marines crept into *mi mente.* The more I thought about it, the more I realized that there was nothing keeping me in Pomona.

When I mentioned the idea to my *jefito* and asked if he would cosign for me when I turned seventeen in May, he couldn't have been happier.

"The Marines will teach you responsibility and discipline as a young man," he said, "and get you off the streets."

The next time my *carnal* came home, I asked him about the Marines. He recommended that I go into the Army. I don't know, maybe he knew that the Marines wouldn't accept my rebellious nature as much as the Army.

On May 2, 1976, my seventeenth birthday, my jefito cosigned the papers and I was in the Army. The local recruiter congratulated me for making the right choice. I spent the rest of the month with *mi familia,* but I didn't know how to tell Sandra that I was abandoning her, so I avoided her as much as possible. I didn't know what Sandra thought, but I was going through so much stuff myself that I wasn't in any kind of position to consider what she might need and how I might help her.

On June seventh, I found myself headed to LAX with twenty other green recruits to catch our flight to Fort Leonard Wood, Missouri, for basic training. This was my first trip in an airplane and I didn't know what to expect. As the plane sped down the runway, I felt the power of the engines force my body back into the seat.

It was a trip to watch from my window and see the ground move further and further away as we lifted off into the sky. Los Angeles and Pomona soon became an insignificant speck in the distance. Suddenly, I realized that I had never before traveled this fast or ventured this high or this far from the *barrio*. All kinds of thoughts raced through *mi mente*. I wondered about what I was leaving behind and what lay ahead.

Till now, *Los* Sharkies *Calle Doce* had been the only world I knew, but with each passing minute, my world was rapidly expanding. I thought about how the chain of events that placed me on this plane started that evening at the L.A. County Fair Grounds in the Fun Zone when Li'l Capone caught sight of me as the crowd squeezed in between us like the wedge that would eventually drive us apart. It's funny how one situation over which you have little or no control can change the entire direction of your life. I wondered whether the next time I saw Li'l Capone, I would want to thank him or kick his butt. It was a thin line we strolled between love and hate.

Calle Doce homeboys pose for a picture at the entrance to Sharkie Park.

Homeboys kick back with some *pisto* in front of a wall tagged with *Los* Sharkies *placasos*.

A Pomona *ruca* proudly shows off her Sharketts sweatshirt.

Homeboy savors a *pisto* in the backyard of his *cantón*. The middle sweatshirt on the clothesline shows original *Los* Sharkies *Calle Doce* Pomona design while the two on the sides are designs brought in by the youngsters.

Calle Doce homeboys gather in front of old Catholic Church before a meeting.

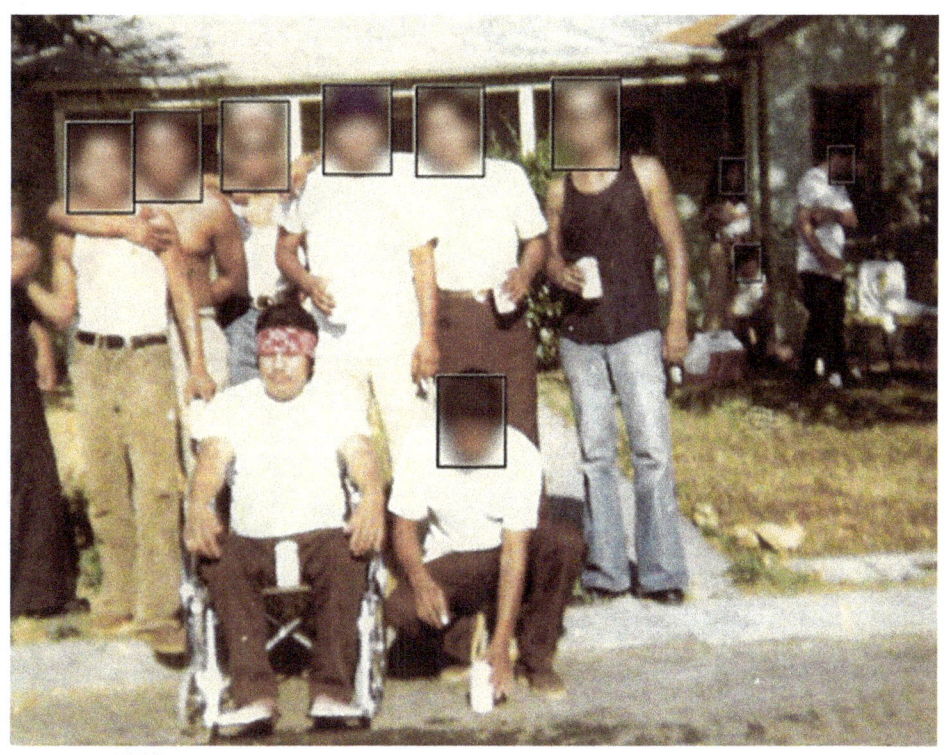

Los Sharkies homeboys enjoy good times and cold *pisto* at a homeboy's *cantón*. Homeboy in wheelchair was paralyzed by a *bala* during a movida from a rival *barrio*.

Los Sharkies *Calle Doce* homeboys gather for a photo. The two youngsters in front display the "XII" arm gestures representing 12th Street.

Homeboys pass the afternoon with some *pisto*.

Los Sharkies homeboys remain *trucha* for *vatos* from a rival *barrio*.

Street shooting in valley leaves 1 dead, 2 injured

Police Friday were investigating a Chino street shooting which left one man dead and two others injured.

Moments after the shooting, Pomona police arrested a suspect and turned him over to the Chino Police Department.

Booked into the West End Sheriff's Department jail in Ontario on a charge of suspicion of homicide was Henry R. Avila, 20, Pomona.

Pronounced dead on arrival at Chino General Hospital shortly after the 11:16 p.m. shooting Thursday was Albert Martinez, 21, Chino.

Rodrigo Nava, 18, Chino, was taken to Chino General Hospital for treatment of gunshot wounds. He was treated then transferred to Kaiser Foundation Hospital in Fontana in stable condition.

Gilbert Martinez, 17, Chino, was given emergency treatment for minor gunshot wounds at Chino General Hospital and sent home.

Robert Ceja, 17, of Chino, was an occupant of the car in which Martinez, Nava and Gilbert Martinez were riding when the shooting occurred. He was not injured.

In reconstructing the shooting, Chino police said they received a call reporting a traffic accident on 2nd Street between C and D streets.

Immediately officers received additional information that shots had been fired at the accident scene.

They arrived to find a car, occupied by the four young men, had jumped the curb and rammed into the side of a house.

Officers were told the four had been shot at by a man in a car who sped away.

Police plan to question more people in slaying of Marine

Pomona police today planned to contact again several persons they questioned earlier in the brutal slaying early Saturday of 17-year-old Marine Pfc. Arthur Garcia.

Police Lt. Jack Blair said that some persons already interviewed were to be recontacted in an attempt to straighten out some discrepancies.

Blair said there have been no arrests in the young marine's killing.

Garcia, of 470 W. 12th St., Pomona, was beaten to death by four youths using tire irons or jack handles. A coroner's office deputy described it as one of the worst beatings he has ever seen.

Garcia was attacked in front of the Towne Shoppe Liquors at 1201 S. Garey Ave. as he was leaving the store. A companion managed to get away.

Garcia, a former Garey High student, had been in the Marine Corps since September.

Permission to reprint these articles granted by *Pomona Progress-Bulletin*.

Gun blast puts man in hospital

One of four young men wounded by shotgun blasts fired from a small pickup truck passing in front of a home in the 12800 block of Wright Street in Chino early Saturday morning remained hospitalized this morning with pellet wounds of the upper portion of his body.

Frank Melendez, 20, according to a Chino General Hospital spokesman, was listed in satisfactory condition this morning recovering from multiple shotgun wounds. Also wounded and treated at Chino General Hospital Saturday morning were Phillip Orosco, 20; Erick Rucker, 17; and Randy Gallegos, 17; all of Chino.

Police said that about 1:30 a.m. Saturday a group of youths were attending a party in front of the Wright Street home. A small white Datsun pickup truck drove in front of the home and one of its passengers suddenly opened fire with what is believed to be a 12-gauge shotgun loaded with birdshot. Four to five shots were fired into the group of youths and adults. Pellets struck the four young men and a car parked on the street.

Police said the motive for the shooting incident was unknown. The youths attending the party, according to police, had no previous connection with any inter-city gang rivalry between Pomona and Chino youths.

Shots fired at police officers at Sharkey Park

Pomona police are seeking clues today in the aftermath of a shooting incident involving three officers at Sharkey Park.

Sgt. Richard Hannibal and officers Reed Laney and Dale Le Fleur were shot at late Friday night after they stopped a car in the park at Grand and Park avenues, police said.

The three policemen had halted a car they believed was involved in a shooting on White Avenue, officers indicated.

While they were placing four juveniles under arrest for possession of marijuana and carrying a concealed weapon, shots rang out, they said, from an undetermined location.

The bullets apparently passed over their heads and no one was injured. Officers believe the weapon used was a .22 caliber rifle, but they have no suspects yet. They did hear loud muffler pipes of a car leaving the park after the incident.

Permission to reprint these articles granted by *Pomona Progress-Bulletin*.

Fresh primer hides the holes made in a homeboy's *ranfla* by *balas* from a rival gang during a *movida*.

Drawing of *cholos* in the 1970s by Don Armijo.

Calle Doce veteranos hanging strong for the *barrio*.

Homeboys doing time at correctional facility.

12

A.W.O.L.

The flight from Los Angeles to Lambert Field in St. Louis, Missouri, took about three hours. Upon arrival, we immediately hopped a bus to Fort Leonard Wood. The bus trip was pretty boring until I woke up after a brief nap to find that we were heading down a big old hill on a scrawny little road that wound its way through the Ozark Mountains in Southern Missouri. I couldn't believe what I was seeing. Los Angeles was surrounded by hills on the east but these hills were so thickly covered with trees that it looked like we were cruising through a South American jungle.

I let my eyes soak up the panorama, and before long a sign at the front gate announced that we had arrived at Fort Leonard Wood, named for some *gavacho* general. I found out during orientation that he had fought against Geronimo in the late 1800s, commanded Theodore Roosevelt's so-called "Rough Riders" regiment, and was the Military Governor of Cuba after the Spanish American War. None of these facts impressed me. I favored the name used by some of the recruits that had been there for a while, "Fort Lost in the Woods."

During the first week, we lived in temporary quarters and were shuffled about as we were issued uniforms, completed more paperwork, got our hair cut, and endured a good number of quarantine shots. My hair was already short, so I didn't spend much time in the barber's chair, but if I never saw another hypodermic needle during the rest of my tour in the Army, it would have been too soon.

There were *gavachos*, *mayates*, and even some *Chicanos* in our ranks. Dudes from all over the country were there. Some of them were already complaining about life in the Army and we hadn't even started basic training. These dudes spent a lot of time counting out pushups, peeling potatoes, and cleaning the most undesirable seats on the entire base. The plain fact was that we all missed home or something that we'd left behind. *What a weak bunch of chavalas,* I thought to myself.

After two weeks of processing, we were loaded onto big trailers with long wooden benches running along each side to take us to the barracks that would be our home for the next twelve weeks.

As we bounced along, I noticed several *placasos* written on the inside wall. One identified "Sleepy *de* Lomas," a gang from East L.A. What was this *vato* doing making his mark way out here? I couldn't believe it. So far from L.A. and homeboys were still throwing up their *placasos*. Back in *Califas*, I would have crossed out that *vato's barrio*. It didn't matter, I thought and just wrote *"Braso de* Pomona *Doce"* on the wall next to "Sleepy *de* Lomas," since I was actually glad to see that other *Chicanos* had taken this ride. Now, when another *vato* climbs into this trailer on their way to basic training, they'll know that they are not alone.

The trailer finally jerked to a stop and the doors flew open.

"You slimy worms got five minutes to get out of my trailer, and two minutes are up!"

The voice boomed at us and everybody scrambled for the door at once. A couple of *gavachos* fell trying to get out.

"Who gave you worms permission to fall on my dirt? Get up and get out of my sight, you slimy worms!"

I've never seen anybody move as fast as those two *gavachos*. When I finally had a chance to quickly look around, I noticed two drill sergeants, stationed on either side of the trailer doors, yelling at everybody who was still trying to get out of the trailer.

"Move it! Move it! I want you worms out of my trailer, now!"

Six other drill sergeants were spread out around the back of the trailer, getting in our faces and telling dudes who looked confused to drop and give them twenty on the spot. Anybody that hesitated got forty. I never heard so much profanity in one day. The confusion continued for a couple minutes until we figured out they wanted us lined up in four rows.

The first couple weeks were the hardest, as I struggled to adjust to this new routine. Every day started early and ended late. It was hot going into July, and most of my time was spent marching, hiking, running, or doing some kind of physical activity, usually with a full field pack. All I could figure is that they wanted to make sure we were asleep as soon as our tired butts hit the bunks in the evenings. No problem. I've never been so tired in my life.

I enjoyed survival training and the time we spent on the rifle range. The fresh smell of gunpowder reminded me of my first *movida* with Nite Owl and Slim after getting jumped into *Calle Doce*. All I had to do was imagine the target hanging round the neck of a *jura* or some *vato* from Chino or Cherrieville and my *balas* always hit their mark.

Unfortunately, most of the time we spent running somewhere just to sit and wait, doing calisthenics, or on some stupid drill. It was interesting how the drill sergeants were teaching us to be killing machines. They weren't that different from the *veteranos* who taught homeboys how to pull the trigger in the *barrio*, but this time it was in service to America. Go figure!

What I did figure out early on was that the best way to get through this was to keep my mouth shut and do what they said. The *gavachos* and *mayates* that didn't snap to that conclusion had the drill instructors screaming in their faces on a daily basis.

Sandra's letters were the only thing that kept me going. In her first letter, she said she had called The Huggy Boy radio show and had made a dedication in my honor. I can't tell how many times I've heard someone dedicate "Greetings, This is Uncle Sam" by the Monitors to a homeboy that had joined the ranks. It was a tradition in the *barrio*, and now it had been played for me. I missed Sandra and my *familia* so much.

My *carnala* also wrote. Her letters kept me updated on what was going on in the *barrio* with the homeboys. In one of her letters, she wrote that Rudy's *familia* won the wrongful death lawsuit against the Pomona Police Department. She also sent some news clippings from the Progress Bulletin, one with a headline that read, "Sniper Fires on Pomona Police." Homeboys had been given the green light to hit the *juras* in payback for what they did to Rudy. I wished I was back there so I wouldn't miss out on the fun, especially now that I knew how to shoot a weapon and hit the target. I could see how this training could payoff.

As each day passed, I noticed more and more of *La Raza* in our ranks. There were *vatos* from New Mexico, Arizona, Texas, Colorado, Nevada, Kansas, and Utah. *Shoot! I never even knew they had a state named Utah, let alone that Chicanos live there.*

There were a lot of *Chicanos* from the Los Angeles area in basic training at Fort Leonard Wood, many of them homeboys just like me. One day while shopping in the PX, I met a *vato* named Mendez who bunked in the barracks across from mine and was from, of all places, Chino! He knew all the *vatos* from D Street. It was a trip because here we hung out together and downed *pistos* whenever we had the chance, as though we were old friends. It made the time go faster. We even formed our own little *qlica* with the other *vatos*. Back in the *calles* of East L.A., we would have been throwing blows or shooting *balas* at each other.

Finally, after twelve weeks, the day I had been waiting for arrived. Graduation from basic training was one of the happiest days of my life. It was the first time I had really accomplished something on my own. I had decided to join the Army, and although there were a number of times that I was just one pushup or one step away from quitting, I actually stuck it out and boot camp was behind me. I was now a Private First Class in the United States Army. Even I was amazed at how much I had changed since signing those papers at the Army Recruiting Station in Pomona nearly three months ago.

After graduation, I stayed at Fort Leonard Wood and completed Field Wire Man training before taking a plane home for a two-week leave. The view of Los Angeles as the plane crested the mountains on the east side of the San Bernardino basin was the most beautiful sight I had ever seen. City lights stretched out forever in all directions as the sun dipped into the dark waters of the blue Pacific.

Sandra and my *familia* met me at LAX as I got off the plane. I could see that they were all as proud of me as I was of myself. Even my *jefito* couldn't help but smile at the sight of his youngest son in a crisp, new Army uniform. I could see by the look in his eyes that he was the proudest of all. Needless to say, I was happy to be home again.

Although it seemed like I had been away on an adventure to the other side of the globe, everything looked pretty much the same on our drive home from the airport. I spent the first couple days with Sandra and hanging out with my *familia,* but it wasn't long before I had to venture into the *barrio* to see what was up with the homeboys.

As I strolled past Sharkie Park, all the memories of the good times I had shared with the homeboys flooded *mi mente.* I missed those times but realized they were now just memories.

A sense of loss fell over me. Somehow, I understood that while everything looked the same, something was very different. Whether it was the situation with Li'l Capone or the fact that I had been away for several months, I didn't know. All I knew was that I looked at Sharkie Park and saw the ghosts of my childhood like an old man looking at the faded pictures in a scrapbook. There was a sadness in looking back and an uncertainty in looking ahead. Right now, I didn't know which was worse.

Marty was kicking back when I arrived at Nite Owl's *cantón.* He was surprised to see me and I was happy to see a familiar *cara.* We drank a few *pistos,* and he told me that Nite Owl, Li'l Capone, *Payaso,* Black Crow, and Fat Joe had all been busted. Some on drug charges, others for breaking into gun shops or for *movidas* on the *juras,* Cherrieville or Chino. *Man, the juras have been taking care of business!* I didn't know what to think.

Nite Owl and Li'l Capone were stopped by the *juras* after a drive-by in Cherrieville. *Payaso* and Black Crow along with another homeboy got busted with heroin found in their *ranfla.* Fat Joe had broken into a gun shop that had a silent alarm and the *juras* arrived while he was still inside. All of them were now serving time in a youth camp.

A good number of the *veteranos* had also been busted and were doing hard time in *la pinta.* Though the war with Cherrieville, Chino, and the *juras* was taking its toll on homeboys, a lot of them were still taking care of business on the home front. Marty also told me that a lot of youngsters were coming up, so there were plenty of new recruits to continue the battle. Marty asked me about life in the Army. I told him so far so good and mentioned some of the *vatos* I had met from *Califas,* even the one from Chino, but I didn't feel the need to tell him that during basic training I had tipped a lot of *pisto* with him.

That afternoon, I headed over to J-Bird and *Travieso's cantón* to visit their parents. They were glad to see me and said that J-Bird was getting out soon, having served his time on the burglary conviction, and that *Travieso* had to do six months on a drug charge.

I could relate to what J-Bird, *Travieso*, Nite Owl, *Payaso*, Fat Joe, Black Crow, and my other homeboys were going through at youth camp. In a way, it felt like I had just been released after serving twelve weeks at Fort Leonard Wood for getting caught in a situation that was out of my control. I had two weeks off and then I'd have to go back and complete my three year sentence.

Two weeks wasn't enough time to catch up on everything that was happening in the *barrio*. Though I still felt connected, at the same time, I felt distant. It was weird.

When it came time to leave, I said goodbye to my *familia* and Sandra, then caught a plane from LAX to my new assignment at Fort Riley in Northeastern Kansas. In route, we had a two-hour layover in Kansas City. It was late October; the sun burned brightly through the large plate glass windows of the terminal building at the Kansas City Airport. I decided to step outside for a breath of fresh air before the short flight to Junction City, a few miles from the fort.

When that first blast of artic air hit me, it cut through my uniform like a sharp *filero*. My butt nearly froze on the spot. I could see my breath and was certain the little hairs in my nostrils had curled up and died. I couldn't get back inside fast enough, and as soon as I did, I wrapped myself around a big steaming cup of coffee. It took two cups before I stopped shivering.

On the flight to Junction City, I saw large white patches all over the ground. *Snow*. I had seen snow in pictures but this was the real thing. I didn't know what I had gotten myself into this time.

Fort Riley was a mixture of old and new. Built in 1853 to keep the Indians from killing settlers who were stealing their land, it was now the home of the Army's First Division, better known as the Big Red One. It intrigued me how similar the Big Red One was to *Calle Doce*. The Army had generals and officers; we had *veteranos* and shot callers. The Army had MPs and Special Forces; homeboys had enforcers and *vatos locos*.

During processing, I was happy to run into Mendez, the *vato* from D Street, and find out that he, too, was stationed at Fort Riley. At least, there would be someone there that I knew.

I was assigned to a tank artillery battalion headquarters. Every day, as the months stretched into the new year, was pretty much the same. We had physical training, what we called P.T., then morning chow and formation. Afterwards, we marched to the motor pool where all the field wiremen in my platoon worked on our equipment. When lunchtime arrived, we hurried to the mess hall, quickly ate then gathered for noon formation and marched back to the motor pool. One final formation before evening chow and the rest of the evening was ours to do whatever we wanted.

Life at Fort Riley was boring and the only town nearby worth mentioning was a little hole in the wall called Junction City which wasn't that different from being on base because you'd see soldiers everywhere. So I passed a lot of time kicking back with Mendez and a few *Chicanos* and Puerto Ricans from New York and Chicago. The *mayates* who had connections to hard-core gangs in New York and Chicago were down for theirs. They had *cora* and knew how to carry themselves, so I didn't mind partying with them. Having to work side-by-side with them showed me what kind of people they were. If we had to go to war, I knew they'd have my back.

Back in L.A., homeboys wanted nothing to do with the *mayates* in the Crips and Bloods who always tried to be like us but didn't know how. The only thing they knew was how to talk loud without really saying anything! Homeboys outnumbered them nearly ten to one and had absolutely no respect for them.

We went through a lot of *pisto,* and I discovered that drugs were easier to get at Fort Riley than in the *barrio*. Speed, cocaine, T.H.C., hashish—which was my favorite, and *yesca* were all readily available. This was some of the best *yesca* I had ever smoked. It hadn't been that long since the end of the Vietnam War, and veterans who had established strong drug connections in the jungles of South East Asia ensured that a constant flow of product came onto the base.

Sometimes it seemed like everybody was doing drugs, and I do mean everybody. Life on base was boring, morale in the military was at an all-time low, and racism between noncommissioned soldiers flourished.

In June, as I passed the one year mark, I received a sad letter from my *carnala* saying that Li'l Capone, who had completed his sentence in youth camp, had been shot to death in the *barrio*. The news hit me hard. I couldn't imagine that a homeboy like Li'l Capone could be killed. It just didn't seem possible. He was a hard-core *vato loco,* and in spite of the difficulties we'd had, I had loved and respected him. I only wish he could have known and understood that.

In the next several months, I received a string of letters from my *carnala* letting me know that homeboys were hitting Chino and Cherrieville hard in payback for Li'l Capone's death. The carload of *vatos* that killed Li'l Capone didn't call out their *barrio*. Since homeboys didn't know whether to blame Chino or Cherrieville, they had to hit both *barrios*. As a result, homeboys introduced a Chino Sinner and two *vatos* from Cherrieville to the grim reaper.

Cherrieville hit back and killed homeboy Lizard, so homeboys took out another *vato* from Cherrieville. Meanwhile, homeboy *Oso* got busted for killing a *vato* from Cherrieville and some of the homeboys got into *pleito* with the Black Angels, so the Sharks were busy blasting on them, too.

Los Sharkies were under attack on three fronts, four if you count the *juras*. It didn't sound any different from the stories I was hearing of firefights in the rice paddies of Vietnam. War is war no matter where it's fought.

After a couple months at Fort Riley, I was transferred within the same battalion to 1st Platoon, Company B. While out in the field, my job was to provide wire line communication between headquarters and the M109, a 155mm self-propelled howitzer that looks so much like a tank that we called it a tank. The M109s were the biggest, baddest, most powerful killing machines I had ever seen. When these beasts fired a round, they caused a rumble that shook everything. I was right in the middle of it. A man from each tank would bring me their communications line and I would hook them all up to a central box. When it came time to move out, I would disconnect all the lines and climb back into the lead tank.

Sergeant Gonzalez, a *Chicano* from *barrio* Dog Patch, known as *Kilo* for his size and stature, was in command of my tank. Dog Patch was a section of Paramount, located in southeast Los Angeles. *Kilo* and I quickly became good friends.

Autumn was rolling in again when we received orders to fly out to Fort Irwin near Barstow, California, for desert training. This was great news as this was only two hours from Los Angeles. If things worked out right I might get a weekend pass.

The second night at Fort Irwin, we were all in the barracks and dead to the world. Suddenly, smoke and tear gas grenades exploded a few feet from my bunk; then some dudes ran through the barracks shooting in all directions. After I soiled my boxers, I ran around in a panic like everyone else trying to get out. I don't know whose idea of fun this was but if it had been the real deal we'd have all been tagged and bagged. We found out later it was Special Forces units who had parachuted in just to mess with us.

Most of us spent our evenings kicking back in the only bar on base. You had Special Forces and grunts alike sporting their unit emblems and colors. Once the *pisto* began flowing, it wasn't long before someone was throwing blows. Fights were so frequent it reminded me of the Fun Zone at the L.A. County Fair.

I was glad when we finally got our paychecks on Friday and a weekend pass. *Kilo's jefito* gave me a ride down to Pomona. My *jefitos* had already left for a two week vacation in Mexico City and left me the *llaves* to the *cantón* and *ranfla*. I immediately picked up Nite Owl and we drove over to J-Bird and *Travieso's cantón*. Homeboys had served their time and were out on the *calles* again. We all drove down to Whittier Boulevard in East L.A. This is where all the baddest lowriders cruise and some fine *rucas* hang out.

We met some *rucas* from East *Los* and partied with them till Sunday when I was supposed to return to Fort Irwin. I called up *Kilo* and told him I had a ride back, and I'd see him at base. Little did he know that I had no intention of going back. Given a choice between a fine *ruca* and an Army bunk, I'll take the *ruca* every time.

Homeboys and I partied with the *rucas* for another week. We would have partied longer but our *feria* was running low, so we said *al rato* to the *rucas* and drove down to Sharkie Park to hang out with the other homeboys. I can't tell you how good it felt to be back.

I was passed out on the sofa when the front door opened and a burst of sunlight hit my bloodshot eyes.

"What are you doing here?" my *jefito* demanded with a look of shock on his face. "Aren't you supposed to be back at base?"

I shook off the hangover and told him I had gone A.W.O.L. for the moment.

"For the moment!" he shouted. He looked so disappointed that I don't think he knew what else to say.

I stayed in the *barrio* for another three weeks and partied with the homeboys. I think it took that long for my *jefito* to calm down but eventually he did. One evening he called me into the living room and we had a serious talk. It was the first time that we really talked to each other man-to-man. He didn't yell or get mad and I actually listened.

He suggested that I get my act together and think about what I was doing. If I wanted to stay in the Army then I needed to go back and take care of this business. He told me it was better if I took responsibility for what I had done because if it was left up to the Army, I might as well kiss my butt goodbye.

I knew he was right. I had heard how poorly the Army looks upon deserters. Besides, I had to get out of Pomona before Sandra caught wind of my madness. I hadn't called her or gone by to visit her the whole time I had been back. I knew what she would say and didn't want to hear it.

On day twenty-nine of being A.W.O.L., I walked into the Pomona recruiting office. The same sergeant that signed me up came out from behind his desk when I walked in. He recognized me and seemed glad to see me but wondered what I was doing there. His smile faded as soon as I told him what I had done. He gave me the same look my *jefito* had when he asked me if I wanted to stay in or wanted out. I told him I wanted to stay in, so he immediately got on the phone.

The next day he picked me up at home and drove me to the Coast Guard station where they gave me a plane ticket back to Fort Riley. My parents took me to LAX but there was some kind of delay, so we said our goodbyes and they left. I don't know how things got mixed up, but the lady at the counter said my flight would be announced over the intercom. I waited and waited. No announcement, so I went back to the counter to the same lady.

"That flight took off an hour ago."

I couldn't believe it.

On the bus ride home, I tried to think of what to tell my *jefito* but nothing I thought of sounded good enough.

The look on his face proved me right. Nothing I said made a difference.

"You're wetting your pants 'cause you don't want to go back and face your responsibility. That's why you missed the plane!"

I didn't blame him for being mad. I was scared but I didn't miss the plane on purpose.

The next day I called up the sergeant at the recruiting office and we went through the same procedure as before, only this time my *jefito* stayed at the airport and made certain that I got on the plane.

My *jefito's* last words before I boarded the plane were, "I hope they kick your butt for me."

I love you, too, dad, I thought, *and thanks for the reassuring words.*

When I arrived back on base, I reported to Sergeant *Kilo*. He took me straight to the captain who asked, "What's your excuse for going A.W.O.L?"

"No excuse, Sir. I wanted to party, Sir."

"I hope you got enough to last you 'cause it'll be a long time before you party in the company of another female," he barked back.

Even though the captain was mad, he wanted to let me off with an Article Fifteen which was a step down from court-martial, but since I had been gone for thirty-one days his hands were tied.

I was confined to my barracks for the next two months. At the trial in January of 1978, I pleaded guilty and it was all over in less than fifteen minutes. The Army sentenced me to twenty-four days in the stockade, loss of rank, and assignment to the Retraining Brigade. They were going to give me a second chance. If I successfully completed retraining, I could finish out my three year contract with the Army and receive an honorable discharge with all benefits.

Kilo received the assignment of escorting me to the stockade. Once my bags were packed and in the jeep, we went directly to the bar and he bought me a couple cold *pistos*. After leaving the bar, he parked in a secluded area of the base and broke out a fat joint filled with *yesca*. We sat there and smoked the whole thing.

The stockade didn't look any different from the rest of the buildings, except that it had a tall chain-link fence with coils of razor wire at the top. Inside the front door, two MPs stood behind a tall podium-type desk. *Kilo* gave them my paperwork, then we shook hands and said our *al rato*. I didn't know when or if I would see him again.

One of the MPs stepped around the podium and looked me over as though I was something he'd wipe off the bottom of his shoe.

"Stand at attention with your back against the wall!" he ordered in a firm voice. I knew this MP wasn't about to take any bull from anyone, and he had the build to back it up.

As I stood against the wall, he grabbed the private first class patch on my left shoulder and ripped it right off my fatigues. Then he tore loose the rank and company patches from my right sleeve. I'll never forget the sound as the threads snapped loose.

I couldn't help but think of a television series that I remembered seeing as a kid called "Branded" staring Chuck Connors as Jason McCord, the only survivor of the Battle of Bitter Creek in the 1880s. Rather than defame an Army commander who was actually to blame for the massacre, McCord kept silent and was court-martialed. The Army stripped him of his stripes, broke his sword. and kicked him off the fort. He spent the whole show traveling the Old West trying to prove that he wasn't a coward. At this moment, I knew exactly how he felt.

The MP dumped the contents of my duffel bag on the floor and ripped the rank insignias off all of my uniforms. He separated my stuff into two piles. He told me to put one pile back into my duffel. The other pile he put in a bag and made me sign for it. He said that I'd get it back when I finished serving my time.

"Pick up your duffel and follow me, Private."

Steel clanked against steel as a set of heavy iron doors slid open. He led me through them and down a long corridor. The sound of the heavy steel slamming shut behind me sent chills up my spine. From there, we entered a holding cell.

"Drop your duffel bag and disrobe, Private. Skivvies, too," he ordered.

There's nothing more humiliating than having to bend over and spread your cheeks while another man looks up your butt for contraband.

I spent the night alone in the cell. It was the loneliest night of my life. I knew it was my fault for getting myself into this mess. As I lay there on the bunk, I began to regret my decision to stay and party with the *rucas* from Whittier instead of returning to base on time.

The next day, I was processed into a cell with fifteen other soldiers. Most of them were there for the same reason I was. Now we were paying for it and the price was chopping wood, eight hours a day, every day, in the freezing cold with nothing but a chisel and sledgehammer or a two-man saw. At the end of the day, I was glad to get out of the cold. A hot meal, a hot shower, and a warm bunk never felt so good, knowing that the next day we would have to do it again. I wasn't what you would call a religious man, but I thanked God for Sunday and the reprieve it offered from the chisel and sledgehammer.

One of the soldiers in the cell was a *gavacho* from Los Angeles named Casper who reminded me of homeboy Spooky. A *Chicano* from Chicago also shared the cell.

"Chicago!" I said. "There's *Chicanos* in Chicago?"

He laughed and told me that *Chicanos* were holding up the flag for *La Raza* big time in Chicago. They were gangbanging hard against the Puerto Ricans. They followed more of an east coast style and didn't have any lowriders. I never knew *La Raza* stretched so far east. It made me feel good to hear that they were hanging out there as homeboys were doing in Pomona.

On my tenth day in the stockade, orders came down for the other fifteen soldiers to transfer to the Retraining Brigade. The MPs told me my orders would come down in a few days. While everyone else shipped out, I chopped wood for another three days.

Finally, my orders came through. I was quickly processed and put into a van. We drove to the south side of the base and stopped at the guard shack. The MPs showed the guards my paperwork, and we proceeded over this little bridge and into what looked like a miniature World War II prison camp deep in the German woods. I had driven past this location many times before and wondered about the old barracks peeping through the trees. My curiosity was about to be satisfied.

The van stopped in front of one of the buildings in the little camp. The MPs directed me to stand at attention against the wall near the door while they went inside. It was cold standing there as the Hawk whistled around the edge of the building, carrying the sound of soldiers singing cadence. For some reason, that cold, sharp northern wind that blew all winter long was known as the Hawk. I stood there hoping that the MPs would hurry back and tell me to go inside but that never happened. The MPs came back out and left without a word. A few minutes later, the door opened and a sergeant poked his head out.

"At ease, Private. Come inside!" he commanded in a firm voice.

I followed him inside. He immediately topped off a cup of lifer juice, the non-career enlisted man's term for coffee, and stepped back behind a long counter.

"That Hawk is kicking my butt today, Private."

I didn't know what to say, so I kept my mouth shut.

He eyed me up and down as he tossed two blankets, two sheets, and a pillow on the counter. Then he grabbed a bag of toiletry items and tossed them on the counter, too.

"Welcome to the United States Army Retraining Brigade, Private. Your first ten days here will be for processing. Then you'll go across the road for ten weeks of training. Do you have any malfunction in understanding that, Private?"

"No, Sergeant!" I responded crisply.

"Good answer, Private!"

He then had me gather my stuff and wait outside for the barracks sergeant who escorted me to what would be my home for the next ten days.

As I stowed my gear in the barracks, I heard the sound of cadence growing louder.

"Platoon, halt!" shouted a drill sergeant outside the barracks. "Right face! You slimy worms got fifteen minutes to prepare for chow! Dismissed!"

The barracks quickly filled with the rumble of soldiers' boots stomping on the old wooden floors as men poured into the barracks. I was happy to see Casper, the *vato* from Chicago, and the others from the brig. Being a soldier was lonely enough but serving time in the brig by myself was nearly unbearable. Having someone around who understood where I came from made the time go faster.

After ten days of processing and some of the best chow I've ever eaten, we started our retraining. From this point until graduation, we weren't privates any longer. We weren't even soldiers. We were hoodlums, the lowest of the low. We had a drill sergeant just like in basic training. As I stood in formation with our new drill sergeant, it hit me that it was like I had just joined the Army and I was starting all over again.

Our drill sergeant, a short stocky man with thick, black eyebrows and a fat cigar, stood there sizing us up with his dark, beady eyes. In a way his look reminded me of that cold, dark stare that Li'l Capone used, detecting even the slightest little weakness that a homeboy might be harboring. I didn't know what our drill sergeant was looking for as he expelled a smoke ring then took another puff on his cigar.

"I'm Drill Sergeant Vinzer! I will be your drill sergeant for the next ten weeks. I will be on you day and night until you hoodlums can get your act together and be productive for the United States Army! And, when you hoodlums are too old to get a hard-on, you will look back and thank me for making you into soldiers again. Is there any malfunction in understanding that?"

"No, Drill Sergeant!" we all spouted from deep within our souls.

At 0400 hours the next morning, the lights flashed on in the barracks and Drill Sergeant Vinzer blew through like a tornado. He threw trash cans, kicked foot lockers, and tossed hoodlums off their bunks if they didn't get their butts up fast enough.

"Get up, hoodlums! Get up! You hoodlums got five minutes to prepare for P.T. and two minutes are up!"

Every day started out at 0400 with calisthenics, then a four-mile run and morning chow. After that, we'd learn to rappel, run the obstacle course, attend some class, or do whatever else the Army thought we needed to do to deserve the honor of rejoining the ranks. It was hard but I was determined to get through it. I had messed up once and that was enough.

That wasn't the case for a skinny hillbilly *gavacho* from Tennessee who Drill Sergeant Vinzer called Gomer Pyle. Gomer was a natural disaster. He couldn't even do one pushup. Some of the guys wanted to kick his butt because he was making it even harder on us, but Drill Sergeant Vinzer made it very clear that if anything happened to Gomer, none of us would graduate. I didn't care about Gomer's sorry butt, I just wanted to get out of this hole and move on.

I must have been doing something right because during the third week, Drill Sergeant Vinzer was having problems with the new squad leader. He jerked the blue arm band off the squad leader's right arm and tossed it to me.

"Here, hoodlum. Be a good leader for your men!"

I was shocked and at the same time, honored and proud. No one had ever trusted me with that kind of responsibility. I didn't let him down.

The next few weeks were some of the toughest I've ever faced. They made boot camp seem like a picnic. Finally, we entered our last week of training. With only five days left, I was more determined than ever to graduate.

Monday morning after chow, we marched to the armory to pick up our M-16s and some ammunition.

"Alright, you hoodlums. Listen up! You will be issued a weapon and six clips of ammunition. Although they are blanks, they are still dangerous. When you get those six clips of ammunition, you will put them directly into your ammo pouches until further instructed. Do you hoodlums understand?"

"Yes, Drill Sergeant!" we all yelled in unison.

Those who had received their weapons stood in formation outside. We were allowed to smoke, talk, and move around as long as we kept one foot in place. I immediately put my ammunition clips in my pouch and strapped my M-16 over my right shoulder. Casper and I were talking about the fact that once we completed three days of combat and survival training, we were done and would soon be assigned back to a regular Army unit, when all of a sudden, BAM!

Drill Sergeant Vinzer came flying out of the armory. I had never seen him so mad. He grabbed his hat and flung it on the ground as he ran up to Gomer Pyle and snatched the smoking weapon from Gomer's hand.

"I can't believe this! I gave you strict orders to put your clips away!" He screamed like a mad man in Gomer's face. The rest of us regrouped in formation and kept our traps shut as Drill Sergeant Vinzer continued his verbal barrage.

"See those woods?"

"Yes, Drill Sergeant!" Gomer replied.

"I want you to take your sorry butt into those woods and don't come back until you find a weapon! Do you understand me, Gomer Pyle?"

"Yes, Drill Sergeant!"

"Move it!" Drill Sergeant Vinzer commanded, still fuming.

While Gomer took off for the woods, the Drill Sergeant bent down, picked up his hat, and positioned it firmly on his head.

After about ten minutes had passed, Gomer came out of the woods carrying a small branch about four feet long. He ran up to Drill Sergeant Vinzer and stood at attention with the branch held across his chest like a long rifle. The Drill Sergeant grabbed the stick and broke it in two pieces and tossed it aside.

"You call that a weapon? That isn't a weapon! I said, don't come back until you find a weapon! Do you understand me?"

"Yes, Drill Sergeant!"

"Move it!"

This time, Gomer emerged from the woods carrying a log, four inches in diameter, that was a little longer than the branch the Drill Sergeant had easily snapped in two. Everybody watched to see if this was sufficient but Drill Sergeant Vinzer grabbed the log out of Gomer's hands and tossed it aside.

"What is your malfunction, boy? I said a get me a weapon! Do you call this a weapon?" Drill Sergeant Vinzer yelled as he moved close to Gomer's ear. "You take your sorry butt back into those woods and you better come back with a real weapon, Gomer Pyle! Now, move it!"

Gomer started to ask a question but the Drill Sergeant interrupted him with "Move it!"

In a few minutes, Gomer came out of the woods dragging a big tree limb with all the branches and leaves still attached. The whole thing was more than twice Gomer's size and he had to wrap both arms around it to make it move. We couldn't hold back any longer. The whole platoon burst out laughing. Even Drill Sergeant Vinzer let a smile spread across his face.

"Now that's a weapon!" the Drill Sergeant announced.

Gomer Pyle just stood there, proud as a peacock, clinging to this stupid tree limb with a silly grin on his face.

"By the end of this day, Gomer Pyle," Drill Sergeant Vinzer said, "I am going to make a soldier out of you that will give the Army a hard-on. Do you understand me?"

"Yes, Drill Sergeant!" Gomer responded.

"Good. Do you know how to say bang!"

"Yes, Drill Sergeant!"

"Then say it!"

"Bang!"

"I can't hear you!"

"Bang!"

"Louder and don't stop!"

Gomer must have yelled "bang" for more than a half hour before Drill Sergeant Vinzer confiscated Gomer's ammo clips and told him whenever he got into a firefight during the next two days that he would have to yell "bang!"

During combat and survival training, we humped our way through some rough country terrain. Toward the evening of the first day, we were ambushed by Company B in a small valley. When the shooting stopped and it got quiet, all you could hear was Gomer's voice echoing through the hills, "Bang! Bang! Bang!"

I graduated from the Retraining Brigade in April, 1978, as first squad leader. I felt proud that I was able to accomplish something during this intensely challenging time in my life. As our bus headed back over that little bridge, my eyes focused on the road ahead and I never looked back.

After graduation, the Army sent me to Fort Ord in northern *Califas*. It was only six hours from Pomona, six hours from Aztlan *con La Raza*. While there, I got my first *ranfla*, a powder blue 1973 Buick Regal, which I lowered to the bone then added some nice rims and white walls.

On weekends, I cruised down to Pomona. I had been away from the *barrio* for nearly two years. It seemed like a long time, but in some ways I was lucky that I had been away since a lot of *veteranos* had been busted as a result of the war with the *juras*. My short time in the brig was nothing compared with the hard time some of them faced. In spite of all that, my trips to Pomona allowed me to repair my relationship with Sandra which was steadily improving, even while the situation between *mi jefita* and my *jefito* remained rocky, mainly due to my *jefito's* affection for the bottle.

Some weekends, I'd hit San Jose where *vatos* were low riding hard on Story and King Roads. The *vatos* from San Jose were starting to do a lot of gangbanging, like East *Los* in the early '70s. There were a bunch of *barrios* up there.

On one of my trips home early in June, I received some sad news. I don't know exactly how it came down, but from what I had heard, a few of the homeboys were kicking back in front of Sad Girl's *cantón* late one night when a carload of *vatos* from Cherrieville did a drive-by. They left one homeboy severely wounded and Sad Girl dead where she fell. This was the first time one of our homegirls had been shot.

On the drive back to base, I couldn't get the thought of Sad Girl out of *mi mente*. I could picture her pretty *cara* and that killer smile. She was also very hard core for the *barrio*, like the female counterpart to Li'l Capone. I remembered her throwing blows with those two black girls at Simons Jr. High, and she stood right beside us dishing it out in the Fun Zone at the fair. She definitely had *cora* and could kick some butt.

Unfortunately, her *placaso* didn't reflect her true nature which was to be joyful. She always liked to clown around and had a way of making everybody laugh. As was often the case, *placasos* told the opposite story and it was Sad Girl's *placaso* that now reflected how we felt. It saddened me to wonder who was taking care of her little daughter.

Sad Girl's death had the same impact on the *barrio* as when Tudy, Rudy, and Li'l Capone were killed. The homeboys were still at war with the *juras,* which only compounded the level of hatred when homeboys extracted their revenge from Cherrieville. Homeboys hit Cherrieville so hard that they completely shut them down to the point where they couldn't even hang out in their own *barrio*.

The remainder of my time in the Army flew past in a blur and before I knew it, it was August of 1979, I was twenty years old and cruising in my Buick south on the Pacific Coast Highway. A warm wind blew in off the Pacific and the "Happy Feelin's" of Frankie Beverly and Maze filled my *ranfla*. This trip home was different from all the others. I had my honorable discharge and once again, I was a civilian.

Three years of Army life was enough for me. I was headed back home to what I knew best. As we used to say, "You can take the homeboy out of the *barrio* but you can't take the *barrio* out of the homeboy!"

13

Weasel's *Wila*

I knew by now that I wasn't meant to be a career soldier serving Uncle Sam. *Thank you very much for the experience* but that whole military scene with rules governing what time you could use the latrine and for how long was just too messed up for me. That wasn't my idea of being a freedom-loving American. Life in the *barrio* meant sharing *carne asada* and a cold *pisto* with the homeboys. That was my picture of freedom.

But since I had been in the Army, the *barrio* had changed. Most of the older homeboys who had been heavy into gangbanging when I joined the Army were now doing hard time in *la pinta* and getting "qlicked up" with *La Qlica*. Joining *La Qlica* required a serious irrevocable decision. Inside the walls, *La Qlica* controlled the flow of heroin and other drugs. They had the *jugo*. Nothing happened unless they said so, and anyone who crossed them usually didn't live long enough to complete their sentence.

On the outside, *La Qlica* also had a lot of influence. Their strong connections with the street gangs gave them the muscle to bring down the wrath of God on anyone, whenever and wherever they wanted. I knew that some of the *Calle Doce veteranos* were qlicked up with *La Qlica*, but I also knew enough not to ask any questions.

Other homeboys that I knew had married and moved out of the *barrio*. Those that remained were heavy into dealing heroin and some of the new drugs like PCP that had appeared on the *calles* since I had been gone. PCP raged through the *barrios* like wildfire devouring dry autumn timber on the hills of Southern *Califas*.

Homeboys had several methods for preparing PCP, but the most popular involved marinating mint leaves, better known as "angel dust." We called it *polvo*.

As destructive as heroin was with its long term effects, PCP was faster and wreaked more havoc, as it quickly became the drug of choice among many of the younger homeboys. This caused a rift between the homeboys who used and those who didn't.

With some military training behind me, I had an idea of how the government gathered intelligence and the tactics they used against the enemy, whether on some foreign battlefield or in the *barrio*. I realized how effectively drugs could be used as a "chemical weapon" against the homeboys, to neutralize them as a significant threat. If we had had a way to hook the Vietcong on animal tranquilizers, our troops could have strolled victoriously into Hanoi during the height of the Vietnam War.

Whether I liked it or not, the *barrio* was changing. Since I'd been gone, the *juras* had become less confrontational, opting to use undercover cops, or narcotics officers which we casually referred to as "narcs," to cruise the *barrios* looking for signs of trouble in their unmarked cars. Even so, we could spot them a mile away.

But the winds of change were blowing through the *barrio*. Even the youngsters brought in a new sweatshirt design and a baggy look, though their Khakis still had a crease. Black and white Nike "Tennie" shoes replaced the shiny Imperials and Stacy Adams. All this was taking *Calle Doce* in a new direction that I wasn't sure I liked.

After being home for a few weeks, my *jefito* suggested that I apply for work at the foundry in West Pomona where he used to work. I also found out that he was moving into a small apartment near his work, as he and *mi jefita* were splitting up. While I was surprised, it didn't completely catch me off guard. They had been arguing and fighting for as long as I can remember. My *jefito* would come and go as he pleased on weekends, and when *mi jefita* asked him where he had been and with whom, thinking he might have been cheating on her, she would explode. I just thought that was part of being married. I never guessed they would actually split up. While it was sad news to hear, there was nothing I could do about it.

On my first day of work at the foundry, I was assigned to a hard-core *vato loco*, who was supposed to show me the ropes. As I approached him, my eyes fell upon a big

"D ST." tattooed on the right side of his neck. This was the *tac* used by the Chino Sinners from D Street. *What have I gotten myself into now! De volada*, he noticed the "XII" *tac* on my right hand. Both of us hesitated. I could see the same thoughts that I had racing through his *mente. Do I mad-dog him or let it go?* To break the impasse, I extended my hand as I said, *"Braso,"* purposely omitting where I was from to minimize any sound of a threat. I was relieved that he did the same, introducing himself as Wizard, a *placaso* homeboys earned by doing a lot of *movidas* and surviving a lot of close calls. We both smiled and exchanged a friendly, respectful handshake.

Luckily, the seven-year war had come to an end because the parents in his *barrio* had finally gotten fed up with all of the violence and joined together in an effort to stop it. This caused friction within the gang since it was homeboys' *jefitos* and *jefitas* policing the *calles* not the *juras*. One night, one of the *jefitas* was shot and killed by a Chino Sinner. This sparked turmoil within the ranks of the Chino Sinners that proved so self-destructive that continuing the war with us proved impossible.

It seemed crazy but somehow, after all those years of hatred between us, we now had respect for each other. This was the kind of respect that a soldier has for a formidable but honorable adversary. Through all the violence and in spite of all the blows and *balas* we had thrown at each other, as far as I knew, neither side had ever snitched to the *juras*. We had held our mugs and fought a good fight. I told Wizard about kicking it in the Army with his homeboy Mendez. He said Mendez was out of the Army and had since gotten married and moved out of the *barrio*.

During my time at the foundry, I met another *vato* who worked in our area. Shady was a member of Big Hazard gang in East *Los*. His *familia* moved into a *casa* on *Calle* Palm Place northeast of our *barrio* in what was considered neutral territory. Shady's wife's sister was married to Big Owl, one of our older homeboys who was doing his last year in *la pinta*.

At work, just as in the Army, which *barrio* you were from didn't seem to matter. We were all *Chicanos* and were always outnumbered by the *gavachos*, so we stuck together.

A couple of months passed and Sandra and I patched up of our differences. I was impressed that she had stuck with me through my time in the Army and especially in spite of all the madness in which I had involved myself. In my book, that was grounds for love. We celebrated her eighteenth birthday and made plans for the future. Actually, she was the only one who had plans, and they all involved us getting married. I thought, *why not?* Within a week, we were on our way to Las Vegas to tie the knot. When we got back, we set up house in a small apartment on the east side of Pomona.

At the same time we were getting married, Sandra's parents were going through a divorce. Sandra's *jefita* moved to a *cantón* near 7th and Polamares Street in *Calle Doce* territory. Sandra's older *carnal* Robert was out of the Marines and living at home because he, too, was going through a separation from his wife. Betty, one of Sandra's older sisters, lived there as well with her young daughter and longtime boyfriend Weasel, a handsome, stocky man, about five-foot six-inches tall with a light brown complexion. Although only in his mid-twenties, heroin abuse made him look much older.

In November, Weasel and his four *carnales* were relaxing in the backyard of Sandra's *jefitas* pad, drinking *pisto* and smoking *polvo* with Robert and another homeboy, Tito, who was my age. As the afternoon surrendered to evening, an argument developed between Weasel and Tito and quickly escalated into blows. Weasel's *carnales* immediately jumped in. Robert tried his best to stop it, but Weasel and his four *carnales* were too much and they worked some heavy damage on Tito. It was all Robert could to do to get Tito back to his *cantón* still in one piece.

The next day, Tito went into the *barrio* and talked with some of the *veteranos* about what had come down. Tito wanted homeboys to call a special meeting and have Weasel and his *carnales* attend. Tito wanted to fight Weasel one-on-one to resolve this before the issue got out of hand.

The *veteranos* respected Tito's older *carnal* who had been killed during a drug robbery nearly four years before and therefore, granted his request for the meeting. Since Weasel was my *cunado*, the homeboys called on me to deliver the *wila* to Weasel. When I told him what the homeboys wanted and asked if he'd be there, he shrugged and gave me an unconvincing "yeah!"

The day came for the meeting and I waited along with Tito and the other homeboys. Weasel and his *carnales* never showed. Tito was determined to have his day in court. Homeboys discussed it and decided to set up another meeting and again, I was instructed to deliver the *wila* to Weasel.

The day of the second meeting came and again Weasel didn't show. At first, I didn't mind being the messenger, but Weasel and his *carnales* were showing their weakness and disrespect for the homeboys. The worst part of it was I was getting caught in the middle.

A third and final meeting was called. *This is it!* I told the homeboys that I would deliver the *wila*, but after this I wasn't going to be anybody's messenger.

This time Weasel's response was "So, what!"

Man! All Tito wanted was a fair fight and may the best man win, but Weasel was disrespecting the homeboys big time by not showing up. I knew something was going to come down, I just didn't know what or when.

That Friday, Sandra and I were kicking back at her *jefita's cantón* watching television. Weasel and Betty were in the kitchen fixing something to eat, and Sandra's younger sisters were playing in the front yard when one of them leaned in the front door.

"Weasel, your friends are outside in a white truck. They want to talk to you!" she yelled.

Weasel stuck his head in from the kitchen.

"Tell them I'm not here," he replied.

He glanced briefly at me before returning to the kitchen. We both knew it was Tito with some of the homeboys.

Sandra wasn't fully aware of what was happening, so she thought it a bit strange when I said, "I'll go tell them."

Not realizing it, I became the messenger again. Even so, I didn't think it was right for Sandra's younger sister to have to deliver Weasel's response. As soon as I stepped out the door, I recognized Tito with a *veterano* we called Trigger riding shotgun. Homeboys didn't get a *placaso* like that for nothing. I knew they meant business. Even so, I strolled up to the truck and casually leaned in the window.

"*Q-vo*," I said acting as though I had no idea what they really wanted.

Tito wasted no time in getting to the point, "Where's Weasel?"

"I don't know, Homes," I replied.

"Is Weasel inside, *ese*?" Trigger plied as he stared deep into my eyes. As I stared back, all I could see was darkness in his eyes. I hoped he didn't see doubt in mine.

"*Chale*, Homes!" I said.

"*Sabes que*, Homes. Don't be lying for that *chavala*, *ese!*" Trigger warned.

"I'm not, Homes. He's not here."

I tried to be as convincing as I could.

"Weasel's inside, *ese*! We know he is!" Tito countered sharply.

Suddenly, Trigger raised a .38 Special that he had hidden between the seat and the door and held it menacingly in front of him so I could see it.

I took one look at the *cuete* and thought, *this mess just got deeper and Weasel's dragging me to the bottom with him*. Once again, I was in the middle like a pigeon with a *wila* tied around my neck!

"*Órale*, Homes. We know he's here, *ese! Sabes que*, we're going inside and if you're lying for that *chavala*, you're going down first!" threatened Trigger.

My thoughts were racing. *I'm no rata but forget this. I'm not going down for that vato!*

"Look, Homes. Weasel's in the kitchen," I offered, "but the kids and . . ."

"We just want Weasel, *ese!*" Trigger interrupted sharply.

Tito pushed the driver's door open as I slowly backed away. Trigger got out and grabbed the back of my collar then shoved his *cuete* in my back. The three of us strolled to the porch.

Trigger prompted me through the door. Tito quickly followed. I saw the shocked look on Sandra's *cara* as she grabbed for the comforting arms of her *jefita* who was equally surprised. All I could do was offer them a look of helplessness. I was the one with the *cuete* in my back.

Trigger made certain everyone saw the *cuete* as he motioned for Sandra and her *jefita* to keep clear. Betty was standing by the stove. When she saw us, her *cara* turned as white as a ghost. Weasel nearly wet his Khakis. *De volada*, he jumped to his feet and glanced at the back door. It was too far away. Trigger immediately shoved me against the counter and focused his attention on Weasel.

"*Órale*, Weasel. Now, it's your turn, *ese!*" Tito shouted and lit into the poor bastard with both fists. Weasel didn't fight back, since he didn't want to provide Trigger with any excuse to unload on him.

Tito beat on Weasel until he wore himself out, then he stuck a finger in Weasel's bloody *cara* and stated with a sense of satisfaction, "*Órale, Chavala!* Now, you know what it feels like!"

With that, Trigger and Tito strolled out through the front.

"Hey, Weasel. There was nothing I could do!" I told him.

"Don't worry about it," Weasel said with a little warble in his voice.

Obviously, his jaw and other body parts were causing him some pain as he grabbed a towel off the counter and wiped the blood off his *cara*. After things calmed down, Sandra and I headed back to our *cantón*.

The next day, we returned to check on Sandra's *jefita*. Sandra stayed in the house to talk with her *jefita*, who still seemed to have been quite rattled by the whole event, while I joined Weasel and his *carnales* in the backyard. As soon as I stepped out of the back door, they wanted to know all the details of how it came down. I wasn't in the mood to rehash it, so I gave them the quick version of events then made up an excuse saying we'd just dropped by to check on Sandra's *jefita* and couldn't stay.

I went back into the *cantón* and told Sandra, *"Vamomos!"*

She kissed her *jefita* and, *de volada*, we went back to our *cantón* where we kicked it the rest of the day.

Little did we know that, soon after we left, Weasel and his *carnales* loaded up on artillery and headed into the *barrio* looking for Tito and Trigger. At the Macias's *cantón*, they found about twenty homeboys kicking back with some *pisto* and enjoying the evening. It seemed that nobody knew what had happened the night before, so when Weasel and his *carnales* burst out of their *ranfla* like the cavalry with their *cuetes* cocked and aimed at the homeboys, nobody expected it.

"Nobody move! Where's Tito and Trigger?" Weasel's oldest *carnal* shouted.

Trigger was in the back. He heard the commotion and strolled to the front to see what was going on. *De volada*, Weasel's oldest carnal drew a bead on him with his *cuete* and told him, *"Caiga, ese!"*

Most *vatos* would be soiling their Khakis by now but not Trigger. He casually strolled up to the Weasel's *carnal* and coldly stared down the barrel of the *cuete*.

"What, *ese*?"

"*Sabes que*. You don't mess with us, *ese!*"

It's not clear what happened in the next few seconds but suddenly a tense silence was broken with . . .

BAM!

Trigger went down, blood streaming from his *cara*.

"Don't move!" Weasel's *carnales* yelled as they nervously fanned the *cuetes* back and forth, then *de volada*, they jumped back in their *ranfla* and burned rubber around the corner.

Homeboys had their own *cuetes* stashed in the bushes but by the time they retrieved them and raced into the *calle*, Weasel's *ranfla* was gone. They quickly loaded Trigger in a *ranfla* and rushed him to the hospital.

Meanwhile, Weasel and his *carnales*, like *pendejos*, returned to Sandra's *jefita's canton*, parked in the backyard, and strolled in brandishing their *cuetes* and bragging about what had just come down. Sandra's *jefita* sensing that this wasn't the end of it, grabbed her granddaughter and told Betty and her other *hijas* to follow her to the neighbor's *canton*. No sooner had they stepped inside the neighbor's door, than four carloads of homeboys surrounded her *canton*.

"*Caiga!* We know you're inside!" homeboys shouted out.

Weasel and his *carnales* responded by shooting out the front window.

Wrong answer!

Homeboys had come packing, and unloaded everything they had on the *canton*, then drove off. Weasel and his *carnales*, thinking the coast was clear, tried to sneak out the back.

BAM! BAM! BAM! BAM! BAM!

Homeboys in the back alley unloaded their arsenal on those *pendejos*. *De volada,* they ran back inside.

In a few moments, six more *ranflas* full of homeboys arrived and shot all their *balas* into the *canton*. Then things quieted down for a few seconds. Suddenly …

BOOM! BOOM!

Several homeboys had worked their way up to the back door and cut loose with a couple shotgun rounds. They tried to kick the door in but return fire from inside forced them back under the protective cover of the *ranflas* as another pack of homeboys arrived and unloaded on the *cantón*.

All Sandra's *jefita* could do is watch the destruction of her *cantón* as she peeked cautiously through the neighbor's window.

Finally, the homeboys ran out of *balas* and left. *De volada*, Weasel and his *carnales* ran to their *ranfla* and fled the scene before another round of homeboys showed up.

* * *

It was late morning. Sandra and I got dressed and ready to go visit her *jefita* for Sunday morning *menudo*, something that had become somewhat of a ritual for us. As we rounded the corner on to 7th Street, we noticed the police cars in front of her *cantón*; then we saw the damage. It looked like an Army platoon had sprayed the *cantón* with several boxes of 50-caliber machine gun cartridges. There wasn't a pane of glass left in any of the windows and the walls looked like Swiss cheese.

As we entered the front door, a *jura* confronted me, "Who are you?"

Sandra's *jefita* explained and he went back to taking pictures and writing on his little note pad. I had nothing to do with this, and he's getting bad with me just because I'm all *cholo'd* out.

"All I could see was this thick, dark cloud of gunpowder hovering over my house like some demon!" Sandra's *jefita* exclaimed. She was still in shock.

Nearly everything in the *cantón*, which was still standing, had a bullet hole or a bullet lodged in it somewhere. The house was a complete wreck. Even the back door had holes in it the size of a man's fist.

I was amazed that Weasel or one of his *carnales* wasn't lying in a pool of blood on the floor with a sheet draped over the body. Sandra's *jefita* and the girls were lucky they got out of there when they did.

After the *juras* left, Robert and I traced some of the bullet holes and found several objects hit by the same bullet before it came to rest in a wall or piece of furniture.

One bullet even went through two walls, the refrigerator, and lodged itself in the wall behind the refrigerator. The *cantón* looked like a war zone; it was crazy!

Robert had been in the *cantón* when homeboys started shooting. The whole time we're tracing bullet paths, he's telling me how it came down. He had me busting a gut as he described his ordeal.

"You should've seen me, *Braso*." Robert explained in a drunken-cowboy accent. "I got out of a side window and then I low-crawled next door like a worm through the grass. Shoot! I thought I was in Vietnam or someplace like that. I could just about feel those bullets kissin' my keester. I knew I had to get to greener pasture as fast as my little knees would craw!"

It was a crazy thing for Robert to do, crawling to the neighbor's house, but he was a Marine and had a gung-ho attitude about this kind of stuff. Good thing none of the homeboys saw him. They would have likely thought he was Weasel or one of his *carnales*, and he would have gotten the full treatment.

We found out later that Trigger had survived and that Weasel and his *carnales* had come out of this deal without a scratch. To me the whole thing was simply amazing. Considering all the *balas* that went through that *cantón*, I couldn't believe that no one had gotten shot, either inside or outside.

Homeboys soon found out that Weasel, who had lived up to his name throughout this entire mess, was still on the run with his *carnales*. All this drama could have been avoided had Weasel taken his medicine like a man instead of acting out of fear and betrayal. Now, *Los* Sharkies had the scent and weren't about to let this one go.

I was tired of getting *wilas* tied around my neck but there wasn't much I could do about it. The truth was I was in too deep and on the wrong side to stay around. So, after Sandra and I helped her *jefita* and her sisters move into an apartment on the north side of Pomona, we decided to get out of town.

Sandra's brother Robert had already moved back with his ex-wife in Denver and was trying to patch things up with her. He urged us to move out to the "Mile High City" with him. He said he had a good job and could get me one, too. Sandra reminded me that I had relatives out there who could help us get by until we got on our feet.

At first I was reluctant, having spent enough time fighting the bitter cold winds of "the hawk" at Fort Riley, Kansas, but Sandra persisted, and I finally agreed that we had to go somewhere since it was impossible to stay in Pomona as long as homeboys were after Weasel.

Sandra and I quickly packed up everything we could fit into my *ranfla* and gave the rest of our stuff to her *jefita*. We said our goodbyes to my parents and were off to Denver which was recording eighteen inches of new snow and a wind chill off the scale. Just the thought of snow made me shiver.

14

The Town I Live In

Upon arrival in Denver, Sandra and I moved in with Robert and his ex-wife. Within a week, I got a *jale* working construction with my *tio* who also lived in Denver but that didn't last long as winter quickly shut down what construction was still going on. Luckily, I found another *jale* driving a truck for a company that made furniture for banks and offices. This gave me the opportunity to learn my way around town.

Meanwhile, another *tio* offered Sandra and me the job of managing some apartments that he owned just south of downtown. I quickly accepted the offer without hesitation, since sharing the house with Robert and his ex-wife was getting on my nerves.

Overall, I liked Denver. It reminded me big-time of Los Angeles, from the downtown skyline to the huge population of *Raza* that lived there. The north side of Denver was just like East *Los*. The *Chicano* movement was strong and had been active since the sixties, but the *Chicano* youth were just now getting into the *cholo* and lowrider scene.

Things ran smoothly for Sandra and me for a while, but before long I missed hanging out with the homeboys, and 38th Street was the closest thing Denver had to our *barrio*. The *cholos* had marked out their cruising territory along a stretch of 38th Street near *Chicano* Park. That's where everyone kicked back. There were a few gangs coming up but nothing to match the mentality of *vatos locos* in Los Angeles. The weakest gang in Los Angeles could kick butt in Denver.

Spring in Denver brought out the *gente*. One afternoon I decided to cruise *Chicano* Park. I had all the fine *rucas* scoping me out to the tune of "More Bounce to the Ounce" by Zapp and Roger as I cruised slow and low in my *ranfla*. The Denver *rucas* loved *vatos* from *Califas*, and I was taking full advantage of the notoriety. Before long, I noticed a *ranfla* with California plates cruising up next to me. I knew the three *vatos* in the *ranfla* had noticed my plates by the way they were checking me out. When they pulled up beside me, they nodded *"q'vole"* and I motioned for them to pull over. We parked and introduced ourselves. The two *vatos* in front were *carnales* from a *barrio* in *El Monte* known as *Monte Flores*. The other *vato* came from a *barrio* called *El Hoyo Mara* in East *Los*. All three of them knew a lot of my homeboys from *Calle Doce*. We all respected each other due to the fact that we were from legit *barrios* back in *Califas*.

I started hanging out with these *vatos* every chance I got, and as time went by we got to know each other pretty well. The oldest *carnal* from *Monte Flores* was a Vietnam vet who had done a couple of tours in the jungle. His younger *carnal* and the *vato* from *El Hoyo Mara* were both fresh out of *la pinta* back in *Califas*. Both had that hard-core *vato loco* look.

The one from *Monte Flores* was a big *vato* in his late twenties with rough brown skin and a thick *brocha*. He had served five years for selling drugs. The *vato* from *El Hoyo Mara* was about my height at five foot six but with a muscular build. His skin was light brown and he had shaved his head bald. I liked the way his *brocha* tapered down around the sides of his mouth. He looked like he was in his mid-twenties even though he was well past thirty. He had done fifteen years in *la pinta* for shooting a security guard during a bank robbery back in 1965.

The situation between Sandra's brother Robert and his ex-wife wasn't improving, so Robert decided to take off for Dallas. Sandra and Robert were born in Dallas and their older *hermana* still lived there.

Sandra and I weren't getting along that well either. She wanted me to stay home and act like a husband. I couldn't see it, so I sent her back to her *jefita* in *Califas* with a broken heart. Our marriage had resulted from a moment of weakness and seemed doomed from the start. The more I thought about it, the less I wanted to think about it. To tell the truth, I didn't care anymore. With Sandra gone, I was free to come and go as I wanted.

It wasn't long before my *tio* lost faith in my ability to manage the apartments. I had left that job up to Sandra, and with her gone, it simply didn't get done. I soon found it easier to put some distance between me and *tio*.

I still had my *jale* delivering furniture, so I had *feria* coming in and was living off and on with one of my *primos* or kicking it with the *vatos* from *Califas* and partying heavy. The *vato* from *El Hoyo Mara* told me that he had been sent to Denver to represent the interests of *La Qlica*, so we were low riding hard and setting up connections with the local *vatos locos*. For a few weeks everything seemed good, but deep down in my soul I missed Pomona and started to regret what I had done to Sandra.

One day, I had had enough, so I told the three *vatos* from *Califas* "*al rato*" and they thanked me for helping them further the cause of *La Qlica*. Then instead of heading to my *jale*, I packed up my *ranfla* and hit the highway with "You're Still A Young Man" by Tower of Power keeping time with the tires.

*   *   *

It was early April of 1980 and I was back in Pomona. It felt really good to be home. Sandra was living with her *jefita* and although I wanted to see her, I wasn't sure she'd want to see me, so I let her be and went down to Black Crow's pad to see what was up with the homeboys.

"*Q-vo*, Homes. Where you been, *ese*?" Black Crow asked as we shook hands.

"Denver."

"Denver, Homes! We were wondering where you disappeared to, *ese*," he said nodding his head.

"Eh, Homes. When all that mess came down with Weasel and his *carnales*, I didn't want nothing to do with it," I explained, then added, "By the way, how's Trigger?"

"Homeboy is still kicking it," Black Crow responded. "The *bala* hit him in the front of his jaw and went clean through his mouth then ricocheted out of his neck. He lost some teeth but nothing a *dentista* couldn't fix!"

"Can homeboy talk?"

"Can he talk?" Black Crow laughed. "Since he got out of the hospital, he hasn't stopped talking about killing them *vatos!*"

"How do I stand with him and Tito?"

He paused a moment, then shrugged, *"De aquellas*, Homes."

"*Órale*," I said with a sense of relief. I had hoped things had cooled off with my being out of sight and was happy to hear that they had.

"What happened to Weasel?" I inquired. "Has anyone seen him and his *carnales?*"

"*Chale*, Homes. Nobody's seen them but they're around, *ese*. Homeboys will put them *chavalas* out of our misery when we find them."

"*Que sí!*" I agreed. "Let's get some *pisto*."

We both climbed into my *ranfla* and headed to the liquor store on 12th Street.

"*Órale*, Homes. What's been happening with the homeboys?" I asked Black Crow.

"Same-o, same-o, *ese*. Most of the homeboys are locked up, and the ones who are on parole were put on this new program where they can't hang around known gang members or they'll get violated."

"That's messed up, Homes!"

"*Sí mon, ese*. It's messed up! *Mi jefito, mi carnal, tios, tias,* and *primos*, we're all from the same *barrio*, Homes. How can they throw a homeboy back into the *pinta* for hanging out with his *familia* and friends?"

Just the thought of what Black Crow was saying made me mad.

"We lived in the *barrio* our whole life, *ese*," he continued. "Now, all of a sudden the law says you can't hang out together! What kind of law is that?"

"What about our civil rights?" I questioned.

Black Crow laughed.

"C'mon, Homes. Nobody cares! You know there's never been any civil rights in the *barrio!*" He paused to pat a bulge on the side of his waist before adding, *"But, you better believe, ese*, I'm not giving up the right to carry a *cuete!"*

A moment of silence gave me a brief opportunity to ponder how the *barrio* had changed yet again. I didn't like it. I didn't like the idea of the *juras* telling us who we could or couldn't hang out with. *It wasn't American!* But then, when did *La Raza* ever figure into what was or wasn't American?

The music of Thee Midniters filled my *ranfla* with "The Town I Live In" as Black Crow started telling me how Nite Owl had to leave the state. He said Nite Owl happened to turn up in the wrong place at the wrong time and witnessed the wrong murder. The trigger man was a general for *La Qlica*. Homeboy had to disappear, *de volada*, or *La Qlica* would have made sure he disappeared permanently.

Black Crow filled me in on all the homeboys. J-Bird had been in and out of *la pinta* on drug violations. *Travieso* had hooked up with some *ruca* from Ontario and was living at her *cantón*. I was glad to hear that Fat Joe and *Payaso* were still hanging tough for the *barrio*, as was *Conejo* when he wasn't working.

As we rolled past Sharkie Park, I noticed that it was empty.

"Where's all the homeboys?" I asked.

"Everybody's down at Big Jerry's *cantón*, Homes."

I was anxious to get back into the routine, so we picked up a couple cases of *pisto* at the liquor store and headed over to Big Jerry's. I was happy to see some homeboys kicking back in front of the *cantón* but there weren't as many as I thought there would be. Even so, I shook hands with everyone as they grabbed a *pisto*. I was glad to be back.

As the afternoon slipped away, more and more homeboys arrived. Near evening, Trigger pulled up. *De volada*, he saw me and strolled in my direction. I wasn't sure what he had in mind until he reached out and we shook hands.

"*Órale*, where you been, *ese*?" Trigger asked.

"Eh, Homes. When that *pleito* with Weasel came down, I didn't want anything to do with it. I didn't know if you and Tito were mad at me or what, so I split to Denver."

"*Órale, Braso*. It didn't have anything to do with you. We wanted Weasel, *ese*."

"*Sí* mon, Homes, but it got too crazy for me!"

"*No hay pedo*, Homes."

No big deal! Maybe now, but at the time it was my neck dangling out in the middle of that mess. I was, at least, glad to see that I had stayed away long enough for things to settle.

Trigger and I shook hands again, and as he turned into the porch light, I couldn't help but notice a little round scar about the size of a nickel just below his Adam's apple. Other than that scar, you'd never know he had gotten shot with a high caliber pistol.

As night overtook the day, a lot more homeboys drove up and the minty fragrance of *polvo* filled the air. I took my first toke and it hit me like stepping in front of a freight train. It took immediate control of my body and *mente* to the point where I wasn't sure where I was or what I was doing for the next couple hours. When I finally broke free of its grip, I knew I didn't want to do that again. I liked knowing what was going on around me at all times.

*   *   *

My *carnal* had been out of the Marines since 1978 and was now driving a bus for the R.T.D. One day, he told me that the R.T.D. was hiring. He said the pay was good and the work easy. That was the kind of *jale* that interested me, so I cruised to the R.T.D. office in downtown Los Angeles and filled out an application. They said they'd let me know.

While I was in Colorado the *juras* had established the "Gang Task Force," and it turned out to be just that—"a gang whose task it was to administer force!" They were always looking for new ways to control how homeboys behaved. This time they had the full support of politicians and lawmakers. These Gang Task Forces or Gang Units were set up in the police departments of each city. Officers came from within the departments and most of them were already well known amongst the homeboys for their flagrant brutality. To me, it seemed like putting the Ku Klux Klan in charge of Harlem!

Homeboys didn't cry about it when the gang units came down on all known gang members because we knew it came with the territory. They kicked in doors and arrested everyone. Those who had weapons or drugs were arrested. Those that didn't were set up. The *juras* were already experienced at planting drugs on homeboys who were clean. They had been doing that for years but not with this level of enthusiasm. Lucky for me, I was in Denver when all this started, otherwise things might have gone differently for me.

Nonetheless, this was nothing new. From zoot suiters to *cholos*, it's always been the same, a battle for control of the *barrios*. One group wants to control the other and is willing to use physical force in order to do so. You'd think that the *juras* and their Gang Task Force would have figured out by now that *Calle Doce* homeboys weren't going to give up control of our *barrio*. To me, what the Gang Task Force needed most was what they were trying to exert upon us in regard to controlling our behavior. From where I stood, they were the ones that were out of control.

The *juras* new plan slowed us down some as we took a hit with declining numbers but it didn't stop us. We simply conducted our meetings in complete secrecy and restructured them somewhat from our open meetings in the early and mid-seventies, but otherwise our unity and leadership remained strong, and we handled any opposition *de volada* before it got out of hand.

The real blow to our *barrio* came from within. A *Chicana* who was very active with the Pomona City Council and extremely vocal on behalf of our *barrio* was somehow convinced by City Council that the *Cinco De Mayo* and Mexican Independence Day festivals, which homeboys had held at Sharkie Park for as long as I could remember, needed to be moved to the park behind City Hall. Stabbed in the back by one of our own, homeboys were stripped of all control over the festivals. While there may have been some valid concerns that prompted moving the festivals, the reality of the situation was that the one thing that brought unity to our *barrio* had been stripped from our grasp. Now, we had nothing to bring pride to our community. Nothing to fill Sharkie Park with *gente*. Nothing to bring us together, except *Calle Doce* and homeboys' unified hatred of the *juras,* and we had plenty of that to go around.

15

Doing It To Death

Halfway through April, I received a call from the R.T.D. to come in for an interview. I went in the very next day and the interview seemed to go well. They hooked me up with a physical which I easily passed. and in a couple days they called back and said I was hired, and they would let me know when I would start training. I was so happy I called my *carnal* and *mi jefes* then I went over to Black Crow's *cantón* to celebrate.

Homeboys Fat Joe and *Payaso* were already at Black Crow's *cantón*. I told them the good news, Black Crow busted out a bottle of *Tequila,* and we all toasted to my new *jale*. While I was there, Black Crow got a call from Big Owl who told him that he had just been released from *la pinta*, so we all loaded into our *ranflas* and headed up to the *cantón* he shared with his *esposa* on Palm Place.

Big Owl was standing on his porch with six other *vatos* when we arrived. I didn't recognize any of them, except Shady, the *vato* I worked with at the foundry who was a member of Big Hazard gang in East *Los*. At first, I wondered why he was there; then I remembered that his wife's sister was married to Big Owl.

Big Owl left the *vatos* on the porch and met us as we got out of our *ranflas*. I immediately remembered his big smile framed by his coffee-colored face, and short black hair which he had neatly combed back on his head. I hadn't seen him for several years and was surprised that he was now in his mid-twenties and how much he'd changed. Homeboy was tall and muscular and what I would consider handsome.

"*Q'vole*, homeboys!" Big Owl shouted joyfully as he shook hands and hugged everyone. He had always respected the *barrio* and there was much love and respect amongst the homeboys for Big Owl.

The *vatos* on the porch were checking us out as Big Owl led us back to onto the porch. Black Crow and each of us carried a case of *pisto*. We set the *pisto* down and all shook hands out of respect for Big Owl, but an air of distrust lingered between us. All of them were from the Big Hazard gang and one of them was Shady's *carnal*. We had never had a problem with the *vatos* from Big Hazard, but there was no love lost either.

Everyone grabbed a *pisto* and we kicked back for a while, then Big Owl wanted us to take him to the *barrio* so he could see the rest of the homeboys. We respectfully said our *"al ratos"* to Shady and the Hazard homeboys and cruised back to the *barrio* where we partied all night with Big Owl at Black Crow's *cantón*.

Monday morning started early. It was my first day of a three-month training program with R.T.D and I was excited as I cruised to *El Monte*. The time went quickly and each day I learned a little more about how they run their system and how to operate those big old busses. They were easier to control than I thought, and the best of all, I liked driving them.

The following Saturday, I went back over to Black Crow's *cantón* to kick back with the homeboys. While I was there, homeboy Slim and Fish drove up with three carloads of homeboys. They seemed excited about something and were eager to let us know what it was.

"Check it out, Homes. Homeboy Evil got kidnapped by Cherrieville last night, *ese*," Slim offered.

We couldn't believe it.

"But somehow he got away!" he continued.

"What!" Black Crow and I exclaimed simultaneously.

"*Sí mon*, Homes. *Matón* wants a meeting."

Black Crow made some phone calls to the rest of the homeboys to inform them about the meeting; then everybody at Black Crow's *cantón* climbed into the *ranflas*. Black Crow sat shotgun and I had four youngsters in back. I threw "Take Me To The

Next Phase" by The Isley Brothers in the tape player as we caravanned in five *ranflas* to the meeting.

We rode low and slow through the *calles* of our *barrio*, swerving to the right through the dips at each intersection then left back into the lane, just as I remembered as a youngster, when I'd caravanned to a meeting for the first time in 1974. Back then, I had to sit in the back; now I was driving. It seemed like only yesterday. I thought about how far I had come and knew I still had a ways to go to earn the respect that was reserved for *veteranos*, but I knew that's what I wanted.

Sixty or seventy homeboys showed for the meeting and gathered in a circle with *Matón* at the top. He sat proudly in a chair, leaning back slightly with his head and chin raised in a posture we commonly called the "gangster lean." He sat casually, with his right leg crossed over his left leg and his hands resting comfortably on his right knee, but there was nothing casual about his look. His light brown face projected the deadly serious look of a stone cold *vato loco*. His dark piercing eyes reminded me of Li'l Capone, but *Matón* was tall and thin. He was in his mid-thirties, and homeboy had just finished doing six years in *la pinta*. He had a lot of *jugo* from *La Qlica*, so when he got out, it was natural that he became the shot caller.

Malo soon arrived with Evil whom *Matón* directed to the center of the circle. The late afternoon sun highlighted his bronzed skin. Evil, in his mid-twenties, was short but stocky, clean-shaven with thick eyebrows and neatly combed hair.

"*Órale*, Evil. Tell us what came down last night." With that, *Matón* began the meeting.

"Check it out," Evil began. "These *rucas* I know from East *Los* came to my *cantón* yesterday and wanted me to go with them to the Boulevard to throw some rounds."

I knew he was talking about Whittier Boulevard.

"While we were there, we stopped at a liquor store to get some *pisto*. As I strolled in, Rascal, *Raton,* and *Chango* from Cherrieville strolled out. *De volada*, we started throwing blows. Some *vato* hit me from behind and knocked me down. Then, all kinds of *vatos* came from out of nowhere and bum-rushed me into this van!"

"*Qué paso con las rucas?*" asked *Matón*.

"*Sabes que*, Homes. The last thing I heard was one of them yelling to call the *juras, pero* everything was happening *de volada*, ese."

"*Órale*," added *Matón*.

"So, I'm in the back of the van and these *chavalas* got a *cuete* in my face. They're are telling me they're going to dump my body on Twelfth Street if I don't tell them where homeboys live and give up phone …"

"What did you tell them?" interrupted *Matón*.

"I told them *chavalas nada*, Homes," Evil was emphatic, *"Nada!"*

"So, then what happened?" *Matón* invited him to continue.

"Next thing I know, the *juras* are stopping us. They told me to keep quiet, but as soon as the *juras* came up to the van, I started yelling and throwing blows with them. *De volada*, the *juras* dragged us all out of the van. They knew what was up. The *juras* busted them for the *cuete* and sat them all on the curb in a line. I told them I wasn't going to forget their ugly *caras!*"

"*Órale*, Evil. *Sabes que* I believe you, and you got my back up, Homes," vowed *Matón*.

As Evil proudly strolled back to join *Malo*, I was thinking how closely he had cheated death. If it hadn't been for those *juras*, I'm sure we would've found homeboy lying face down on Twelfth Street. Evil had held tight and hadn't "ranked out" on his fellow homeboys by giving up addresses and phone numbers. Looking around at the *caras* of all the homeboys, I wondered who among us would have ranked out if we had found ourselves in the same situation. Even with my military experience in P.O.W. training, I wondered what I would do in a similar situation. I wasn't sure of the answer.

Matón cocked his head back and immediately commanded everyone's attention.

"I want Cherrieville hit!" he ordered. "And, I want homeboys in the County to move on them."

It was open season on Cherrieville again both in their *barrio* and in the L.A. County Jail, commonly known by homeboys as "the County."

Just when I thought *Matón* was about to adjourn the meeting, he invited one of the youngsters to the center of the circle. The youngster informed us about a group of youngsters on the south side of Pomona who were calling themselves Southside Lamp

Post and were trying to come up. Everyone broke into laughter when they heard the name of the wannabe gang, Southside Lamp Post. *Who do they think they are?* South Pomona has always been Twelfth Street territory and always will be. Not only that, but we have a lot of homeboys that live in that area, including myself.

"They crossed out our *placasos* and jumped Li'l Puppet," the youngster told Matón.

I couldn't believe it. *These youngsters don't know who they're messing with, because if they did, they'd know they can't disrespect the Shark and escape the jaws of death.*

Matón wanted these *vatitos* dealt with *de volada*, then he adjourned. After the meeting, everyone pitched in for *pisto* and we kicked back and laughed about the youngsters who thought they could move in on our territory without getting slapped down. Later that night a carload of homeboys hit Cherrieville and wounded one of their *vatos* but didn't get to chalk up a kill.

Sunday morning I decided to visit Sandra. I had heard that she wanted a divorce and wanted to talk with her about it. It was funny because when I arrived at her *cantón*, she pulled up with her older sister Betty. I could see that they had just gotten in from a long night of partying. I was jealous because Sandra looked really sexy in her short skirt and blouse, but I knew there was nothing I could say or do since I was the one that pushed her away. While Betty went inside, we stayed on the porch and talked. She told me that she wanted a divorce and added that she might be pregnant from some *vato* that she had been seeing for a couple of weeks now. I told her she could have the divorce and that I wouldn't bother her anymore and left it at that. "Smile Now, Cry Later" by Sunny and the Sunliners broke through on a cassette of oldies I was playing as I cruised to the *barrio*. Sandra was moving on with her life. She must have known that I was a dog with bad habits and was not about to change for her. I felt sad and knew in my heart that it would be a long time before I would find another good woman like her.

I found homeboys kicking back at Sharkie Park. Talk centered on last night's hit on Cherrieville. I also found out that homeboys had spoken with the homeboys in the County by phone. Homeboys in County had stuck four of the *vatos* that kidnapped Evil and put them in the infirmary, leaving them to lick their wounds. The rest of those *chavalas* "locked it up" and were in protective custody. This brought weakness and dishonor on them and their *barrio*. Word was out on those *vatos* from Cherrieville who were now known as "no good." This was the "jacket" they now had to wear, and as a result, all of them were going to catch trouble from the rest of the *Chicano* gangs both in the County and in *la pinta. It's a dog eat dog world*, I thought.

The Shark now turned its attention to the youngsters from the so-called Southside Lamp Post gang. No one moves in on *Calle Doce* territory without paying the price. A couple of our youngsters drove up and told us that there were about twenty Southside wannabes hanging out in front of their *cantóns* on a dead-end *calle* between East Philadelphia and the 60 Freeway. We all loaded up in eight *ranflas* and headed south ready to stick that lamp post where the sun don't shine.

As we caravanned south, we were careful to avoid the *juras*. My *ranfla* was the sixth in the pack of eight. Black Crow rode shotgun and I had four younger homeboys in the back seat as the Isley Brothers' "The Heat Is On" fanned our passion for blood.

When we turned onto their *calle*, we were halfway down their throats before they even noticed us. *Some big gang they are!* By the time they knew something was up, we were toe-to-toe with them and they didn't even know what to say.

"*Somos Calle Doce Los* Sharkies *rifamos!*" we announced.

As soon as they realized who we were, they tried to act like they weren't scared, but I had been around long enough to know how to sense fear in the eyes of your prey. I could tell these *vatos* were scared. Most of them were in their early to mid-teens and I knew they hadn't been in any heavy *pleito* before. The oldest one wasn't more than twenty but none of that made a difference to me. I flat out didn't care. If these *vatos* wanted to talk the talk, then they better be ready and able to walk-the-walk.

We didn't wait for them to react; we attacked!

I went straight for one *vato* but he didn't even know how to fight. It was too easy and I was getting a lot of good shots in when another homeboy laid him out with a blow to the back of his head that sent him to the ground, then the two of us tried to break a hole in the pavement with the *vato's* head.

Some of the Lamp Post *vatos* tried to make a run for it but the Shark had them securely in its jaws and no one was getting out without a severe beating. Homeboys who weren't throwing *blows* were busy busting out windshields with crowbars and tire irons. Li'l Puppet was getting his payback big time.

When we were done, those *chavalas* were all laid out. One of our homeboys pulled out a *cuete* and some homeboys grabbed the older *vato* and stood him upright. Homeboy pressed the barrel of his *cuete* up against the forehead of the *vato* and warned him, "*Te acuerdas! Porque*, next time *Calle Doce* comes down, we come down to kill! *Entiendes? Los* Sharkies *y-que!*"

Homeboy stepped back and whipped the butt of the *cuete* across the *vato's cara* leaving a bloody gash above his eye. Homeboys let him drop like a rag doll to the ground.

To the sound of distant sirens, we all jumped back in our *ranflas* and, *de volada*, sped away in different directions knowing that the *juras* couldn't chase us all.

Black Crow and I were laughing with the other homeboys in my *ranfla* as we headed back to our *barrio*. I doubt those *chavalas* will ever forget who broke them in.

Darkness was falling as I took the last of the homeboys riding with me to his *cantón*. On the way, homeboy Evil flagged me down from his front yard, so I stopped to see what he wanted.

"*Órale*, Homes. Dónde *vas?*" he asked.

"Taking homeboy to his *cantón*," I replied.

"Let's hit Cherrieville!" Evil suggested.

"*Vámonos!*" I responded. I didn't have to think twice. Besides, what's another *movida* to cap the day.

The youngster who had been riding shotgun swung the passenger door open and climbed in back and Evil hopped in the front. As soon as he closed the door and I headed out, he pulled out this shiny .38 "Snub Nose" Special and held it over his heart.

"Loves to kill, Homes!" Evil chanted with a chilling glare in his eyes.

Neither I nor the youngster said a word; we knew he was dead serious.

I drove north on Highway 71, exited on Holt Avenue and headed east, then made a right on Hamilton Street. I knew we could catch them with their Khakis down by coming in from the north. Evil finished checking the *cuete* and seemed satisfied that it was fully loaded and ready for action. As I turned west into their *barrio* on Monterey

Street, my headlights swept across three *vatos* strolling along the sidewalk. *De volada*, homeboy Evil had his *cuete* out the window.

BAM! BAM! BAM!

"*Calle Doce!*" he yelled as the *vatos* dove for cover while he unloaded his last three *balas* on them.

I shut off the headlights and punched the accelerator making a quick left onto Newman Street. One more left and we'd be headed back out of their barrio, when . . .

BING!

A *bala* ricocheted off my rear quarter panel. Within seconds, two more shots hit home. *De volada*, I buried the gas pedal in the floor mat and we skidded into the next turn with tires spinning. More shots rang out but missed. I kept the accelerator floored and jammed through the stop sign with a quick right on Hamilton Street. Luckily, no trains were coming as I raced across the railroad tracks. I could almost visualize the sparks flying from my undercarriage as we bottomed out on each of the three sets of tracks. Another quick right onto First Street and south on the 71 brought us safely back into home territory.

We went to Big Jerry's *cantón*, parked in front and went inside. Big Jerry had a police scanner. We told him what had gone down and he turned up the volume. The *juras* were reporting that one *vato* had been hit and they were looking for a blue *ranfla*. *De volada*, I hurried outside and pulled my *ranfla* around to the seclusion of a carport behind a nearby apartment building.

As I was strolling back to Big Jerry's *cantón*, a *jura* slowly cruised around the corner and came to a stop. We locked eyes and I just about crapped on myself. I thought for sure he knew I was the guilty party. I knew the worst thing you can do at a time like this is look guilty so I kept my cool and strolled on into homeboy's *cantón*. I let a few minutes pass before I peeped out the window and was relieved to find that he was gone.

Evil, the youngster, and I kicked back all night at Big Jerry's *cantón*.

I rose early and strolled around to the carport before the morning sun crested the horizon, so as to head home while it was still too dark to see any damage to my *ranfla* from last night's *movida*. The *calles* were empty and the *juras* were changing shifts, so I wasn't worried. When I got home, I walked around my *ranfla* to see where the *balas* had hit. I expected at least a couple bullet holes but was pleased to find only a small dent, which seemed to have been caused by 22-caliber *bala*, on the right rear fender above the tire well, another one on the trunk, and a third dent above the back window on the chrome stripping. I was pleased that the dents weren't large enough to be noticed by the *juras*.

Later that day the shooting hit the front page of the *Pomona Bulletin* that reported a fifteen year old from Cherrieville had been shot in the eye and was in critical condition. As I read the story, I thought, *an eye for an eye!* I had hoped it was going to report when and where his funeral was going to be held, but had to settle for taking the *vato* out of commission for a while.

The whole experience of catching those *chavalas* in their *barrio* with their khaki's around their ankles was a natural high. We had executed the *movida* with military precision and had achieved good results. The element of surprise had been on our side and made the whole thing seem so easy. I couldn't forget the look on their *caras* when homeboy announced "*Calle Doce!*" It was priceless. Like a bunch of *pollos* with their heads cut off, they didn't know which way to run.

I finished the article and put the newspaper down then smiled to myself as I reflected on this *movida*. I didn't feel nervous the whole time. We were prepared and had gone in to take care of business and that's what we did. I felt good like a soldier who had just returned from a successful raid into enemy territory.

* * *

May 2, 1980, was here and I was now twenty-one years old. I headed over to Black Crow's pad to celebrate with the homeboys. When I arrived, several homeboys were out in the yard and strolled over to greet me. One of the youngsters gave me a fake human skull. Jokingly, I set it on the panel inside the rear window. Everyone was tripping out on the skull and the dents from the *balas*. The dents were considered marks of honor by the homeboys and framed the skull which made my *ranfla* look even more "gangsterized."

The next day, I drilled a hole through the bottom of the skull and wired it to the panel in the back window then wrapped a blue bandana around the forehead of the skull just like we wore them. When I was done, I stepped back and checked it out. *Firme!*

I went inside, took a shower and *cholo'd* down. Put on my dark shades or *loc's*, a tradition that dated back to the *Pachucos* in the fifties. I liked the look.

I cruised to Black Crow's *cantón*. Homeboy Larry and his *carnal* were there with a tattoo machine. I told Larry I wanted a tattoo of a *vato* with a trench coat and a hat where the brim falls over the eyes and the rest of the *cara* is a skull. I also wanted the *vato* holding a *cuete* in his right hand pointed straight ahead like the poster of "Uncle Sam wants you!"

Larry turned on his machine and went to town on the lower part of my left arm. At first, it hurt, but little by little the pain numbed and I got used to it. I was amused how people could adjust to pain and get used to it. I was also impressed with the way Larry worked and how the tattoo gradually took shape. After about two hours Larry had completed the main body of the tattoo and we took a break and each drank a cold *pisto*.

After the break, Larry added a brick wall in the background with the word "SHARKIES" on it and one of those old fashioned lamp posts with a street sign showing "12th St." He finished it off with a full moon and clouds. It looked absolutely *bonarood*.

My first *tac*, located just above my thumb on my right hand, showed my loyalty to the *barrio* and the homeboys. This one showed my commitment to *la vida loca*. I knew there was a new level of responsibility attached to this tattoo. It shouted *"Calle Doce Rifamos"* loud and clear but I also knew that I was up to the challenge. I was proud to death of both *tacs*.

After Larry cleaned up, I took the homeboys out to show them what I had done with the skull. They all tripped out with the way it looked and suggested we cruise the *barrio*.

I was tripping as we cruised through the *calles*. I had my left arm angled out the driver's window so everyone could clearly see my new *tac*. We took the dips at the intersections nice and slow to the rhythm of Fred Wesley and The J.B.'s "Gimme Some More" spilling out from speakers mounted under the panel that held the skull in my back window. I knew in my heart and my soul, I was doing it to death!

16

Sly, Slick & Wicked

I completed the R.T.D. training with no problems and was assigned to a division on the northwest side of Los Angeles. They put me on the 42 Line which took me from the anonymous to the famous and back to anonymity several times in one day. The route ran from downtown L.A. to the Fairfax District of Hollywood and back. Since I was a new driver, I shared the driving with a line instructor until I learned the route.

I liked the *jale*. It was a breeze driving back and forth across town and getting paid for it, so I had no complaints.

The uniforms were nice and comfortable. I wore my pants *cholo* style, a little baggy and long to where they covered most of my shiny Stacy Adams. I always kept a clean and neat appearance.

When people got on my bus, they would trip out on me, especially when I wore my dark shades. No one expected a *cholo* to be driving a bus up Broadway.

Even though my route passed through other *barrios*, I was cool with everyone who got on my bus and didn't sweat the small things. One of the perks was getting to meet a lot of fine *rucas* whenever I went through *barrio* Diamond Street. Once I learned the line, they put me on a four-hour "tripper" during the afternoon rush.

Sometimes I would pass my *carnal*, behind the wheel of his bus, heading south through Los Angeles on Vermont Avenue and we would wave at each other. I was happy for him to see me in my own bus and, in fact, proud to be in charge of moving so many people from place to place.

After work, I would head into the *barrio* in my uniform to see the homeboys. I liked showing off a bit but also knew that it made them feel good to see one of their own with a good *jale*.

* * *

During the summer of 1981, the *juras* in East *Los* started blocking off Whittier Boulevard to all the lowriders. The *gavachos* continued to race up and down Bellflower Boulevard north of Long Beach Airport, but the *juras* didn't shut them down.

Blocking off Whittier Boulevard didn't stop *Chicanos* from low riding. The *juras* simply forced the lowriders to find other *calles* to cruise. Many of the car clubs in Pomona and surrounding cities started cruising Holt Boulevard which headed east and west through Pomona about a mile north of 12th Street.

At first, a small crowd cruised Holt on weekends then as word got around, *gente* from all over East *Los* poured into Pomona on Friday, Saturday and Sunday nights. Most of the cruising took place between East End Avenue and Mills Avenue. The adjacent parking space in front of a shopping center anchored by Sears and a Zody's Department Store gave us plenty of room to kick back and check out the bad *ranflas* and the fine *rucas*.

Homeboys were concerned about so many *vatos* from different *barrios* trying to flex their muscles in Pomona, so *Matón* called a meeting. This was our territory and we couldn't let *vatos* from rival *barrios* come in and think that they could control the boulevard. That would make us look weak. After the meeting, everyone understood that for the next several weeks, homeboys would meet at Big Jerry's pad, then caravan to Holt.

That Friday, we loaded up eight *ranflas* with about forty-five homeboys and headed out. Each *ranfla* had a *Calle Doce Los* Sharkies sweatshirt draped over the driver's door for all to see. On Holt Boulevard, which was already filling up with lowriders, we mad-dogged everyone even the *rucas*, and were ready for anything if anyone disrespected us.

We cruised up and down Holt several times then decided to pull into the Tropicana, a nightclub at the corner of Holt and Mills Avenue where homeboys often gathered to dance. When we got inside, the *rucas* looked good and the music had everyone moving to "Take Your Time (Do It Right)" by The S.O.S. Band. *De volada*, Black Crow snags a *ruca* to dance. We weren't looking for trouble, no more than usual, so we were surprised to run into Shady's *carnal* from Big Hazard sucking down a *pisto* at the bar.

After Black Crow got his groove on with his unique dancing, he and the other homeboys who came in my *ranfla* wanted to throw some more rounds on Holt, so we headed out. I knew the homeboys who stayed were packing, just in case of *pleito*, so I didn't worry about them as we headed to my *ranfla*.

As we were finishing a round on Holt, a carload of homeboys cruised up beside us and told us to split, *de volada, porque* homeboys just shot Shady's *carnal*. No sooner than we received the warning, the *juras* swooped down on the Tropicana. We didn't stick around to see if the *vato* was dead or alive.

Back in the *barrio*, we heard what had happened. After we left, Shady's *carnal* had gotten into an argument over some drugs with homeboys and wanted to take it outside. As soon as Shady's *carnal* stepped out the door, the argument was over in a flash and Shady's *carnal* went down with a *bala* in his brain. Homeboys immediately split, leaving the *vato's* lifeless body lying in a pool of his own *sangre*.

It didn't take Shady long to get the news and to find out that it was a *bala* from a *Calle Doce cuete* that brought down his *carnal*. He and the Big Hazard homies on Palm Place immediately declared war on us.

Matón called a meeting and made certain that Big Owl was there.

"*Sabes que*, Homes," *Matón* warned Big Owl. "You need to move from Palm Place, *porque* Shady wants a payback and if he has a hard time getting it you'll be his target, *ese*."

All the homeboys agreed with *Matón*, but Big Owl didn't seem in the least bit worried about Shady.

"*Chale*, Homes. We're *cunados*!" Big Owl replied.

"*Sí mon*, Big Owl, *pero* you're not *familia*, Homes. You're married to Shady's wife's sister. That don't mean *nada* to him!"

"*Chale*, Homes. Me and Shady get along."

"With all love and respect, Homes, we don't want anything bad to happen to you," *Matón* confided. "You do what you want, *pero* I believe your life is in danger if you stay on Palm Place, *ese*."

The meeting ended with those words of caution and *Matón* telling us to be extra *trucha* for Shady and his homeboys. We knew the *vatos* from Big Hazard were down for their paybacks, and it could be a fatal mistake to ignore them.

Matón didn't want this to spill over into *la pinta* where both sides had homeboys qlicked up, so he sent a *wila* to *La Qlica* to explain the situation in order to prevent any type of escalation.

After the meeting, one of the homeboys invited some of us out to his *ranfla*, opened the trunk, and tossed back a blanket. He had a load of *cuetes*, all types, for sale. I looked them over several times and my eyes kept coming back to a chromed .38-caliber "Snub Nose" Special. I liked the way it looked and the way it felt in my hand, so I bought it.

Till now, I hadn't felt the need to pack a *cuete*. Even though a lot of serious *movidas* had come down during the war with Chino and Cherrieville, I could always get a *cuete* if I needed one. Now with Shady and the *vatos* from Hazard acting crazy in our backyard, I wasn't sure when I would need one, because anything could happen at any time, and I didn't want to get caught with my Khakis down.

As Black Crow and I headed back to my pad, I told homeboy I wanted to pack my new *cuete* somewhere in my *ranfla*. I wanted to be able to get to it easily but keep it out of sight so the *juras* couldn't find it. We both started looking around for a space large enough to hold the *cuete*. At once, both our eyes landed on the arm rest between the front seats. It was perfect, just wide and deep enough to conceal the weapon.

When I got home, I made a straight cut with a knife on the top of the arm rest and took out all the foam rubber in the middle. Black Crow helped me hollow out a section of the foam rubber the shape of the *cuete*. Then, we stuck the foam rubber back in with the *cuete* inside and no one could tell the difference.

Surprisingly enough, a couple days later Black Crow and I were cruising in our *barrio* when a *jura* pulled us over, for no reason other than we were *cholos* riding low and slow, and started searching my *ranfla* from top to bottom. When he finished, he begrudgingly let us go because he didn't find a thing. If he'd only known how close he was to my *cuete*.

The next Saturday, my *carnal* let me borrow his four-door '54 bomb. It was a clean, beautiful machine, lowered to the bone, that my *jefito* had helped fix up. I got in and started it up. I loved the roar of the engine and could feel its power vibrating through the accelerator pedal.

I cruised over and picked up Black Crow and we went over to *Matón's* pad. When we got there, Trigger was there, also. Both of them were tripping on the bomb, so *Matón* and Trigger climbed in and with Black Crow riding shotgun we cruised around the *barrio*. Low riding hard and feeling like the "Duke of Earl" as Gene Chandler's voice carried through the speakers. I wanted to tell them about the new hiding place I had for my *cuete* but thought the fewer people who knew about it the better.

"*Te acuerdas*, Homes," *Matón* said to Trigger as he looked out the window. "When we were youngsters in the *barrio*?"

"*Sí mon*, Homes. Those were the days, *que no?*" Trigger replied.

I couldn't help but remember when I was a youngster, what I would have given to ride in the back seat with the shot caller. Now the shot caller *Matón* was reminiscing with one of his Lieutenants in the back seat of my *carnal's ranfla*. I was tripping on that.

"*Sí mon, pero* everything is changing, *ese*. It will never be the same," lamented *Matón*. His voice revealing a sadness I had never heard from him.

"*Sí mon,* too many homeboys are getting locked up, and that *polvo*, "Trigger added, "is messing up the youngsters, *ese*."

"*Me la raya*, Homes. We let the drugs mess us up!" *Matón* concluded.

Although I knew they were right, it made me uneasy hearing them actually talk about it. *Yesca* was one thing but *polvo* was a whole different ballgame. It was the difference between getting high and getting crazy. As much as the *veteranos* talked about how bad it was for the youngsters to get involved with *polvo*, when it came down to it, the *veteranos* couldn't deny that it was the youngsters involved with *polvo* that were bringing in the "fast" money.

If it weren't for the fact that I liked knowing what was going on around me all the time, I'd probably be smoking that stuff and acting just as crazy as the other homeboys who smoked it. Thank God for small favors.

After cruising the *barrio* for an hour, we all went to the Macias's pad and kicked back with some *pisto*. Later that evening, I gave everyone a ride home, took the *ranfla* back to my *carnal*, then went back to my pad and crashed. At about eight in the morning I was awakened by a phone call.

"*Braso*, this is Black Crow. Wake your ass up. I got some bad news!"

"*Qué pasó?*" I asked, struggling to wake up.

"Check it out, Homes. *Matón* was killed last night!"

That woke me up like a bolt of lightning.

"What! No way!"

"*Sí mon*, Homes. Come and pick me up. All the homeboys are meeting, *de volada!*"

"*Órale*, Homes. I'll be right there!"

I hung up and still couldn't believe what I had heard. I was just with homeboy a few hours ago. I rubbed my eyes again and looked around the room just to make certain that somehow I wasn't still asleep. I took a quick shower, then got dressed and headed over to pick up Black Crow.

On my way to his pad, I couldn't help but wonder what had happened to *Matón*. Was it the *vatos* from Chino or Cherrieville? While I knew we couldn't trust them, things with them had cooled recently. If anything, I thought it was more likely Shady and the *vatos* from Hazard. The thoughts just kept circulating through *mi mente*.

When I got to Black Crow's pad, I pulled up in front and honked. Homeboy came out, *de volada*, and we took off for the meeting.

"*Qué pasó*, Homes?" I asked anxiously.

"*Sabes que*, somebody set homeboy up," he replied.

"Set homeboy up!" I couldn't believe it. "What are you talking about?"

"*Nosotros* had a contract on *Matón, ese*. Somebody got paid off," Black Crow explained with a deadly serious look on his *cara*.

"*Órale!*"

I had heard of *Nosotros*. They were a group of hard-core *Chicanos* from Northern *Califas* who rivaled *La Qlica* for control of drugs in *la pinta*.

"*Sí mon*, Homes. I talked to homeboy's wife and she said that somebody knocked on the door last night after we dropped him off. *Matón* picked up his *cuete* and looked out the door to see who it was, but must have recognized the *vato* because he put the *cuete* away before opening the door."

"*Órale*, so he knew who it was," I said.

"*Sí mon*. As soon as he stepped out the door, they blasted him!"

"In front of his *familia*, Homes?"

"*Sí mon*, Homes. They shot homeboy up, *gacho!*"

"That's messed up!"

I couldn't believe it. Homeboys knew that you didn't take someone out like that in front of their *familia*. Something about this wasn't right. Homeboy never had a chance.

"*Sí mon*, Homes. Besides *Conejo* and you, nobody else knows. So *cuidado* and say *nada* to no one. We still have to find out who came up to the door."

"You think one of our homeboys set him up?" I asked.

"*Sí mon,* Homes. It has to be one of us. Who else could it be? Homeboy would've never put the *cuete* away if it was someone he didn't know!"

I was puzzled. *Why would one of our homeboys set Matón up? Who could have done it?* Black Crow was right. It had to be someone he knew, *but why?*

We were both silent the rest of the way to the meeting. As Black Crow and I strolled toward the *cantón* of the *veterano* that was hosting the meeting, Black Crow whispered to me, "After the meeting, I'll let the righteous homeboys know what we know!" Being "righteous" meant that that homeboy was truly down for the *barrio* and could be trusted with your life.

Conejo called the meeting to order. I wasn't surprised to see that he was now the shot caller. While he wasn't qlicked up, he did have the blessing of the *veteranos* and the respect of all the homeboys. With *Matón* gone, it was *Conejo's* time to lead.

"By now most of you know that *Matón* was killed last night in front of his *familia!*" *Conejo* paused. His cold dark eyes sliced through each homeboy looking for any sign of betrayal.

Likewise, I studied each homeboy, looking at how he reacted to the news of *Matón's* death. I was looking for any sign of guilt. In the history of our *barrio*, I had never seen such treachery. Yeah, we've had *ratas* that we've had to deal with, but nothing like this. I still couldn't believe it even as I stood there hearing that one of our own had betrayed us so badly. *Conejo* didn't delve into much detail and didn't have much else to say other than to ask all of us to pitch in *feria* for *Matón's* funeral.

After the meeting, Black Crow invited the "righteous" homeboys over to his *cantón* and told them what he had told *Conejo* and me. He also explained that who we were looking for used to be one of us. Whoever did this was no longer a homeboy in our eyes. *Conejo* suggested that the deed might have been done in exchange for heroin or *feria*. We had our work cut out for us. Find the guilty party and bring him to justice, homeboys' style! I couldn't help but hope that whoever had done this would save us the trouble by overdosing on a syringe full of death.

Matón was buried with full honors. All the homeboys turned out in colors to show their respect for our fallen leader. We collected nearly a thousand dollars to help *Matón's familia* with the funeral expenses.

Black Crow and I did our best to comfort *Matón's esposa* and *familia*. They were taking the sudden loss of *Matón* very hard, and I couldn't blame them. While his *esposa* understood and accepted homeboy's lifestyle, no one could anticipate being snatched away by the grim reaper in such a malicious fashion.

*   *   *

By August of 1981, Shady had recruited those *vatos* who were connected with Southside Lamp Post. He was jumping *vatos* into his so-called Big Hazard Gang *de* Pomona. We knew he was up to something but didn't know what. It didn't matter to us. No way was he going to catch us with our Khakis down.

The hard-core *vatos* from *barrio* Hazzard in East *Los* didn't recognize the new wannabe members that Shady was jumping in, because they didn't get jumped in by them and were therefore considered untested. They couldn't hang when they were Southside something, now all of a sudden they're gangsters. We knew it was weak.

Those new knuckleheads didn't understand that they were being manipulated by Shady, and kept busy crossing out *Calle Doce placasos* with "The Big Hazard Gang *de*

Pomona Palm Place." Guess they didn't realize that they were just stirring up the Sharks with this little game.

To make matters worse, we found out that homeboy Lucky, who was pushing nineteen, had a younger *carnal* called Mugsy who had started to hang out with the *vatos* on Palm Place and was showing a lot of disrespect toward our *barrio*. Homeboys weren't happy about this. The older homeboys told Lucky to put Mugsy in check, or Mugsy would get a major beat down, or end up dead. I personally felt that Lucky showed weakness by letting his younger *carnal* hang out with those *vatos*, and I lost all respect for him.

Meanwhile, some homeboys were released from *la pinta* and brought home the answer to *Matón's wila*. Word from *La Qlica* was that any issues we had with Shady over the death of his *carnal* would remain in the *calles*. This gave us a green light to move against Shady. All we needed was a plan and the element of surprise.

That Saturday night, about forty homeboys gathered out front at Big Jerry's *cantón* to figure out a good time to make our move. We didn't want to go into Palm Place on a dry run that would alert them to their impending doom. We knew we had to do it right the first time.

As we were working up our plan, four homegirls pulled up in a *ranfla*. Slim, *Payaso*, and I, along with a couple other homeboys, strolled up to them.

"*Q-vo*," we offered respectfully.

Slim leaned toward the passenger window and asked, "*Qué pasó?*"

"*Q'vole*, we're going to cruise Holt," replied Lucy from the driver's seat.

Lucy was a true homegirl and dedicated to the *barrio*. She had a certain darkness in her eyes that let you know she didn't mind mixing it up with anybody that was being disrespectful.

Slim turned back to us and said, "*Órale*, they can check out Palm Place."

"Check out what?" Lucy queried Slim.

He turned back to Lucy.

"We need you to scope out Palm Place. We want to do a *movida* on them. When you see all of them together, come back and tell us."

"That's going to take too long," I interjected. "When you see them, go to the nearest phone booth and call Big Jerry's pad," I instructed.

"*Órale!*" said the other homeboys while Lucy smiled with a slow nod.

"*Te acuerdas*," Slim added. "Don't call until you see all of them."

"*Sí mon,*" Lucy acknowledged then drove off with her homegirls.

The warm air grew heavy with tension as we surrounded *Conejo* while he laid down the rest of the plan. Slim would lead the first group of *ranflas* and I would lead the second. We were going to hit them with a six pack from two different directions, the north and the south, so they couldn't escape. We had six sawed off shotguns and four *cuetes*. I picked up one of the shotguns and stashed it in my *ranfla*. The rest of the shotguns and *cuetes* were distributed amongst the older homeboys in the two groups.

Now all there was to do was to wait for the phone to ring. Some of the homeboys calmed their anxiety by passing some *yesca*. I didn't want anything to dull my awareness, so I settled for a cool *pisto*.

When the call came, every head turned toward the sound. I looked at my watch. It was ten o'clock on the dot. Big Jerry appeared in the front door of his pad, "*Vamonos!*" *De volada,* we all headed to our *ranflas*. Like a platoon of tanks warming up before a battle, our engines roared to life and we drove off in order according to plan. Each *ranfla* stayed several car-lengths apart so as not to raise suspicion if spotted by a *jura*.

Black Crow rode shotgun with me and had my .38 Special tucked under his belt. I had the shotgun at my side. Our target was Palm Place, located northeast of *Calle Doce* where Holt crosses Towne Avenue. Towne Avenue was our main route north. When we reached Monterey Avenue, we split up. The first three *ranflas* continued north on Towne, planning to make a right on Holt, then another quick right into Palm Place. Black Crow and I took our group right on Monterey Avenue.

Palm Place was a short *calle*, one block east of Towne between Monterey and Holt. We were coming in from the south and the other homeboys from the north. Shady's homeboys would be sitting ducks with no way to escape.

Adrenaline surged through my veins while the sound of "Another One Bites the Dust" by English rock band Queen flooded the *ranfla*. A quick glance in my rearview mirror confirmed that the other two *ranflas* in my group were in position behind me, so I cranked the steering wheel with my left hand taking us onto Palm Place. My right hand wrapped tightly around the shotgun and my finger rested gently against the trigger.

As I made the turn, my headlights swung across several groups of *vatos* standing on both sides of the *calle*. In the darkness, I couldn't make out how many *vatos* they had, but it didn't really matter. *The more the merrier*, I thought, as we were about to make Shady and his *vatos* bite the dust.

De volada, I hit the brakes. Black Crow and I swung open our doors and hopped out. I quickly positioned myself behind a parked car and aimed the shotgun over the back of the trunk at the front door of Shady's *cantón* while the homeboys in the back seat burst into the crowd of *vatos*, yelling *"Calle Doce!"*

Flaco, who was second in line in his *ranfla*, screeched to a stop, and he and all the *vatos* with him rushed into the fray as did *Malo* who was behind *Flaco*.

The Palm Place *vatos* didn't know what hit them.

Meanwhile, I kept extra *trucha* for any movement from the Shady's *cantón*. The full moon shed plenty of light, so it was easy to see a *vato* slipping around the side of the *cantón*. It looked like he had some kind of weapon. I quickly drew a bead on him and squeezed the trigger.

BAM!

The blast lit up the yard and echoed between the *cantóns*. *De volada*, I pumped another round into the chamber. When I looked up, the *vato* was gone. He must have retreated for cover or went down. I couldn't be certain what happened to him. Just then, a *vato* burst through the front door of Shady's *cantón*.

BAM!

De volada, the *vato* scooted into a U-turn and ducked back into the *cantón* as the blast from my shotgun tore off part of the screen door. I instinctively pumped another round into the chamber. While the shotgun proved to be enough, I couldn't help but wish that I had the M-16 that the Army had issued to me. With that kind of firepower, I could have taken out the *vato* and opened up the entire front door.

Off in the darkness, I could see the headlights from the other half of our six-pack closing in from the north. These *vatos* were surrounded by Sharks, frenzied with the taste of blood and ready to tear them apart.

Homeboys were exchanging blows everywhere and I could hear the discharge of *cuetes* all around. I wanted to join in the fun but held my position. Then in the midst of the madness, the sound of sirens echoed from a far. It was time to go. Those of us that were packing started to yell, *"Ya estuvas, vamonos!"*

I continued to hold my position while the rest of the homeboys moved back to the *ranflas*. There were two homeboys still beating down some *vato* that was already on the ground. It looked like they were landing some good punches into his side, but as they left him and ran by me I could see *sangre* dripping off their *fileros*. They stuck that *chavala* good.

Black Crow and I took a good look around to make sure no one got left behind. Homeboys learned early in life that you looked out for each other, and just like the Marines, you made sure everybody came home. Once everyone was back in the *ranflas*, I handed the shotgun to a homeboy in the back and ordered, "Shoot into the air!"

BAM! BAM!

Then I jumped behind the wheel. The three *ranflas* from the north were already heading in our direction. After they passed, I threw my *ranfla* into reverse and fell in line behind the others as we all hurried away from the sirens.

The next day, I picked up Black Crow at his *cantón* and we cruised to Sharkie Park where the rest of the homeboys were kicking back. I overheard Big Owl telling a couple of the homeboys, who had missed out on the fun, how we hit those *chavalas* with the precision of a search and destroy mission, putting a lot of them in the hospital. I thought to myself, *the hungry Shark has instilled fear in their hearts and is satisfied, for the moment.*

We stayed *trucha* for the next couple weeks, expecting some kind of retaliation from Palm Place. Late one night some *vatos* hit the home of a young Mexican couple who lived in our *barrio* near 7th and San Antonio. They kicked in the front door and stormed in with guns blazing, shooting the man and his wife. Luckily, they left the couple's baby merely traumatized, but otherwise unharmed. By the time the *juras* arrived, the assailants were long gone. The event surprised and shocked all the *gente* that lived nearby and left the *juras* baffled. Nobody knew why this had happened.

Homeboys immediately had an emergency meeting where we were told that Shady had sent some *vatos* from East *Los* Hazard to hit our *barrio*. Somehow Shady found out, probably through Mugsy, that several of our homeboys lived on the same block as the young couple. It became immediately apparent to everyone that the Palm Place *vatos* had messed up and hit the wrong *cantón*. Had they kicked in the door on either side of the young couple, we might be burying another homeboy. As a result of this new tactic, the four homeboys who lived on that block armed themselves with *cuetes* and formed the first "neighborhood watch."

We did find out later that Shady had targeted a specific homeboy for the attack, one who lived one house east of the young couple. Luckily, the young couple survived and soon afterwards moved out of the *barrio*.

To let Palm Place know that we wouldn't tolerate their intrusions, homeboys hit them with drive-bys every chance we got. While a lot of *balas* were flying and we left their sidewalks stained with *sangre*, we didn't score any kills.

Then one morning Black Crow called my *cantón*.

"Eh, Homes. Big Owl was killed last night in Palm Place. All of the homeboys are having a meeting."

At first, I couldn't believe it. Then a cloud of sadness surrounded me, and all I could say was, "I'll pick you up, Homes."

As I drove over to Black Crow's *cantón*, I couldn't help but remember *Matón's* words warning Big Owl to move out of Palm Place. Somehow, I had known it was just a matter of time before Shady would try to take him out.

At the meeting, two rumors surfaced as to how it had gone down. One was that Shady's *carnala* had two *vatos* from Big Hazard come down and set up Big Owl for the hit. The other rumor had some *rucas* lure Big Owl to their *ranfla* where they blew him away. No one could say exactly how it happened. What was certain was, that Shady was frustrated with not being able to hit us, and Big Owl, just by being there, stuffed *Calle Doce* in his *cara* on a daily basis. The attack on the young Mexican couple had embarrassed Shady, who in his sly, slick, and wicked ways had to kill his sister-in-law's *esposo* Big Owl. Everyone knew he had to do something and that was all he could do. It was just as *Matón* had predicted.

As the meeting broke up, homeboys all pitched in enough *feria* to lay another homeboy's soul to rest.

17

All *Ratas* Die

For the next three months, homeboys went on a rampage against Palm Place to avenge the death of Big Owl. We hit them so hard that Shady and his *familia* had to move out, leaving his ragtag gang and Mugsy to fend for themselves.

On a Friday in February 1982, Black Crow called me after work with the news about a certain homeboy who had suddenly acquired a large amount of heroin. The death of *Matón* had hit Black Crow particularly hard and he had taken it upon himself to find the *vato* who had perpetrated this affront upon our *barrio*. His persistence was about to pay off.

After I hung up, I changed clothes and hurried by Black Crow's *cantón* to pick him up. As soon as he slid into the *ranfla*, he said, "Eh, Homes, when we get to Big Jerry's *cantón* you might want to wait outside. The less who know what's about to happen, the better, Homes."

I knew his suggestion came from love rather than distrust. Black Crow has always been like *mi hermano*. He was giving me the option to jump into the *ranfla* if I wanted, but his hint let me know that the *ranfla* was already full.

"*Órale*, Homes," I replied.

When we arrived at Big Jerry's *cantón*, several homeboys were kicking back. *Payaso* saw me and popped in a cassette with a big smile.

"Eh, *Braso*, this *rola* is for you, Homes."

I didn't catch the name on the cassette but when I heard the honking of a bus horn matched to a funky beat, I knew immediately it was "Double Dutch Bus" by Frankie Smith. *Payaso* had chosen that selection in honor of my *jale* with R.T.D. As I joined him in front of the *cantón*, *Payaso* started to dance and draped his arm around my shoulder, so I joined him for a few steps. Black Crow shared a brief look of gratitude with me as he headed for the *cantón* to formulate his plans. I didn't know how he came upon the information about who perpetrated the hit on *Matón,* but it didn't really matter. I knew they'd take care of business, and *Matón's* death would be avenged.

Later that night, three carloads of *rucas* from *barrio* Peaceful *de* Norwalk drove up to Big Jerry's pad and the party began. Peaceful *de* Norwalk was located about thirty miles southwest of Pomona.

My eyes immediately fell upon a *ruca* of magnificent beauty. Black hair framed her *cara*, accented by narrow, dark Asian eyes and lips that formed a warm smile. I was drawn to her and soon found myself *cara á cara*.

"*Q-vo*, what's your name?"

Her eyes traced a line across the features of my face. She seemed to be analyzing, evaluating, and assessing the very depths of my character before making a choice to communicate with me. All the while, my soul lay bare on an altar before her, to torture or soothe as she saw fit.

"*La* Sleepy," she responded revealing her benevolent nature. "What's yours?"

"They call you that because of your beautiful eyes, huh?"

She smiled softly in appreciation of the compliment.

"So, what's your name?" she persisted.

"Homeboys call me *Braso*."

"What do your lovers call you?"

I didn't have an answer for that one but recovered from the surprise of her directness quickly enough to realize that she had just swung wide open the door to her heart. I wasted no time in staking claim to this beauty, if only for the night.

Meanwhile, Black Crow broke the ice for the other homeboys with his special *Calle Doce* dance to the sound of "Bounce, Rock, Skate, Roll" by Vaughn Mason and Crew. I wasn't concerned with all this, as I was already in the pond well over my head.

The beat of the music and the smooth rhythmic motion of *La* Sleepy's body clinging to mine merely reinforced the desire that was already evident in our eyes. We danced and partied well into the night.

As the morning light gently broke through the windows, I opened my eyes to find *La* Sleepy nestled snugly in my arms on the sofa. It was a good feeling that I hadn't experienced since Sandra and I had broken up. I knew I couldn't let myself get used to it, but I saw no reason not to enjoy it a little while longer, so when *La* Sleepy and her homegirls suggested that we all spend the day at the beach, who was I to complain? This Shark wasn't about to let a fine catch like *La* Sleepy swim away.

Once everybody's eyes were open, homeboys headed to their *cantóns* to shower and grab a quick change of clothes. I took *La* Sleepy to my pad where we showered and gathered some towels for the beach. Everyone met back at my *cantón*, and eight *ranflas* caravanned down the Pacific Coast Highway past Dana Point to Doheny Beach, which the *rucas* had suggested because it had fire pits and allowed overnight camping. We were a few miles north of Capistrano Beach which was usually populated by rich *gavachos*, but that didn't concern us. Both beaches had sand and provided access to the same cool, blue Pacific Ocean.

I soaked up the crisp, cool air blowing in off the water as I helped homeboys carry coolers of *pisto* to one of the fire pits. We had plenty of *pisto* and plenty of *carne asada*. We were well prepared for a good time.

It was nice to get away from the *barrio* for a while. I felt free from the worries of *barrio* life. I felt relaxed like I had not felt for a long time. There were no drive-bys and not a *jura* in sight. Nothing but the endless, rhythmic waves rolling up on the sand, then rushing back out to sea, and a group of people who just wanted to partake in the joys of life.

Soon the fragrant smell of *carne asada* floated across the sand. After we ate and darkness settled over the land, several of the homeboys broke out some *yesca* and *polvo*. We gathered around a crackling campfire, rolled some joints and everyone got a good buzz.

Then all of a sudden, Black Crow stood up and shouted, "Skinny dipping time!"

Several homeboys joined in with, *"Sí mon.* Time to get naked!"

We were serious and to show it at least ten of us homeboys stood up. I think we caught the *rucas* by surprise, because for a moment they looked around in disbelief but almost in unison replied, "Sure!"

I immediately put my hand out to *La* Sleepy. She looked beautiful sitting on the sand in the darkness as the flickering flames of the campfire highlighted her lovely curves. I didn't want to show any hesitation or give her any reason not to join in the fun. I was happy to see that she responded with a warm smile as she reached up to take my hand. The two of us strolled confidently toward the surf.

Black Crow and his *ruca* were already at the water's edge and he was shedding clothes left and right. Some of the *rucas* stood and watched trying to seem a bit shy, but nobody believed their act. All it took was for Black Crow's *ruca* to unbutton her shirt and drop her panties for all the others to follow suit.

La Sleepy and I stood close to each other, just out of reach of the waves lapping at the sand. Both of us kicked off our shoes. I took off my shirt and laid it across my shoes. *La* Sleepy carefully unbuttoned her shirt. My eyes were immediately drawn to her beautiful skin and her heavenly contours highlighted by the moon.

Suddenly, I heard a splash and looked up in time to see the pearly white butts of Black Crow and his *ruca* diving into a wave. The sight made me a little self-conscious about how much my skinny butt would glow in the moonlight but there wasn't much I could do about it. I wasn't about to spoil the moment by climbing back into my boxers at this late date, so I grabbed *La* Sleepy's hand and we both ran into the cold water quickly diving into a wave as it crashed over our heads. *Man that water's cold!* As our heads broke the surface, I pulled *La* Sleepy close, her hard nipples pressing against my chest, and kissed her as my hands roamed the naked expanse of her back. Our shared body heat quickly warmed the entire ocean.

For several minutes, we were the only two humans on earth. Then slowly I started hearing homeboys and their *rucas* laughing and splashing all around us. Black Crow and his *ruca* were only a few feet away.

"Let's get out. I'm afraid of the sharks!" she cried.

De volada, all the homeboys broke out laughing.

"*Órale*, baby doll, we are 'The Sharks!'" Black Crow laughingly explained. "Come here and I'll show you how a Shark bites."

Before long, everybody started dragging their soggy butts out of the water. We dried off as best we could and climbed back into our clothes, then huddled around the warmth of a campfire. The crackling flames felt good. The rest of the night we spent passing *yesca* and *polvo* or slipping off into the darkness for a little privacy.

As the morning sun crested the California hills, we gathered everything together and headed back toward Norwalk. We kissed the *rucas* goodbye in neutral territory and took our tired butts back to Pomona.

I saw *La* Sleepy off and on after that for a couple months, but I think she could see that my love was first and foremost for my homeboys and the *barrio*. She seemed to know that, unfortunately, she would always end up with sloppy seconds.

* * *

In March of 1982, homeboys got together for a football game in Sharkie Park. This was just for our entertainment and didn't involve any *vatos* from Cherrieville or any of the other *barrios*. I don't remember who won or even who played on what side. It didn't matter. Everybody had fun.

After the game, a stranger with a camera approached us. At first, I thought he was *loco* or cruising for a good beating or both. I was surprised to find out some of the *veteranos* knew him and that he was a photographer from a magazine called *Lowrider* who wanted to take our picture. All the homeboys knew the magazine, which first hit the *calles* around 1974. *Lowrider* was the first and only magazine at that time to portray *Chicanos* and their *barrios* in a positive light. Homeboys respected the publication because it celebrated the art and culture of low riding, so everyone gladly gathered round for a photograph.

The *vato* took several group shots with a couple of the homegirls kneeling in front, holding a *Los* Sharkies sweatshirt. After the photograph, homegirls went their way and the homeboys went to a meeting called by Slim, who had eleven youngsters between thirteen and fifteen years of age that he wanted to get jumped into *Calle Doce*. As everyone watched, Slim matched up each of the inductees with a homeboy his own size and had them exchange blows for several minutes. They all fought hard. It looked like a miniature gang fight and reminded me of when we used to trade blows with the *vatos* from Cherrieville in the Fun Zone. When it was all over, they wiped off the blood, shook hands, and were cordially welcomed into *Calle Doce*.

I couldn't believe it. Slim had been with me the night I did my first *movida*. He should know what kind of *huevos* it takes for a young *vato* to pull the trigger for the first time. It can make or break you. This was lame. Every youngster should know how to throw blows before they're even recommended. I didn't know if Slim was on some kind of ego trip or just wanted to be a shot caller. But now I understood why some of the older *veteranos* shared a dim view of this kind of initiation. Personally, I didn't trust any of these new youngsters, since they hadn't undergone a serious test.

My suspicions were proven correct a few weeks later when one of these youngsters got into blows with some *vato* from Cherrieville at an alternative school located at the corner of Park and Holt. The alternative school served as a last chance to get a diploma for troubled students from all the high schools in Pomona, which meant that some of our homeboys had to deal with *vatos* from Cherrieville and other *barrios* every day.

One day a homeboy, called Downer because he was always down for action, had some heated words with the Cherrieville vatos about the situation at the alternative school. Downer and a new youngster told Fat Joe what had come down, and got a couple *cuetes*. When they arrived back at the alternative school, students were being dismissed for the day, so they laid low in their *ranfla* while they watched and waited. As soon as they saw the *vatos* from Cherrieville leave the school, they unloaded on them and sped away. They hit three *vatos* from Cherrieville, leaving one of them dead on the sidewalk in a pool of *sangre*.

The *movida* was a good hit except for the fact that it was done in broad daylight. When the *juras* started asking around, they found plenty of eyewitnesses who gave them a good description of the *ranfla*.

After they learned about the altercation between our homeboys and the *vatos* from Cherrieville, it didn't take the *juras* long to decide who was involved. The *juras* busted the youngster first, which turned out to be good for them because with a little pressure he rolled over, becoming a big time *rata* on Fat Joe and Downer. The way the *juras* worked it, they relocated the youngster's *familia* before homeboys knew what was up, then swooped in and arrested Big Joe and Downer. It was a trip because the *juras* were smooth acting to protect the youngster's *familia* after he spilled the *frijoles*. In fact, this was the first time that the *juras* had acted in this fashion, that's why none of us had suspected a thing.

The only deal the District Attorney had to make was with that *rata!* I couldn't believe it. *He had pulled the trigger también!* All the D.A. wanted was Downer and Fat Joe because of their years of hard-core gang-related activity. When the verdict came down, Fat Joe got seven years and Downer, who was only eighteen, twenty-five to life in *la pinta*. They hit Downer especially hard since ballistics showed that it was his *bala* that killed the homeboy from Cherrieville. All Fat Joe did was drive the *ranfla*. We lost two good *soldados* because that youngster couldn't keep his mouth shut.

I felt sorry for Fat Joe, since he had to do serious time. I wanted to kill that *rata*. All the homeboys did, but no one knew where the *juras* had stashed him. Wherever he was, he'd better stay there *porque* if any of us homeboys got a hold of him, his *jefita* wouldn't even recognize the body when we got through.

*   *   *

It seemed like everybody that I had grown up with was in *la pinta* or had done some time. J-Bird was getting out this month but was lost somewhere over the heroin horizon. *Travieso* married his *ruca* from Ontario. Nite Owl was gone. Only *Payaso*, Black Crow, and I were hanging tough for the *barrio*.

Conejo held a meeting and called out Slim. All eyes focused on Slim as *Conejo*, seated at one of the tables, asked with his piercing stare, "I want to know who gave you the green light to jump in those youngsters?"

Slim, dumbfounded, didn't know what to say. I don't think there was anything he could say. The verdict was already in. *De volada, Conejo* rose followed by Trigger, Big Jerry, *Bala*, and Henry. They quickly surrounded Slim.

"*Órale*, homeboys. *Escucha me!* There's only one shot caller in this *barrio*. That's me!" he said looking around at all of us before directing his stare back to Slim. "You were out of line, *ese. Con todo respeto* and love, but you didn't show me any respect or love!"

No sooner than the word "love" departed *Conejo's* lips, *Conejo* sent Slim down with a *gacho* punch into his *cara*. *De volada,* Trigger, Big Jerry, *Bala*, and Henry started kicking Slim something good. When the dust settled, Slim lay on the ground in a bloody mess. *That's a nasty beating he'll never forget!*

Conejo turned toward the homeboys.

"Slim messed up and this is the price he has to pay. I don't ever want this to happen again, *porque* next time," he paused long enough to stare at each homeboy one at a time before he continued with, "you'll be taken out!"

Everyone knew what he meant.

Conejo returned his attention to Slim who was still in the dirt but showing some signs of life. "*Órale*, you're still good, Slim, but never disrespect me or the *barrio* again, *entiendes?*" Then *Conejo* turned back to the homeboys. "Because of all this, homeboys Downer and Fat Joe are locked up. I want you youngsters that got jumped in by Slim to stand in the middle!"

Ten youngsters slowly made their way to the center of the circle.

"*Sabes que* I got a mission for you *vatos*. And, if you don't take care of it, take a look around you." The youngsters looked at all the homeboys surrounding them. *Conejo* continued, "*Porque* these will be the *vatos* who will take care of you!"

This was what should have happened in the first place. Had these youngsters been jumped in right, Downer and Fat Joe would have been sitting here with us at the meeting instead of doing time in *la pinta,* and that little *rata* who sold them out would have gotten his head served to him on a platter for not having the *huevos* to take care of his business and keep quiet about it. That's how it should have happened but it didn't. Now *Conejo* had to make it right. He sent everyone away, except the ten youngsters. The rest of us headed for Sharkie Park where we took up a collection for some *pisto* and kicked back the rest of the day. Nobody said much about what happened to Slim. We all seemed to know that *Conejo* wasn't completely finished dealing with this insurrection.

18

Shark's Teeth

In May of 1982 I turned twenty-three years old. Just like many other birthdays, I spent the evening kicking back with the homeboys and tossing down a few cold *pistos*.

I was still working for R.T.D. but had been assigned to drive a new line. This one ran south on Broadway from downtown L.A. to Olympic Boulevard then west through Beverly Hills past Rodeo Drive all the way to Century City, a large shopping mall. It wasn't much different than before, only now I went from poor to rich to poor again several times in one day. Even so, I liked the change of scenery and seeing all the fine *ranflas* folks drove in Beverly Hills.

One of our homeboys met a *ruca* from Cucamonga, a small city located northeast of Pomona. The *vatos locos* from their *barrio* called themselves Cuca Kings, a *barrio* dating back to the forties with a strong reputation for taking care of business whenever anyone disrespected them. Our homeboy convinced the *ruca* to load up some of her homegirls and meet us at a *cantón* in neutral territory. I was looking forward to partying with them, since *La* Sleepy and I weren't seeing each other anymore.

When I arrived at the *cantón* with Black Crow and a couple other homeboys, I quickly realized that there were some good times to be had with these fine *rucas*. While I would have easily jumped any of them, my eyes fell upon one named Annette. She and I partied the rest of the night. Everyone had such a good time that we decided to have a big party in our *barrio* Friday night.

As soon as I finished my shift, I went home and cleaned up. Then I headed over to Black Crow's pad. Homeboys were already kicking back when I got there. We pitched in for *pisto* and decided to have the party across the *calle* at another homeboy's pad. Before long, four carloads of *rucas* arrived. I was happy to see Annette with them. We took the party inside to the beat of "The Breaks" by Kurtis Blow.

De volada, Black Crow jumped into the middle of the room and immediately captivated the *rucas* with his icebreaker dance and *grito!*

"Shaa-aaaah! The Big Twelfth Street Gang! *Rifamous!*"

His dance never failed. Black Crow was all the way live, and everybody joined in. Meanwhile, Annette and I picked up where we left off earlier in the week and partied till sunrise.

After a couple hours sleep, I cruised to Black Crow's pad. As I neared the front door, I could hear "I Heard It Through the Grapevine" by Roger pounding through his speakers.

"Check it out, Homes," Black Crow said with a big smirk on his *cara* as I entered. "Guess who had a big party last night, *también?*"

"Who?" It wasn't going to take me all day to get this answer.

"The vatos from Cherrieville and Palm Place," he replied.

"Are you serious?"

"*Sí mon, pero* their short friendship ended when the *vatos* from Cherrieville pulled out a *cuete* and started blasting the *vatos* from Hazard. All of those *vatos* were inside someone's *cantón*, so check this out," his smirk started turning to an uncontrollable grin. "Whoever pulled the trigger accidentally shot his own homeboy!"

"What!"

"*Sí mon*, Homes. The fool shot his own homeboy and shot a vato from Hazard. Then when all of them were trying to get away, one of the *vatos* from Cherrieville got ran over by a *ranfla, tambien!*"

"Them *vatos* are dumb, Homes," I added as we both burst out laughing. We just couldn't hold it in any longer.

"*Sí mon*, Homes. They messed up big time and both *vatos* died at the hospital."

Homeboys held a meeting later that evening to discuss what had happened between Cherrieville and Hazard. We found out that the *vato* who pulled the trigger, accidentally shot his own *carnal*, and that in the commotion and rush to escape the *balas*, a *vato* from Cherrieville pulled out of the driveway and ran over one of his own homeboys. These *pendejos* did manage to kill a *vato* from Palm Place but if that's how they take care of their business, it wouldn't be long before they wouldn't have anyone left to take care of business.

Ironically, the two *vatos* that died hating each other, died side-by-side in the emergency room at the Pomona Regional Medical Center as doctors worked on them trying to save them. Personally, I had no sympathy for either of them. In my book, there were two less *vatos* that I might have to deal with at some point down the road.

To add insult to injury, homeboys ran *movidas* and took out *vatos* from both Cherrieville and Palm Place. Meanwhile, the *vatos* from Cherrieville were still catching it in the County Jail.

One of our *veteranos*, whom homeboys called Wino, was found dead in a big drainage ditch near the Pomona Freeway. He had been shot execution-style, several shots to the body with two insurance bullets, one to the head and one to the heart. Wino had been a Sharkie since the early sixties. He had done time for some bank robberies, but recently he'd been into some heavy heroin deals. Homeboy's name wasn't too far off base. Whispers trickled through our ranks that Wino was the traitor behind the death of *Matón*.

También, one of the youngsters who got jumped in by Slim was no longer with us. His body was found in an alley, shot once in the head. Word was that he didn't do his *movida*.

Wino and the youngster were two *vatos* that nobody was likely to miss. *Los Sharkies* didn't need that kind of *basura*. This was what homeboys called "house cleaning." *If you don't take care of business,* I thought, *homeboys will take care of you.*

* * *

All through the summer and into September, the relationship with Annette continued to grow more serious. I introduced Annette to my parents and they liked her. *Who wouldn't?* She had a very friendly personality that clicked with *mi jefita*. I couldn't help thinking of the good relationship between *mi jefita* and Sandra. Despite the choices I made when it came to *rucas*, *mi jefita* was always able to get along with them. Homeboys still came first but Annette seemed to be O.K. with that. She was a homegirl from *barrio Cuca* and was down for the lifestyle.

Before I knew it, it was once again time for the L.A. County Fair. Forty of us homeboys caravanned to the fairgrounds to throw blows in the Fun Zone with rival gangs. But due to all the shootings and killings, drugs, and *la pinta*, there was a noticeable decline in the number of gang members on all sides. Unlike past years, we didn't wear our sweatshirts, since the *juras* were coming down on the colors.

Hate still defined the relationship we had with the *juras*, but over the years some respect had developed. The way I looked at it, we were both just doing our *jale*.

I could easily remember nights when the *juras* wanted nothing more than the opportunity to bust their night sticks over a homeboy's head. I could also remember when I no more than stepped foot in the Fun Zone and I was toe-to-toe with some *vato* that was trying to beat my *cara* in.

This night seemed different. To my surprise, the whole evening was relatively peaceful. We met some *rucas* from Duarte, a small *barrio* tucked in below the San Gabriel Mountains between Pasadena and Azusa. We convinced them to come back to our *barrio* to party with us after the fair closed. Annette and her homegirls showed up in the *barrio* a little later. Everybody was up for a partying through the night, so we made a run for some *pisto*. Someone put "Together" by Tierra on the stereo and we danced till dawn.

The rest of the year rolled past much the same way. Nothing eventful happened and we got in as much partying and *pisto* as we could before winter turned to spring in 1983 and cruising on Holt Boulevard once again picked up.

One evening, Black Crow called to let me know that he had plans to cruise Holt Boulevard Friday night with *Payaso* and a few of the homeboys in Joey's new truck. I could tell he wanted me to go with him, since we always had a good time and knew that we covered each other's back. Unfortunately, I had already set up a date with Annette. After I hung up, I felt guilty that I was putting a *ruca* before the homeboys. But soon after picking up Annette, I forgot all about Black Crow and the homeboys, and I was glad that I had decided to keep the date with her.

Saturday afternoon, I dropped by Black Crow's *cantón*. When his *jefita* answered the door, I noticed something was wrong.

"Is Black Crow here?" I asked.

"*Ay, mijo*," she answered almost in tears. "Him and *Payaso* got shot last night and they're still in the hospital!"

"What!" I couldn't believe it. "Are they O.K?" I asked.

"*Sí, mijo.* They're supposed to get out tomorrow."

I could see that she was torn up inside over this, so I gave her a big hug and kissed her on the cheek. As I headed toward Big Jerry's pad, I felt bad that I hadn't gone with the homeboys that night.

When I got there, Big Jerry gave me the lowdown on what happened. Black Crow and *Payaso* had been riding in the truck bed as they trolled for *rucas* on Holt. Somehow, some *vatos* from *Los Olivos* Outlaws, a *barrio* in Upland next to Cucamonga and just north of Ontario, got into *pleito* with the homeboys. *Los Olivos* pulled out some *cuetes* and started shooting. One of the *balas* went through the side of the truck bed, passed through Black Crow's knee and lodged itself in *Payaso's* knee. *Man! Two homeboys with one shot! I've been wanting to do that ever since my first* movida.

Homeboys kicked back later that evening at Big Jerry's pad but I couldn't enjoy myself knowing that two of my homeboys were laid up while those *vatos* from Upland were bragging about their hit on *Calle Doce*. The more I thought about it, the madder I got. Finally, I'd had it. I saw homeboy Cyclone who I trusted and knew was down for the *barrio*, and a youngster called Babyface who needed a *movida* to get jumped into the *barrio*.

I strolled up to them and said, "Let's hit those *chavalas* from Upland!"

"*Vamonos!*" they replied without a second thought.

"Wait here," I told them. "I'll be right back."

"*Órale*, Homes," they replied.

I made a quick call to *Conejo* who set me up with a homeboy who always had *cuetes* for times like this. Within half an hour, I was back with a small sports car my *jefito* was trying to sell and enough artillery to rock those their world. I calmly strolled back into the party and motioned for the two homeboys. We quietly slipped out and were soon cruising north on Euclid Avenue toward Upland.

When we arrived in Upland, we circled the outskirts of their territory. Upland was arranged, like most low-cost housing projects in the *barrios* of East *Los*, with a maze of disorganized *calles*. If you didn't know your way around you could easily find yourself trapped in a bad situation with no way out.

We all decided it was best to go in on foot. We packed enough firepower to shoot our way back to the *ranfla* if necessary. If we were lucky, we'd catch them with their khaki's down, deliver our *wila*, and stroll casually back to the *ranfla*.

It didn't take long to find a good parking spot that was close to the action but still secluded enough that we didn't need to worry about somebody finding the *ranfla*. I hopped out and popped open the trunk. I laid a sawed-off, double-barrel shotgun in the capable hands of Cyclone then turned to Babyface.

"*Órale*, Homes," I said as I stared deep into his eyes. "You down for *Los Sharkies Calle Doce, ese?*"

I suddenly remembered my first *movida* when Nite Owl asked me if I was down. It didn't seem that long ago. I knew when he asked me that I couldn't show any signs of weakness. But this time, it was my dark eyes that probed the youngster's soul for any sign of weakness.

"*Sí mon*, Homes. I'm down, *ese!*" he responded without a moment of hesitation.

I was satisfied and handed him a semi-automatic .22-caliber pistol.

"Can you handle a .22, Homes?"

"*Sí mon*," he replied again without hesitation.

"Are you sure?" I questioned. "I don't want any mistakes when the show starts!"

Just to be sure, I quickly gave him a lesson on the safe handling of a deadly weapon, which included what to do when it came time to pull the trigger.

I reserved a single-barrel pump shotgun for myself. The shotgun held enough shells for a good fight, and I liked the feel of pumping rounds in the chamber and the way it kicked. Also, there was a sense of satisfaction in knowing that when I pulled the trigger anybody within in range was going down.

I quietly pushed the trunk lid down and said, *"Vamonos,"* then quietly led them off into enemy territory.

We cloaked ourselves in the darkness as we worked our way past the first and second set of projects. A thin layer of clouds covered a Quarter Moon. The street lights in this area had been broken out a long time ago, and most of the city governments in East L.A. had a lot more to worry about than replacing light bulbs in streetlamps. It was deadly quiet with only the distant echoes of life going on elsewhere. It all worked to our advantage. Even so, I held the shotgun firmly with my finger poised lightly on the trigger. I was ready to squeeze off a shot at a moment's notice.

As we approached the third set of projects, I heard music and voices and motioned for my soldiers to hold up while I located the source of the voices. I slowly crept up to the corner of one of the buildings and squatted behind a bush for cover. As I cautiously peeped through the lower branches of the bush, I saw six *vatos*. Four of them were kicking back next to an old *ranfla* listening to "Try Me" by James Brown. The other two were standing out in the middle of the yard. All of them were wearing sweatshirts with "*Los Olivos* Outlaws" printed on the back. *We hit the jackpot*, I thought as a smile quickly crept across my *cara* and I hurried back to where Cyclone and Babyface were waiting.

"Check it out," I whispered. "There's six *vatos* standing in front of a *ranfla*, acting like they don't have a care in the world."

Everyone seemed pleased with my discovery.

"I'll go first; then the both of you come out about three feet apart. When I say *Calle Doce*, we light up their world. *Entiendes?*"

"*Sí mon*," they both whispered back.

I led them back to the bush at the corner and quickly checked to verify that the *vatos* were in the same places as when I'd first spotted them. They were, so we tightened up our ranks. We were ready. I looked back at my homeboys and motioned with my head. I stepped out first, followed by Cyclone and Babyface just as we'd planned, took aim, and yelled, *"Calle Doce!"*

It was a trip because the *vato* I had in my sights was taking a drink of *pisto* and choked on it when he saw me.

HOMEBOY'S SOUL

BLAM!

My blast knocked his whole body into a horizontal position about three feet off the ground. Cyclone targeted the same *vato*. When his blast hit home, the *vato* jerked violently from the impact before his sorry butt dropped to the ground. I quickly pumped in another round and squeezed the trigger. This sent his limp body flying up about a foot off the ground and kicked up a good cloud of dust.

Meanwhile, the other *vatos* were trying to make a run for it. I pumped another round into the chamber and took aim on a *vato* who was making a dash for cover inside the *ranfla*, but I was too quick on the trigger. The blast sent his him flying across the front seat. I kicked in several more rounds and blasted out all the windows until the trigger just clicked. No more *balas!* I couldn't believe I'd let myself run out of ammo. *Man! I wish I had a few grenades. I'd mess this whole place up and these* chavalas *with it!* As I quickly shot a look to either side to see how my homeboys were holding out, I was surprised to find myself alone.

As I spun around, I saw them making a mad dash back to the *ranfla*. I was standing there with my *chones* hanging out, expecting my homeboys to be backing me up, and they were already hauling it out of there. I wasn't going to hang out worrying about it. *De volada,* I took off running back to the *ranfla, tambíen.*

True soldiers don't pull out until everyone in their platoon is clear. You go in together and come out together. While I was disappointed, thinking that they should have waited, I had to remind myself that this wasn't the Army and they hadn't received combat training. I was somewhat reassured by the fact that I had the *llaves* to the *ranfla*, so I knew they couldn't leave without me.

When I got to the *ranfla* they were hunched over catching their breath. I quickly popped the trunk and stashed our weapons. In seconds, we were moving cautiously out of their *barrio*, so as not to draw undue attention to ourselves.

Instead of heading back down Euclid Avenue, I swung onto the San Bernadino Freeway westbound back to Pomona. Timing was everything, and I was tripping that the *juras* were already positioning themselves at the bottom of each off ramp as we passed. It was as if they knew our escape route. I figured I could make it to the Towne Avenue exit before they could cover it, so I sped up. As I headed down the ramp on Towne, a

243

highway patrol cruiser was not yet in position as we headed into the intersection. Luckily, we had the light on our side.

"Don't look at them," I cautioned. "And, don't look back. The *juras* can smell fear."

We calmly breezed past the *jura* as he gave us a quick glance. I figured he was expecting a speeding lowrider with a bunch of freaked out *cholos* hot to escape. Since we didn't fit the profile, we were as good as invisible. As I made a left onto Towne, I glanced in my rearview mirror and was pleased to see that he had stayed put. *We're home free!*

I cruised back to the party and stopped at the curb. I threw my arm over the seat and looked Babyface straight in the eye.

"Check it out, *ese*. Homeboys will hear about this *movida*. You keep your mouth shut."

"*Sí mon*," Babyface answered straight away without flinching a bit.

"*Órale*, Homes. *Calle Doce* don't have no *ratas, ese*."

Again, I could hear Nite Owl's voice telling me how it was after my first *movida*.

"When it comes to *movidas* for the *barrio*," I continued, "you don't discuss what happened tonight with anyone. *Entiendes*?"

"*Sí mon*."

He didn't hesitate a bit as he nodded in acceptance.

"Go back to the party like you never left. I'll be back," I told them. Then we shook hands and they climbed out of the *ranfla*.

I went back to homeboy's *cantón* and made sure the *cuetes* were clean of any prints and checked the chambers for *balas*, so as not to leave a history of the evening's events. Then I returned the sports car and headed back to the party.

When I got back to the party, I casually strolled inside and grabbed a cold *pisto*. Cyclone and Babyface were leaning against a wall and sipping *pisto*. They offered me a brief smile, which I returned to acknowledge that this was a good hit. We caught those *chavalas* red-faced with their Khakis down and let them know *Calle Doce* always takes care of business. The three of us shook hands again, then split up and partied the rest of the night, satisfied that we had avenged the damage done to Black Crow and *Payaso*.

Later that night, when I was alone with my thoughts, I wondered about Babyface. He wasn't afraid to pull the trigger. I had checked his *cuete* and he'd emptied it on those *chavalas*. I remembered my first *movida*. I had been fifteen, just like Babyface. I'm sure he was just as nervous as I was my first time and just like me, he had learned to mask his fear with *machismo*. But there was something different about this *movida* for me, and it wasn't that I was no longer afraid. I had pulled the trigger before and was used to it. If I'd only had a howitzer, I could have blown up their whole *barrio*. What intrigued me was the rush I felt standing over that *ranfla* with my finger on the trigger, pumping round after round into the chamber and squeezing it off with cold calculation. I knew I could kill a *vato* in defense of my *barrio*. In *mi mente*, this put me on a different level than most of the homeboys. For a brief moment before I drifted off to sleep, I wondered how different my life would have been if I hadn't become a Shark.

The next day, the Pomona Bulletin reported that four *vatos* from the Upland gang had been shot. Two of them were in critical but stable condition and two others were treated for gunshot wounds then released. The paper also reported that *juras* believed between eight to ten rival gang members had done the shootings. *Eight to ten!* Nobody knew it had taken only three *vatos locos* from *Calle Doce* to rock their world.

That afternoon, Black Crow called me to say he was out of the hospital and for me to come on over to his *cantón*. When I pulled up, he and some of the homeboys were kicking back on his front porch.

"*Gracias*, Homes. Cyclone gave me the scoop. *Sabes que* I'll never forget it," he said as he gripped my hand in a heartfelt manner.

"That's what homeboys are for, *ese*." I leaned down to give him a quick hug, adding, "Don't worry about it, Homes."

"*Órale*, Homes," he replied.

Black Crow was proud of his wound and eagerly ripped off the bandages to show me where the *bala* had entered his knee and exited on the other side; then he reached into his cooler and handed me a cold *pisto*. "This one's for you, Homes."

In that moment, I felt everything—the ice cold bottle in my palm, the resistance of the cap as it finally twisted open, and the calming sensation of the cool *pisto* as it flowed through my mouth, finding its way to my stomach. I could also see from the stress in Black Crow's eyes that his knee caused him severe pain with every little movement. In that moment, Black Crow and I were two soldiers fighting for the same cause, who were now recovering from a recent skirmish with the enemy. We were blood brothers who reveled in our survival. We shared with each other the bond of love and respect that soldiers who depend upon each other for their lives share on and off the battlefield. I knew that there was no other place I would rather be.

"Just make sure everyone knows that Babyface is down for the *barrio*," I added.

"*Órale*, Homes."

I took another long drink savoring the taste as I savored the moment of love and respect from my homeboy.

That evening we cruised over to *Payaso's cantón* to see how he was doing. *Payaso* was in the same condition as Black Crow and just as eager to show off his wound. He thanked me as well and we all kicked back while *Payaso* entertained us with a reenactment of the shooting.

At our next meeting, I found out that one of our homeboys had some *primos* with *Los Olivos* who had reported on the two *vatos* that got hit. One of them had gone blind and the other was permanently paralyzed. He also said that the Outlaws had had enough and didn't want any more *pleito* from the Shark. *Sí mon, the Shark bites deep!* This was the first time that *vatos* from any rival *barrio* wanted a truce after getting hit by *Calle Doce*. It sent a strong *wila* to *vatos locos* from other *barrios*. Calle Doce Los Sharkies always get their payback!

19

Soul Searching

Annette surprised me by taking me out to dinner for my twenty-fourth birthday. While we often went out dancing, dinner wasn't usually a part of the picture. I was surprised, not only by her idea, but also by the fact that I really enjoyed it. After dinner, we spent some time with my family, then joined Black Crow and his *ruca* Linda at the Tropicana. We danced and partied the night away. Annette was a good dancer but I managed to hold my own. Black Crow, even with crutches and all, accomplished something that resembled dancing and we all had a good time.

By summer, Black Crow and *Payaso* were back on their feet. The truce with Upland held and things had calmed down between *Calle Doce* and Cherrieville. For once, the *barrio* was peaceful and I had time to think about my future. The more I thought about it the more seriously I considered becoming a *soldado* for La Qlica. Word had gotten around about my payback on the *vatos* from Upland. While no one was killed, the *movida* had made a strong point, the kind that La Qlica notices. Death and violence was the language spoken by La Qlica, and I had demonstrated I could speak it fluently. In *mi mente*, it became increasingly obvious that becoming a *soldado* and killing for La Qlica was the next logical step in my career.

One Friday in June of 1983, I took Annette out for a night of dancing. I held her in my arms and we swayed to the music. I loved the feel of her body and the smell of her hair but I still had doubts about how long our relationship would last.

The next day I cruised over to Black Crow's *cantón*. His *jefita* answered the door. She was extremely upset and looked like she had been crying all night.

"*Que pasó?*" I asked.

"The police got my *mijo* in jail," she cried.

"In jail!" I exclaimed. "For what?"

"They said he killed Linda," she sobbed. "They said he shot her."

I couldn't believe what she was saying. Linda was Black Crow's main *ruca*. Why would he kill her?

"Who told you?"

"Slim. I think it happened over there." Tears streamed down her cheeks as she melted into my arms for a reassuring hug. But it didn't help. At this moment, I knew nothing would help except maybe the truth.

"I'll be back," I told her. "I'm going to find out what happened."

"*Ay gracias, mijo!*"

I didn't know what to think as I left her in the doorway. I knew Black Crow would never hurt Linda but something really bad must have happened for the *juras* to lock him up. All kinds of things ran through *mi mente* as I cruised over to Slim's *cantón* to find out what really happened. When I parked out front, I could see fifteen or so homeboys hanging out. Everyone looked sad. Then, I saw Slim.

"*Que pasó*, Homes?" I asked as we shook hands.

"It's all messed up, Homes," he said, pausing for a moment as if he didn't want to relive the painful moment.

"*Sabes que* Black Crow had a shotgun that I wanted to buy. So, I called him up to bring it over. He was kicking back with *Payaso* but said he'd be right over." Slim paused again, taking in a deep breath before continuing.

"When *Payaso* pulled up, Puppet was riding shotgun. Black Crow and Linda were in the back. As I strolled up to the *ranfla*, Puppet gets out and leans the seat forward. Black Crow climbs out then grabs the *cuete* on the floor and as he's pulling it out, it just went off!"

"What!"

Slim paused again. I could see the sadness in his eyes as he held back. I didn't know what else to say.

"It happened so fast, Homes. When Black Crow saw the blast hit Linda, he went crazy! We tried to calm homeboy down but she was hit bad, Homes!"

"Where'd she get hit?"

"In the stomach, Homes! We rushed her to the hospital. When we got there she was still alive, but she didn't make it."

"Man, Homes. How did the *juras* get Black Crow?" I asked.

"Homeboy turned himself in when Linda died," Slim stated. "Right after it happened, I checked the *cuete*, Homes, and found a thread from the *cobija* wrapped around the trigger. When homeboy lifted the *cuete* the thread pulled the trigger. I told the *juras* how it came down but they still want to charge homeboy with murder."

"*Chale*, Homes. Whoever was here last night needs to tell the *juras* it was an accident," I suggested.

"We tried, Homes," Slim offered in full agreement. "The *juras* think we're all lying."

I knew what he was saying. The *juras* saw things as brown and white. There were no accidents when homeboys were involved. If there was an opportunity to lock up another homeboy they took it. It didn't matter what the truth was or what any of us said.

I left Slim and the homeboys and headed back to Black Crow's *cantón* to let his *jefita* know how it all came down. Even with the truth in hand, she was still taking it very hard. I tried to soothe and comfort her, but how could I tell a loving mother not to worry about her *mijo*, when all I could see was her face wrinkled up in pain. How could I understand the years of worry she had endured or the long nights of staying awake, listening to gunshots in the darkness and wondering if one of them had found her *mijo*? How could I understand any of that? I was too much a part of it to know the impact it had on others and ignorant of the damage it might be causing *mi jefita*. I was too much a part of it to care about the pain we caused. I was too busy defending the *barrio* to think about saving it.

One month after Linda's death, the *juras* came to their senses, having realized the shooting was actually accidental, and released Black Crow. I went over to Black Crow's *cantón* as soon as I got the news. He was extremely dejected. I've never seen him in such bad shape.

Linda's parents blamed him for their daughter's demise and took his baby son. Black Crow humbled himself and asked for their forgiveness but their grief ran too deep and they had no forgiveness to give. They couldn't accept that their daughter had gotten caught up in the whirlwind of a *vato loco's* madness through her own choices, and had paid the price with her life. Unfortunately, she wasn't alone. Thousands of *rucas* were caught up in that storm. Some of them, like Linda, paid with their lives. Some paid with the lives of their young children while others mortgaged the future of our *barrio* to pay for a PCP or heroin escape, while raising the children of fathers who were doing time in *la pinta*. Either way, they paid dearly.

As much as I tried, I couldn't help my homeboy recover from this tragedy. Deep down, I knew, Black Crow felt responsible and was unable to offer himself any absolution. After Linda's death, he rarely smiled and I never saw him do his *Calle Doce* dance again.

I didn't realize it, but Linda's death had had a profound effect on me, also. I missed the old Black Crow and could see the other older homeboys dropping like flies. Those of us that were left had to hang even tighter, but what we were supposed to cling to became increasingly obscure.

President Ronald Reagan and California Governor Pete Wilson ganged up like two homeboys on a *movida* to implement their trickle-down theory of economics. The reality of it was that the trickle had run dry by the time it got down to the *barrio*. As I saw glimpses of the two men on the news, I could almost hear Reagan's condescending voice saying, "Well, Nancy, I think we should just forget the poor! How many of them do you think voted for us anyway?"

Reagan and Wilson also tried to implement programs that would curb the flow of drugs and violence into white suburban neighborhoods. It was O.K. as long as the plague stayed in the *barrios*, but they were quickly finding out that what goes around was coming around to threaten their constituency. Something had to be done.

Their solution was to increase penalties and to use federal tax dollars to pay for putting more *juras* on the *calles*. Meanwhile, they tried to shift the blame for America's increased appetite for drugs by taking their so-called drug war on the road with a supply-side attack on countries that provided the magical means for so many American's to escape from reality.

In the *barrios*, Reagan/Wilson programs simply drove up drug prices and increased the potential for profit, while making it harder for competitors that didn't have established networks to get into the business. For homeboys, business was good but for me there was still something missing. In July of 1983, I was to find out what it was.

* * *

Regardless of my doubts, Annette and I hung together. The relationship seemed to have its own momentum, and nothing either of us did to screw it up was enough to slow it down. We had been together for almost a year and Annette thought it was time that I meet her *jefito*. He and her *jefita* had separated when Annette was in high school. The fact that both of our parents were divorced may have been the bond that helped keep us together.

It was a bright Sunday afternoon when Annette came over to my *jefita's casa*. I was still in bed so she let herself in and quietly slipped into my bedroom. She woke me with a gentle kiss and suggested that we go visit her *jefito*.

"I want you to meet him," she said, venturing out onto uncertain territory, not knowing how I would respond. "We'll need to be there by five o'clock."

I glanced at the clock. We had plenty of time.

"Sure. Why not?" I replied, sitting up.

"We'll meet him at his church in East L.A.," she added, taking another step into unknown territory. "Is that O.K?"

"That's fine with me," I replied. "I've been to church before."

She looked relieved. I couldn't see why she didn't just come out with it all at once.

"This church isn't like the Catholics," she explained.

"We're just going to meet your *jefito*, Annette. It's not like they're going to convert anybody!"

"If anybody needs God it's you, *Braso*," she said with a sneer and fake smile, adding, "Besides, God can help you change, so we can have a better life."

"The only help I need is a cold *pisto* and a loaded *cuete*," I declared curtly.

"What about me?" she asked jealously with a feigned pout.

I pulled her next to me and kissed her passionately then stared deep into her dark brown eyes. "You know I love you, baby doll."

I don't know how well she was able to understand that when I told her that I loved her, "love" to me was nothing more than a word. I loved her as long as she served my needs as a man. I loved her as long as she was around when I wanted her around and elsewhere when I needed to take care of business. I loved her as long as she didn't interfere with my passion for life on the *calles* with my homeboys. I had genuine love for my homeboys and everything else was just everything else.

I got up and the two of us got ready for church. I dressed in my best Khakis, making sure the creases were sharp, and a clean Pendleton. Annette wore a long dress that covered her sexy legs. Most of the time, she wore short dresses, since I liked the view they provided. In any case, we both looked *bonarood* as we turned onto the San Bernardino Freeway and headed west into East L.A.

Annette told me where to turn, till finally she said, "Park over there." There was a small crowd of people gathered around a building but it didn't look like the churches I was used to with their stained glass windows and pointed spires. This could have been an office building or market or machine shop. It didn't look like a church. It looked more like just a regular building, nothing big or extravagant.

Even the people were different from what I expected. The ladies all wore nice dresses and had long, dark hair. Their faces were free of makeup, but even so they radiated a natural beauty. The men wore suits and had a peacefulness about them that I couldn't understand. I was *cholo'd* down and stood out like a bloody thumb, but I didn't feel uncomfortable. Most of the *gente* were *raza*; I wasn't getting stares from them because they knew and accepted what I was all about.

As Annette and I strolled into the church, I paused and looked around for the little bowls of holy water, but they weren't there so I kept moving almost as in a dream. Everything was real but nothing seemed ordinary. There was a surreal, mythical quality about what I was seeing and hearing that slowed time and removed me from the present, as though I was an observer of myself.

We passed through a lobby area, then into a larger room that had wooden folding chairs set up in rows. Many people were already seated, others were selecting where they wanted to sit, while still others were sharing in happy conversation. It struck me funny that almost everyone had a Bible in their hands. I was used to old ladies and priests carrying their own Bibles while everyone else would make do with the hymnals in the back of the pews, or wing it as best they could. These people were different.

As we made our way down the aisle, we approached a young *Chicano* who held out his hand to shake mine. I reached for his hand to grasp it but he wasn't going with the motions I had learned in the *barrio*. He shook my hand in the traditional manner then looked me in the eye and said, "God bless you."

I didn't know how to respond, so I just smiled and nodded my head. He greeted Annette in the same manner then offered to help us find a place to sit in the front. That wasn't going to fly. *That* vato *must think I'm crazy!* We were there early enough to get good seats in the back, so I grabbed Annette's hand and led her toward two empty chairs on the back row.

"Where's your *jefito?*" I asked.

"In the front row," Annette responded. She pointed at him but I could only get a glimpse of the back of this head as two ladies took the empty seats behind him.

The young *Chicano* that had greeted us and tried to get us to sit up front was now behind the pulpit leading everyone in song. *Gente* were clapping their hands and swaying back and forth to the music as they joined their voices with his. The song sounded like an up tempo tune by James Brown, but I didn't recognize the words which talked about peace and love and made me feel good. I'd never felt this way in church before. It felt good.

As the music continued, more and more people got caught up in the expression of happiness and joy. Many of them waved their arms in the air and jumped up and down with excitement as they shouted, "Hallelujah!" I couldn't believe what I was seeing. I'd never seen people behave this way in church.

Once the song finished and everyone took their seats, I noticed four rows of benches to the side of the pulpit occupied by *Chicanos*. The older ones were *veteranos*, and the younger ones *cholos* or had been *cholos*. There was something about the *cholo* look that stayed with you no matter how you dressed. When I was in the Army or when I lived in Denver, I could tell if a *cholo* was from Los Angeles just by the way he carried himself.

This group of *vatos* really caught my attention because of the uncharacteristic warmth and peacefulness emanating from their expressions. I had never seen *vatos* act like this before. The *vatos* I knew all had a hardened look that warned off strangers, like the rattle of a deadly Diamondback.

Back in the *barrio* homeboys experienced happiness through music, drugs, and *pisto*, but after the party was over and the last *rola* played, the last toke taken and the final sip of *pisto* swallowed, we were right back where we started.

I'd been so focused on the *vatos* that I didn't notice that the pastor behind the pulpit had begun to preach. Once I started listening, the words were clear and powerful. It seemed like I was alone in this large room—just me and the preacher beaming his message of love, like an arrow straight to my heart. It was like nothing I had ever experienced before. I felt a love that I had never known before. Not the love of Annette or any other *ruca* I had known. Not the love of *mi familia* or the homeboys. This love reached into my heart and beckoned me to search for answers. I suddenly realized that it was God's love I had been missing, and now it was God's love that was embracing the depths of my unworthy soul.

"Repent!" the preacher shouted with conviction. "Repent, and be baptized every one of you in the name of Jesus Christ for the remission of sins, and ye shall receive the gift of the Holy Ghost."

A slight pause as he looked around at the congregation.

"Verily, verily I say unto thee. Except a man be born of water and of the Spirit, he cannon enter the kingdom of God. That which is born of the flesh is flesh; and that which is born of the Spirit is Spirit. Marvel not that I said unto thee, 'Ye must be born again.' Is there anyone here who wants to change?" the preacher asked. "Come now. Come! God wants to work a miracle for you!"

I had no doubt that he meant that God wanted to work a miracle with my life. I had no doubt that God must have heard my soul crying out for redemption. I couldn't sit quietly and let an opportunity like this pass me by.

Annette seemed shocked when I suddenly took my feet, silently slid past her, and slowly strolled toward the front. Something had taken control of my body, directing my movements, commanding me forward. It felt like a host of angels had surrounded me and lifted my feet from the floor letting me float gently toward the pulpit where two *veteranos* joined me. One on each side, they put their hands on my shoulders and started to pray.

As I stood there under the kind gaze of the pastor, a feeling of peace came over me. I felt its warmth penetrate to the ends of my fingers and toes until my whole body was saturated in a peaceful cocoon. But the sensation lasted only a moment. Quickly, the frigid forces of evil with which I had consorted for most of my life, suddenly surged within me and flushed the strength from my body like a dying heart pumping blood from a fatal wound.

I had never felt so frightened and ashamed in my life. Without warning tears gushed from my eyes, and I would have collapsed on the floor if not for the supporting arms of the *vatos* on either side of me. These weren't the misty tears of loneliness that I had shed briefly one night in the Army, when I was away from my family for the first time. These were tears of pain and sadness from a tortured soul. Until now, I hadn't realized how lost I was.

"Young man, do you want Jesus Christ to save your soul?"

I looked up and the pastor was standing right in front of me. I wiped the tears from my eyes and tried to swallow the lump in my throat before answering, "Yes!"

He placed his hands on my shoulders and prayed over me, then stepped back and said, "Follow me."

I glanced quickly at Annette as the music started and everyone joined in singing. I thought I saw her smile, but I wondered what she was really thinking as I followed the preacher down the aisle, out through the lobby, and into an office.

Once in his office, he extended his hand and introduced himself as Pastor Ramirez, then offered me a chair and took a seat behind his desk. I hadn't noticed before, but he sported a portly shape topped with short black hair neatly combed back on his head. Age had etched soft wrinkles into the light brown skin on his face. We sat quietly for a moment as he looked deep into my eyes. I immediately recognized that same soul-piercing stare that I had seen from *Conejo*, Li'l Capone, and *Matón*. But instead of the darkness searching my soul for weakness, I saw light in the pastor's eyes searching for signs of goodness and purity. I had never seen such light in anyone before.

I wondered what he saw in me.

When he spoke, he began by reciting a passage from the Bible. I heard his voice but the words didn't register with me. Only when he began explaining the passage, did what he was saying reach me. It was the same message he had given from the pulpit, but this time it was specifically for me. All the time, he peered directly at me with that piercing stare.

"God brought you here, today, and I can see that you are sincere about wanting to be saved," he said in his gentle voice. "It's my responsibility to you, and to everyone that walks into this church, to explain this change taking place in your life. Your soul is at stake." He paused for a moment before he continued, "*Mijo*, I sense a great battle for your soul. I'll keep you in my prayers. Your soul is precious in the sight of God. Your commitment to accept Jesus Christ as your savior is a commitment you can't take lightly, do you understand?"

I nodded, "Yes" even though I wasn't sure what he meant when he said, 'Your soul is at stake.'" *And what is this battle he mentioned?* None of that seemed to matter. In his presence, I felt a sense of peace that I had never known and I wanted more.

He reached in the desk drawer and handed me his card.

"If you have any problems give me a call and we'll see what we can do for you. What *barrio* are you from?"

"*Los* Sharkies Pomona Twelfth Street."

"Do you have a drug problem?"

"No," I answered without hesitation.

"That's good," he said leaning back in his chair. "You know, I used to be a heroin addict and a gangbanger from Little Valley in East *Los*, but look what God did for me. He can do the same thing for you if you truly want it."

I was tripping. Here's this pastor of a nice church who was once a hard-core *vato loco* from a *barrio* that I knew went back to the forties. To look at him, I'd have never guessed that at one time his life was a complete mess. As I stuffed his card in my shirt pocket, I remembered how I'd felt when I first met *Conejo* back in junior high. I remembered how the other *vatos* at Simons had respected and looked up to him and how impressed I was with his look of self-confidence. I had known that *Conejo* held the key to survival in the *barrio*, and I had wanted that key. I had wanted to be just like *Conejo*, and now that I was, I looked at Pastor Ramirez and realized that there was something more to life than hanging out and kicking down *pisto*.

We stood and Pastor Ramirez once again reached out his hand to me. As I enjoined his firm yet gentle grip, I knew that he held the key to my future.

I followed him out of his office and was happy to see Annette waiting in the lobby with her *jefito*. The service was over and Pastor Ramirez left me with Annette and her *jefito*, then went to the door to offer his congregation strength as they went back out into the world.

Annette took my hand and introduced me to her *jefito*. We shook hands.

"Did you like the service?" he asked.

I knew his question reached deeper than whether I had enjoyed the service. His eyes told me that he wanted to know whether I was serious about making a commitment to a new way of life.

"Yes, I did," I replied, not knowing if I was answering both of his questions.

"That's good," he said smiling. "The pastor has a good program called 'Life Line' for young men like yourself. It helps them get away from the gang scene and the drugs, so they can grow strong in the Lord and eventually stand on their own two feet."

I just nodded in response. My brain was full of new thoughts and I felt exhausted.

We stood around a while longer as Annette shared small talk with her *jefito*, then we said our goodbyes and headed back to my *ranfla*.

I realized this was a turning point in my life. For the first time since getting jumped into *Calle Doce*, I began thinking about my feelings toward my homeboys and my *barrio*. I never thought for a moment that I could be on the outside looking in; I had always been on the inside striking out. But now, those dark shades that I always wore to complete the hard-core *vato loco* look, were coming off. Without them, my soul was free to bathe in the warmth of the Lord's light. At the same time the protective shield they provided was gone, and I was vulnerable to retribution for all the sins I had perpetrated in my life. I was scared and in need of comfort but Annette had no comfort to give.

As we drove back to Pomona, I sensed a distance between us. She didn't say too much, and I didn't know what to say. I think we were both surprised by my reaction to the service and didn't know what to make of it. I had hoped that she would share in the happiness of my discovery, but the unknown is like a great ravine. Once you leap into it, there's no going back and no guarantees for a safe landing. I had just leapt into that ravine and wanted Annette to take the plunge with me. As I rapidly descended into my unknown future, I could see her feet still firmly planted in her world as she peered cautiously over the edge. Somehow, I couldn't blame her.

I kept my eyes focused on the road and searched my soul as I wondered what would become of us.

20

Slippin'

"Wash your hands, *cochino!*" *mi jefita* scolded as I grabbed for the fresh stack of tortillas.

She busily pulled another batch of the fragrant treats from the oven and stopped to look at me in a studied manner. "Why are you so happy, *mijo?*"

"I went to a church in East Los Angeles this week and accepted Jesus Christ as my personal savior."

"Jesus Christ?"

The news definitely caught her off guard.

"Yeah, I want to be a Christian and get baptized." I told her.

"Baptized! You were baptized when you were a baby, *mijo*," she said slightly confused.

"No, Mom," I explained, "you have to be baptized as a man, like Jesus."

"Well, I don't understand everything you're telling me," she said, "but it's good you are going to church. Maybe now you'll stop hanging out with those gangsters and stay out of trouble."

I was curious, but I had never known for certain exactly how much she knew about my activities with *Calle Doce*. I suspected that she knew more than she let on, but we had a silent agreement that seemed to work for both of us; she didn't ask and I didn't tell. She seemed to be consoled with the idea that "boys will be boys. They mean well but sometimes they're not as good as they should be." I don't know who she thought was behind the *movidas*, but whoever it was, according to her way of thinking, it couldn't have been me or any of my friends.

I gave her a quick kiss on the cheek and said, "I love you, Mom."

Before I could get out of reach with a handful of hot tortillas, she put her arms out and drew me close to her. For the first time in my life, I could feel the damage all my years of disobedience had done to her. I understood the toll it had taken on Black Crow's *jefita* as she lay awake all the nights listening to gunshots in the darkness and wondering whether the phone would ring with the dreaded news that her *mijo* had passed to the next world. It was a strange sensation, but I could sense that a heavy burden had been lifted from her heart. If there were angels in Heaven I'm sure they rejoiced when *mi jefita's* happiness reached them.

I wanted to share my new found excitement with my homeboys. I wanted to share my feelings of joy with them and to let them know that we didn't have to feel trapped anymore. I wanted to tell them my new-found truth, but was afraid that they would laugh or think I was showing signs of weakness, so I kept my mouth shut.

Payaso was the only one that I trusted enough to tell about my new experience.

He just said, "I hope you're real, Homes," with an air of uncertainty in his voice, then we shook hands and he left.

I knew he was taking the wait-and-see approach. The homeboys were always uncertain about one of their own deciding to take that stroll down the straight and narrow path of Christianity. Some took it as a slap in the *cara*. Others wished them well. Until now, I had always viewed it as being weak. That's probably why I was so self-conscious now that it was me headed down that road.

Payaso was giving me the benefit of the doubt. I also knew that the word was out now. While *Payaso* wasn't about to go out and make a public announcement, the word would slowly spread. I guess that's what I had intended, for the word to spread. I guess that's why I told him. I told *Payaso* so I wouldn't have to spread the word myself and face that look of disbelief that I knew would come from some of the homeboys. It was easier this way.

For the next couple of weeks, I went to church as often as I could. I wanted Annette seated beside me in the *ranfla* as I went in search of salvation. Sometimes she would go, but often I found myself going alone. Even so, I still went and kept going. I got myself a Bible and studied it every chance I could. I even took it on my bus routes and read it during my breaks. I even had thoughts of following in the footsteps of Pastor Ramirez by going into the ministry.

As word got around the *barrio*, I started getting phone calls from various homeboys. They wanted to know why I wasn't hanging with them anymore. I told them about my new commitment to Jesus, but that wasn't good enough for them. I could understand why they reacted that way but it didn't make it any easier for me.

Finally, I decided to face the music and headed into the *barrio*. It was a warm evening and the wind blew lightly through my hair as I cruised down Grand Avenue and turned onto the *calle* next to Sharkie Park. Several homeboys were kicking back amongst the trees as I parked near several other *ranflas*.

At first, I noticed an uneasiness amongst the homeboys as all eyes turned in my direction and watched as I strolled toward them. I didn't know what rumors had been spread about me and wasn't sure how homeboys would respond. It reminded me of when I returned from Denver. Then, I hadn't seen anybody for several months. Even though this time I had been gone only for a short time, in the *barrio* things can change overnight and survival depends upon being ready for anything at any time. I was glad to see that as I got closer everyone seemed to relax and acted as though they were glad to see me.

Even so, something seemed hauntingly different. I didn't feel the blanket of love and respect that usually surrounded me when I got together with the homeboys. As I glanced from *cara á cara*, I tried to discern what had changed, but I couldn't pinpoint anything specific. Everyone looked and sounded the same, but nothing anyone said interested me, so I listlessly roamed, passing up several offers for a cold *pisto* even though I really wanted one. I had made a promise to Pastor Ramirez to swear off drinking as long as I was attending his church.

Maybe it was that Black Crow was in the clutches of the *juras* again, having gotten busted for heroin. I missed not having him around. Most of the homeboys were youngsters and I didn't have much to say to them. I could have shared the message that Jesus loved them, but I wasn't ready for that and figured that they weren't either. I learned early on that talk is cheap but at this point that's all I had. I had decided that it was time to leave when *Conejo*, Trigger, and Big Jerry drove up. They shook hands with everyone than strolled over to me.

"*Caiga, Braso*. We want to talk to you," *Conejo* said, asking, but at the same time, you knew it was a request you couldn't refuse.

I followed the three of them behind the stage. My heart beat faster with each step. I didn't know what to expect. I had seen plenty of *vatos* take this stroll and end up in really bad shape as a result of such a discussion with these three homeboys. If they had come with bad intentions, there wasn't much I could do about it now.

Once out of sight of the others, *Conejo* turned toward me with that piercing stare which he had honed to a fine art. I suspected the first blow would come from him but stayed ready for something coming from behind. *Conejo* spoke first.

"We heard you turned *Christiano?*"

The circle around me closed in tighter. I knew they knew, so there was no benefit in denying it.

"*Sí mon*. I'm going to church," I replied directly.

Their stares burned into my soul from all sides.

"Eh, Homes," *Conejo* stated as he stepped in even closer. "I remember when you were wet behind the ears at school, *ese*, when my *primo* introduced us. Who showed you how to shake hands the *Raza* way?"

"You did, Homes," I quickly acknowledged.

Conejo laughed as he turned to Big Jerry and said, *"Te acuerdas,* Homes?"

"*Sí mon,* Homes," Big Jerry agreed.

"Eh, *Braso*, that day I shook your hand, I knew then you were going to be down for yours. *Sabes que* nothing has changed, *ese*. I'm glad you're trying to do something right."

"*Sí mon*. Don't stop, *Braso*," Big Jerry enjoined as he slapped me on the shoulder, "Keep going to church, Homes."

The tension in my body subsided as *Conejo* and Big Jerry shook hands with me. Then they headed back to the other homeboys and Trigger reached for my hand. I could feel the power in his fingers, especially as he held the last movement longer than normal and stared directly into my eyes.

"Don't let me catch you slippin', *ese!*"

My heart began pounding again as strongly as ever. I hoped Trigger couldn't hear it, even though I was sure he could sense it. As I returned his cold stare, I knew I was looking into the face of evil. I can't say why it was so clear now, or why I had never seen it before. I felt like a kitten that had opened his eyes for the first time only to gaze upon the evil jaws of a devil dog himself.

I knew I didn't wear the cloak of innocence myself, but I had seen the light of a new day and there was no going back. Even so, I didn't fully understand why *Conejo* and Big Jerry had given me a green light to stray from the pack. These were two *vatos locos* who had devoted their lives to the *barrio* and were well respected among the ranks. I couldn't tell if they were proud or jealous or both. All I knew is that if it had been up to Trigger, I might be lying unconscious or dead on ground soaked with my own *sangre*. Instead, I shook hands and returned to the other homeboys.

That night as I lie in bed, *Conejo's* words echoed through *mi mente*.

"I'm glad you're trying to do something right," he kept repeating. Only Trigger's warning interrupted his reassurance.

"Don't let me catch you slippin', *ese!*"

As I drifted just out of reach of sleep, the two voices began merging and the words became jumbled.

One voice offered, "Don't let me catch you trying to do something right," while the other responded with "I'm glad you're slippin', *ese!*" I struggled to straighten the phrases out but the harder I tried the more jumbled they became. By the time sleep overtook me, I was exhausted and ended up sleeping through my alarm. I had to hustle and even then I was fifteen minutes late to work.

During the next few weeks, I stayed out of the *barrio* while continuing to go to church on a regular basis. I even spoke to Pastor Ramirez about the program he had to help gang members. It sounded like a good idea. I told *mi jefita* that I had decided to give the program a shot and she was so happy she nearly cried in front of me.

My *jefito* and *carnal* weren't as enthusiastic about my decision. They didn't like the idea of anyone in the family being a true Christian. They both went to church on Christmas and Easter, but past that they were more comfortable keeping as much distance from religion as possible. They both said that Pastor Ramirez's program sounded like I was being drawn into some kind of cult. My *jefito* equated priests to money-hungry leeches, and since Pastor Ramirez wasn't even a priest or connected with what he called a "real" church, he must be the worst kind of leech.

Needless to say, I was very disappointed with their reaction. As many lectures as I had received from my *jefito* about the dangers of hanging out with my homeboys, I expected a more positive reaction from him regarding my plans. I was slowly learning that there was very little in life that my *jefito* could bring himself to be happy about. Perhaps he had been beaten down by society so many times that he was incapable of comprehending my joy and simply had no words of encouragement left in him.

While the reaction of my *jefito* and *carnal* hurt me, it wasn't enough to detour me from continuing down this path. For the first time in my life, I felt love, and I was saddened by the fact that my *jefito* and *carnal* couldn't see it. But what hurt me the most is, the person that I most wanted to share this love with, couldn't see it either. Day by day, Annette was growing increasingly distant. When I told her of my decision to join Pastor Ramirez's program, she seemed jealous of my new commitment, and in turn I wasn't certain about her faithfulness. The irony of the whole situation is that Annette was the one who had preached to me about another way of life on the day that I met her *jefito*, and for the first time in my life, I wanted to love a *ruca* the right way. It just goes to show that you need to be careful what you pray for, because you just might get it.

*   *   *

In September of 1983, I quit my *jale* with R.T.D. and drove to the church to begin the program. When I arrived, I parked and looked around. I saw another *cholo* strolling toward the door. He had jet black hair combed back over his head and a dark complexion. He reminded me of Fat Joe, since they were both about the same size. We introduced ourselves. His name was Thumper. He was from the *barrio* Peaceful *de* Norwalk and about my age. I told him I was from *Calle Doce*, and he mentioned that he remembered the time we had partied with his homegirls.

Inside the church, several *vatos* milled around, shooting the breeze. Chairs were arranged in a circle. Pastor Ramirez welcomed the new members and invited everyone to take a seat. Pastor Ramirez started out with the ground rules. We were not allowed to do any drugs or have any alcohol while we were in the program. We were to treat everyone with respect and listen to what they had to say. We were all here to help each other discover a new way of life, and it would be difficult at times but we could get through it together.

After the Pastor had his say, we all introduced ourselves and said what *barrio* we were from. No one was allowed to make any bad comments about or boo someone else's *barrio*, and no one did. The Pastor was right, we were in this together. None of us could make this journey alone. I think everyone there understood the importance of the steps we were taking.

Even so, I was glad that there weren't any *cholos* from Cherrieville. I knew this was church and we were in this boat together, but bad blood is bad blood and the fact was that I could just as soon do without having to see some of those *vatos* ever again.

After a dinner of tortillas and *caldo de res*, we all pitched in to pull out some old Army cots which we arranged in rows. Thumper and I placed our cots next to each other so we'd have the opportunity to talk. As we sat on our cots, he told me that he had been a *tecato*, an addict, since he was sixteen. I could see that he was hard core and had been down for his *barrio*, but was surprised to hear that he shared my disillusionment with the endless cycle of violence and the way the youngsters didn't have respect for what we had gone through. I inquired about his homegirl, *La* Sleepy. He said he hadn't seen her for a while but had heard that she was shacking up with one of his homeboys. I told him I hoped that things would go well for her, and decided to leave it at that.

While we were talking, Thumper's face turned pale and began dripping with sweat as he clutched his stomach. I could tell immediately that he was going into withdrawal. Although we didn't know that much about praying, we both fell to our knees and prayed from our hearts for God's help. Thumper suffered through the next day and the following evening after lights out, we again fell to our knees and prayed. It was on the third night that I witnessed my first miracle of God's healing power.

Thumper turned to me with a glowing look of joy on his face.

"I'm free!" he cried. "Can you see it? I feel something, a power flowing through my veins. I've never felt like this before. The last time I felt this good was before I got hooked and that was seven years ago."

Even in the darkness, I could see the excitement in his eyes. With God's help, Thumper had been freed from the clutches of heroin. I shared in his joy. I had never gotten into that madness, but just the same, my soul had its own demons to purge and if prayer could free him from heroin, maybe it could help me.

During the next couple weeks, we read the Bible every day and I learned a lot of things about myself. I also learned about the choices I had made that brought me to where I am today. Pastor Ramirez said that just because we had made some wrong choices in the past, we didn't need to continue to make those choices.

"God gives us the free will to choose right from wrong," he said. "Which one we choose is up to us."

I was glad that I had made the choice to join this program. I could see it guiding me toward a different way of thinking. I wanted to share my new discoveries with Annette, but Pastor Ramirez said that she couldn't visit me during the week. I didn't agree with him and couldn't see why I wasn't free to see her whenever I wanted. *He's messing with my personal life,* I thought. It had only been a month but it seemed longer, and I missed her so much that I even thought about leaving the program, but I didn't.

I was glad to see Annette at the Sunday service. She looked beautiful even though there was a look of sadness on her face that she tried to hide. After the service, we had a chance to talk for a while. She told me how lonely she was with me gone all the time and begged me to go home with her. She must have known how much I missed her because with only a little enticement she had me biting into the forbidden fruit.

The moment we stepped inside the door of my room, I was on her like a caged lion that was now free to ravage his lioness.

When Monday came, I decided not to go back to the program. Within days, Annette and I moved in with my *carnal*. I looked for a *jale* but it wasn't easy, and I soon began regretting my decision to quit the R.T.D. No way would they hire me back now. The more the doors of opportunity slammed shut in my *cara*, the more frustrated I became.

It didn't take long before Annette and I were arguing and fighting over every little thing that happened. Inside, I blamed her for coaxing me away from Pastor Ramirez's program, when she was the one that had encouraged me to start going to church in the first place. I wanted to go back to the program, but I felt stupid and ashamed that I had been drawn away so easily. I tried talking to Annette about the good things God could do for us if we shared a common belief, but she wasn't going for it.

I don't know if Pastor Ramirez had had a bad feeling about Annette or not. Maybe this was what was behind his reason for not wanting her to visit me very often.

But if he felt this way, he was wise to keep it to himself, since just his warnings would have placed some unneeded distance between me and his spiritual insight.

One hot day when my hunt for a *jale* had gotten me nowhere, I went home tired and hungry. Annette was busy putting on makeup when I asked her to fix me something to eat.

"Wait, I still have to finish my mascara," she returned.

Man! That's not what I wanted to hear. I was hungry as a bear and all she can say is, *WAIT!* It was like a short fuse on a stick of dynamite and the spark raced toward the powder. In a fit of rage, I struck out at Annette and hit her *gacho* in the *cara*. Months of anger, frustration, and shame drove my fist when all I really wanted her to see was the difference between evil and good. I just wanted her to realize that good is better and that I wanted her to share in my happiness, but all she saw was my rage. Somehow, I snapped out of it almost as soon as it happened, and saw Annette holding her jaw as tears flowed down her cheeks.

I couldn't believe what I had done to the one person I loved the most, so I stormed out of the *casa* and drove around for hours, not really going anywhere. That's how my whole life had been, just driving around aimlessly day after day, year after year. Not really going anywhere. I was angry but when it came down to it, there was no one to blame but myself. *No one to blame but myself.* That thought circled aimlessly in *mi mente*.

Suddenly, I felt the tension of my foot pressing on the brakes and my *ranfla* came to a dead stop next to Sharkie Park.

"*Órale*, Homes. What are you doing back in the *barrio, ese?*"

I looked up from the steering wheel into the cold, dark eyes of Trigger who was leaning on the driver's door as the dragging rhythm of "Backstrokin" by Fatback Band spoke to me from the speakers mounted in the back window. I was looking for the good stuff, but the backstroke had tightened its grip on my soul. I didn't know what to say.

21

Matón

I had let everyone that I cared about down, by returning to the *barrio*, but I didn't know where else to go. I didn't know how to face Pastor Ramirez after dropping out of his program. I couldn't go back to Annette after venting my rage on her. Even *mi jefita* would have been disappointed to learn that I had retreated on my path to salvation.

The one person that didn't seem the least bit shocked to see me was Trigger. So when I pulled up to Sharkie Park and he strolled over, leaned in the window of my *ranfla*, and said, "What are you doing back in the *barrio, ese*?" I knew he was simply confirming what we both already knew; I couldn't make it outside of the *barrio*.

As though it were written all over *mi cara*, I couldn't hide the depth of my madness from his steely-eyed stare. I was a *matón*, and as far as he was concerned, it was public knowledge. What else did he need to know about me? Nothing, I was just like him. As they say, it takes one to know one. So it was understandable why he wasn't surprised to see me. He knew I'd be back.

"*Qué pasó?*" I said, choosing to ignore his question.

"*Órale*, Homes. Cherrieville hit Big Jerry's *cantón* last night."

I couldn't believe they had the *huevos* to move on Big Jerry's *cantón*. "Did anybody get hit?"

"Big Jerry took a *bala* in the chest," Trigger reported. "It missed his heart but we don't know if he's going to live."

I remembered when *Solo* got shot and I had immediately jumped into the nearest *ranfla* to deliver retribution, even though I had conflicted thoughts on what I was getting myself into. That time, with *Solo,* we ended up driving around without finding anyone till our hot tempers cooled enough to head back to our *barrio.*

This time was different. There were no conflicted thoughts and no hot temper at all. I knew exactly what needed to be done.

"What are you going to do, *ese?*" Trigger quipped, still probing my eyes for any glimmer of weakness.

"*Tu sabes,* Homes. I know what time it is, *ese,*" I said sternly returning Trigger's icy stare.

His stare melted into a slight, yet accepting smile when I reached down and put the *ranfla* in gear.

"Let's do it," he said without hesitation as he climbed into my *ranfla.*

Word was out on who had led the hit on Big Jerry's *cantón,* and Trigger knew where the *vatos* that did it hung out.

He explained to me that *El Gato,* a wannabe shot caller from Cherrieville, was trying to overcome the *jackete* they had been wearing since they shot and ran over their own homeboys during their little party with Hazard. He knew that taking out Big Jerry would be enough to erase that memory.

Trigger and I headed for Cherrieville but first swung by a homeboy's *cantón* to pick up some extra firepower for insurance.

It was late afternoon, and while those *vatos* would be expecting some major retaliation, they wouldn't expect to get hit in broad daylight. They were probably thinking the Shark would wait till later and slip in under the cover of darkness. *Forget that, I don't need no cover of darkness!* I figured Trigger and I could stroll right in, take care of business, and get out before any of those *chavalas* even knew they were dead.

I was tired of this senseless violence that had been going on for years and was ready to terminate as many of those *vatos* as I could. Frankly, I didn't care what happened to me as long as *El Gato* and a good number of his *soldados* faced the wrath of God. Between the Trigger and me, we had enough *cuetes* to fill a couple dozen caskets with corpses.

As we headed up Garey Avenue and turned west on Holt, Trigger's eyes tracked in on a brown '64 Impala low riding two cars ahead of us.

"That's them," he said as surprised as I was with our chance encounter. "*El Gato's* driving."

I dropped back, keeping in line with the two cars in front of us so the *vato* from Cherrieville wouldn't spot us and take off. As we stopped for the light at Park Avenue, Trigger and I checked our *cuetes*. I stuck one under my belt and laid the other in my lap. I wanted to be ready for anything.

When the light turned green, the '64 Impala hung a slow right on *Calle* Illinois next to the Catholic High School. I could tell by the way they were driving that they had no idea they were being stalked. I nodded to Trigger that this was it and immediately punched the gas pedal. We flew around the corner slamming into the rear end of their *ranfla*, shoving it forward and pinning it between my front bumper and a telephone pole. They weren't going anywhere.

Our doors swung open and almost in unison, Trigger and I sprang into position on opposite sides of the *ranfla*. Suddenly, the driver's door flew open and *El Gato* stepped out into the *calle*. I looked him directly in the eye and said, "*Calle Doce!*" then cut loose on him.

BAM! BAM! BAM!

I watched with pleasure as my *balas* penetrated his Cherrie black heart. He went down and I immediately turned my wrath on the *vatos* in the back seat. When Trigger and I quit firing, *El Gato* lay dead on the pavement and there were no signs of life inside the *ranfla*.

Trigger and I calmly strolled back to my *ranfla*. I shoved the transmission in reverse and we carefully swung a U-turn back onto Holt then turned south on White Avenue and we were home free.

I dropped Trigger off at Sharkie Park. He got out of my *ranfla*, turned and leaned in the passenger window.

"Don't let me catch you slippin', *ese!*" he said with a smirk.

I cruised over to *mi jefita's casa*, where I stashed my *ranfla* and the *cuetes* in the garage then went inside and took a shower.

The next day I got dressed and checked the front of my *ranfla*. The damage was minimal, a few dents and scratches on the bumper that needed some quick attention. I went to the back of the garage where I had stashed the *cuetes* the night before. I made certain to leave behind the one that had taken down *El Gato*. While I knew the *cuetes* were hot and were enough to put me away if I got busted with one, I wasn't so *loco* as to get caught with the murder weapon on me. But just the same, these were dangerous times and I felt the need for protection, so I grabbed a *cuete* and headed into the *barrio*, stopping at Big Jerry's *cantón* first. Trigger and some of the homeboys were keeping *trucha* while kicking back out front, as I parked and strolled up.

"*Órale, Braso,*" Trigger said as he slung his arm around my neck. "*Conejo* wants to talk to you."

I expected *Conejo* to join us for a trip to visit Big Jerry in the hospital, but instead Trigger ushered me and the other homeboys in front around to the back. I couldn't believe it. Big Jerry was sitting in an easy chair drinking a *pisto*. The only thing different about him was a big bandage on his left shoulder but otherwise he looked fine. He put his bottle down and reached out to shake hands with me.

"I heard what you did for me, *ese*. I won't forget it," he said with an air of sincerity.

Conejo stood up and shook hands also.

"Sunday's our next meeting," he announced. "We want you to be the shot caller for the *barrio*, Homes."

I had learned a long time ago to control my reactions and did so on this occasion even though the news caught me by surprise and accented my shock at seeing Big Jerry alive and doing fairly well.

"If a homeboy gives you a problem, don't worry," *Conejo* continued. "We'll take care of it."

I realized he was serious and the deal had already been sealed with the Shark's stamp of approval. They were simply letting me know what time it was. We all knew that *matónes* make the best shot callers, not because they're so smart or have the innate ability to develop and implement strategies. *Matónes* make the best shot callers because they have the willingness to pull the trigger. That's what separates the men from the *chavalas*. *Matónes* inspire allegiance through a kind of do-or-die attitude. Homeboys do what they say or homeboys die.

HOMEBOY'S SOUL

There wasn't any discussion, congratulations or condolences. The word wasn't even out yet. That's just the way it was. We all shook hands and I strolled back to the front with a thousand thoughts racing through *mi mente*, like calling a truce with Cherrieville and all of the other rival *barrios*. I would make them believe I was tired of all this violence, and just when they started trusting me, I would blow them all away. I could then implement a tax on all drug deals in Pomona. Those who paid up would be allowed to stay in business. Those who didn't pay would disappear from the landscape.

I knew enough about the world of business to realize that true power required controlling the flow of the almighty dollar, and in the *barrio*, with drugs flowed *feria*. Control the flow of drugs and I could control the flow of money. Of course *La Olica* would get their cut, but I could see our new expanded territory in *mi mente* as clearly as if they were R.T.D. routes highlighted on a city map.

I was still deep in thought as I rounded the corner of homeboy's pad. Suddenly, someone grabbed me and slammed me hard against the wall. It happened so fast that I couldn't see who did it, let alone grab my *cuete*. All I could do was ease my head, which was pinned against the house, around slightly.

"That's him," shouted a *jura* standing near the front of my *ranfla*. Then I felt my wrists being forced into a pair of handcuffs by the *jura* who had control of me. He started to pat me down and I knew I was busted. When his hand hit the *cuete,* he just about wet his pants. It was an easy find, tucked under my belt and hidden from view only by my Pendleton. He quickly yelled something in code to the other *juras*. They immediately drew their weapons and herded all of the homeboys at gun point around to the front of the *cantón*.

Man! What can I do now? The *juras* had me, they had my *ranfla* with the dents and scratches in the front bumper, and they had one of the *cuetes*. I was busted and I knew it. Reality took a big shark bite out of my soul, chewed it up, and spit it out. Homeboys just stared as the *juras* shoved me into the backseat of their patrol car.

It was a short ride to the police station at Park and Mission. Even so, it seemed that everyone we passed had time to take a good long look at me. I could see in their *caras* a look of curiosity. I knew they were wondering to themselves, *what did he do?* I tried to blow it off but there was no hiding the fact that I was headed to jail.

Upon arrival at the police station, I took some pleasure out of seeing all the security measures that the *juras* had implemented on the station, a result of the homeboys shooting up the place after the *juras* beat up a carload of homeboys for no reason at all. I was attending Simons Junior High at the time and the thought of going to jail was the furthest thing from *mi mente*. Now as the *juras* pulled me out of the patrol car, it was the only thing on *mi mente*.

I had never been inside this police station or any police station for that matter. For some reason, I didn't count the time I did in the brig when I was in the Army, all that seemed different. I had joined the Army and, as a personal choice, had decided not to follow their rules, so I deserved what I got. This was somehow different. I hadn't decided to be born and raised in the *barrio*. I hadn't decided to get jumped into *Calle Doce*. All that just seemed to happen. In fact, to me, it was just part of growing up in Pomona but none of that seemed to matter right now.

The *juras* looked happy as they dragged me from the back of the police cruiser. My capture was a crown on their head and they were going to wear it proudly. I knew enough about the *juras* to realize that they really would use anything I said against me, when my case went to trial, so I keep my mouth shut. What was I going to tell them anyway? I'm innocent? There was no denying the facts. They had plenty of evidence and it all pointed right at me.

I remained quiet as they ushered me into a small room with no windows, just inside the side door of the station. They made me empty my pockets onto a plain wooden bench; then an overweight *jura* scooped my stuff into a large manila envelope. After a strip search came fingerprinting. The *jura* took my hand and rolled each finger, tapped it on the black ink pad and rolled it carefully across the paper card. Another *jura* confirmed the name and address information on my driver's license while writing in a large, oversized ledger. And that was it; off to the large holding tank with a dozen other drunks, burglars, murderers, and thieves. I didn't know exactly where the dozen or so other prisoners fell in that mix, but I didn't see any of them that looked like they wanted to mess with me, so I kicked back against the wall. A few hours later, they hauled me down a hallway to a private cell.

Steel clanging against steel echoed off the concrete walls of my cell as the bars slammed shut across the doorway. That familiar sound reminded me of the Army stockade, but only for a moment, as I stood there staring at the toilet and a stainless steel bench which doubled as a bed. A cold chill shot through me as I sat down on the hard surface, not noticing the thin mattress rolled up in the corner. I thought about that first day in church where I'd hoped that now that I'd found the Lord, life would be a bed of roses. I didn't realize that I had only planted the seeds. Without the care and nourishment provided by a commitment to a new way of life, the roses would never bloom. Now, I was up to my eyeballs in thorns and had no one to blame but myself.

22

La Pinta

The first thing I heard the next morning was the sound of heavy metal keys rattling in the steel lock of my jail cell. I squeezed my eyes open and saw a big *jura* staring at me through the bars.

"Let's go for a walk," he commanded.

I got up, still half asleep, and followed him down the corridor between the long rows of cells, not knowing where he was taking me. His footsteps echoed off the gray walls in the otherwise quiet hallway. It was early and most of the other prisoners were still asleep. At the end of the hallway, the *jura* instructed me to sit on a wooden bench while he unlocked a heavy metal door. I sat down and yawned while trying to wipe the sleep out of my eyes. As the door swung open, I saw two detectives waiting on the other side. I knew immediately they were there for me.

The *jura* ushered me into an interrogation room with nothing but a table and three chairs, then the *jura* left me with the detectives. *De volada*, the detectives kicked into their Good Cop, Bad Cop routine. The good cop politely invited me to sit down. He was the younger of the two and seemed well suited for the role. I complied knowing full well how to play this game. At the moment, they had the upper hand and there was nothing I could do but play along.

It didn't matter to me that these detectives were just two white boys with guns and badges who had nothing but contempt and hate for *Chicanos*. I'd seen that look before. I had seen it when I was only eleven years old and witnessed the *juras* getting their butts kicked in Sharkie Park. I remembered seeing the *jura* who stared at me after losing his prey between some houses, and since then I had seen it many times. It was that look of hate, branded into my memory through continued encounters with the *juras* that had guided most of my decisions over the years. Now it was that same look of hate that I saw in the eyes of the two *juras* that sat across the table from me in the interrogation room. Even the good cop couldn't contain his contempt for me and what I stood for.

Even so, I listened patiently as they carefully explained that I was facing charges for first degree murder.

"All I'm saying is we've got enough evidence to lock you up for twenty-five years to life," the good cop pointed out before offering me an opportunity to reduce the charges if I ratted out the other homeboys involved.

Yeah, right! I'm going to rat on Trigger and end up with a filero stuck in my neck, I thought to myself.

The detectives tried to make me believe that they were trying to do me a favor and that they couldn't help me unless I helped them. I felt like spitting in their faces but I knew it was a good way to get a beating, so I kept cool.

The detectives seemed to know that I wasn't alone during the hit on *El Gato*, but I could tell they had no idea how many homeboys were involved or which ones. They certainly weren't going to weasel that information out of me, no matter what tactics they pulled. The only thing these *juras* were getting from me was name, rank, and serial number. Army survival training had prepared me well for being captured and interrogated by the enemy. When they finally realized that I wasn't going to spill any useful information, they called the uniformed *jura* and had me taken back to my cell.

As I reclined on the hard bunk in my cell, I once again found myself alone with my thoughts. I realized what a mess I was in and that it was my mess. I had created it. Those two detectives had nothing to do with that, and they certainly weren't taking time out of their busy schedules to help out a hard-core *vato loco* like me.

In the morning, the *juras* escorted me and a dozen other prisoners through several locked doors, down into a tunnel under the Pomona Police Station to the municipal court building, located next door, where they ushered us into a courtroom.

A white-haired, white-skinned judge looked me over with disdain as he said, "Under California Penal Code 187, you are hereby charged with murder in the first degree. How do you plead?"

"Not guilty," I stated as directly and authoritatively as I could, as if I was going to convince him of anything. I must say that standing tall before the "man" was a very humbling experience to say the least. I was relieved when the judge shifted his attention to the next unfortunate. I was just a tickle in the day in, day out irritation of his burning hemorrhoids.

That was it. I was officially charged with first degree murder.

They brought up the next prisoner as the *juras* led me away to a large holding cell with twenty or so inmates outfitted in blue uniforms tagged with L.A. COUNTY on the back. *De volada,* I saw homeboys Slim and Cyclone who happily greeted me. I was happy to see them, but Slim more than anything because I had the chance to talk with him. Slim told me he was getting released today. Ever since being arrested, I had been concerned about the *juras* finding where I had stashed the *cuetes*, so I told Slim where they were and asked him to have Trigger get rid of them and let homeboy know I'm no *rata.* That would take care of two things that weighed heavily on *mi mente.* The *juras* wouldn't be able to get the *cuetes*, and Trigger could relax about whether the *juras* were looking for him.

By mid-afternoon, I was herded onto a bus with a dozen or so other *vatos* and carted off to the L.A. County Jail. As the bus geared up and headed out onto the freeway, I remembered seeing *Conejo* after he and five other homeboys had spent three days in jail. Everyone wanted to hear his stories and he was more than willing to tell them. It was as though he was some sort of hero, having survived a close encounter with the *juras*. But I also remembered the look in his eyes that hung like a shroud behind the excitement of regaining his freedom and sharing his experiences.

I remembered him saying, "One's not a *Calle Doce* homeboy until you've received a horse beating and live to tell about it."

He could have just as easily said, until you've been to jail. I suddenly realized that he was talking about the reality of being a caged animal at the mercy and whim of the *juras*. I couldn't escape the fact that this was now my reality.

Once the bus stopped, we were immediately corralled into the processing area. The guards wanted to know what gang I was from and if anybody was out to get me. Now that was a funny question, since I knew L.A. County Jail was the easiest place in the County to do a hit on somebody and get away with it. If they weren't smart enough to know that the *vatos* from Cherrieville would just as soon like to see me face down on a catwalk, I wasn't going to be the one to educate them.

They finally finished with the questions. We got our dress blues were led upstairs to the 9000 floor where they gave us each a bedroll and told us to sit on the floor and wait until we got assigned to a housing unit. At least the bedroll made a nice pillow to cushion our butts from the hard concrete floor. *Man, I thought the Army was slow. This place makes the Army seem fast and efficient.* At least in the Army you got some love from the other homeboys who were there putting in their time for their country. Here, I was alone and not about to turn my back on any of these fools.

I was soon to find out that all the cuss words that I had heard on my first day in Boot Camp could not adequately describe the Los Angeles County Jail. It was noisy and crowded. The food sucked, and to say the place stunk is a gross understatement. The stench was unbearable. Simply put, the L.A. County Jail was society's way of getting even with a massive congregation of the worst demons that existed within the confines of the county lines.

I don't know if it was day or night, but finally we were transferred into a huge dorm, which held well over one hundred inmates. *La Raza* stayed together and picked bunks at one end of the room. *De volada,* I met three *veteranos* from surrounding *barrios*. We seemed to have a lot in common and I felt safe kicking back with them. They noticed my XII *tac* and I confirmed I was from *Los* Sharkies *Calle Doce*. They knew a lot of my homeboys and the respect was automatic. Everyone knew we were down and had a reputation for taking care of our business. *Thank God for that!* Now, I was the new link in the long chain of homeboys who had done time in County, and it was my turn to pull the load for *Calle Doce*.

The three *veteranos* were like angels from Heaven as they took me under their wings and schooled me in the protocol of life in jail. "Don't fraternize with the *mayates*," they instructed me. Tension between *Chicanos* and *mayates* was at an all-time high and

La Qlica had passed word down from *la pinta* to expect a green light on all Crips. *Chicanos* were sharpening their *fileros,* pending the go-ahead from *La Qlica.*

When I told these *veteranos* that I had been charged with first degree murder, they smiled and had some ideas on how to beat the rap. Class was in session and I was all ears. They also told me what to expect from the district attorney and how to help make the system malfunction in my favor.

"Did you admit to doing it?" one of the *veteranos* asked.

"I'm not *loco*," I responded.

"Good," he said. "Don't make it easy for them."

"Any witnesses?" another *veterano* asked.

"None that are still breathing."

A smile spread across their faces. They continued by advising me that I could say that I found the gun which had probably been discarded by whoever did the murder. And if, by chance, the *juras* could place me at the scene, I could claim self-defense.

They pointed out that there were a lot of "ifs" surrounding this case. The more "ifs," the weaker the case for the D.A. and the better for me. They also explained that the D.A. wants a conviction no matter what, and the amount of time I would serve was irrelevant.

During the next few days, I settled into my bunk and met a few more *vatos* assigned to the 9000 floor. Luckily, there were no *vatos* from Cherrieville. That was my primary concern. Unfortunately though, there were no homeboys from Twelfth Street either.

During the next week and a half, my education continued. I soaked up every bit of information I could from the *veterano,s* who seemed more than willing to impart their wisdom and advice to the new kid in county blues.

There were a lot of "don'ts." Don't make friends or help anyone other than *La Raza*. Don't use the phones that are designated for *mayates*. Don't spit in the sinks. Don't mess with other people's business. Don't buy drugs unless you can pay. Don't raise your hand for a *movida* even if the command comes from *La Qlica*. There are plenty of youngsters that'll raise their hands for that. Don't deliver a *wila* for someone you don't know, and if you do, don't read it and make sure it is delivered *de volada*. Don't disrespect anyone unless you are ready to deal with it, and if someone disrespects you, it's a challenge that must be dealt with. Don't disrespect the guards because, more likely than not, they will help you.

There were far fewer do's. Help homeboys whenever you can and do everything you can to keep yourself out of trouble.

By the end of my third week in County, I was transferred into a module and put into a six-man cell. It was one of several dozen that lined a long, dark corridor with a walkway in the center for the guards. The air in this wing was even fouler than what I had endured in the dorm room.

I shared the cell with two other *Chicanos*, two *mayates*, and a *gavacho*. The *gavachos* had it the worst at County. They were always outnumbered and would end up paying rent or getting punked out. The stories of rapes flourished and I didn't want word getting out that I shared a cell with a *maricon*, so I kept out of that. I don't know how the *gavacho* would have fared if I hadn't been there.

I had been in jail almost a month before catching the chain back to Pomona for an appearance in Superior Court. The D.A. had picked up the case and I was appointed a faggy looking public defender. He meant well but I could tell from the start that he didn't have the experience or the *jugo* to get me off. *What can you expect for free?* It wasn't as though I could afford a real defense attorney.

I stood there with my "high powered" public defender hanging silently at my side while the D.A. told the judge, "because he does not hold a job and has no significant local ties, the People believe that the defendant poses an extreme risk of flight."

He double-locked my cell by adding, "With his lifelong gang affiliation, combined with his military experience and the heinous nature of this crime, he poses a serious threat to society."

The public defender stood there silently as the judge said, "Bail denied!" and slammed his gavel.

Man! Who's fooling who? I couldn't muster the *feria* to make bail even if it had been an option. Sounded like the D.A. was already trying the case and he did a good job of making me sound as bad as bad can be.

The sad part of my appearance in court was having to stand there in front of the judge with *mi jefita, hermana,* and Annette sitting behind me. I was happy to see them but couldn't imagine the thoughts that must be circulating through *mi jefita's mente* as she saw her *hijo* facing a lengthy prison term without the possibility of parole. How meaningless she must have thought all those times were when she sent me off with a kiss and her caution for me to stay out of trouble. Lord knows, I was in trouble now.

As I stood there listening to the D.A., I thought about how happy *mi jefita* had been when I told her that I wanted to get baptized, and how devastated she must feel now. I couldn't think about anything but how her sadness was all my fault. I wanted to turn around and hug her and tell her, *it's all a big mistake. Let's go home now.* But it wasn't a mistake. It was real. And to make matters worse, my *jefito's* words echoed in *mi mente.* "When your butt is sitting in jail, where are your friends going to be?"

He was right. My homeboys couldn't do a thing for me now, even if they wanted to. As the bailiff escorted me out of the courtroom, I stole a quick glance at my family. They smiled and waved, trying to be supportive, but I could see the tears in their eyes and tried to hide the ones that wanted to escape from mine.

On the bus back to the L.A. County Jail, I realized that there wasn't a man on this earth who could help me. I was floundering alone in a tumultuous sea of guilt and circumstances, and my options were limited. I could sink under the weight of my situation or hold my head up and take my punishment like a man. As they say, *don't do the crime if you can't do the time!*

The District Attorney was determined to see that I was going to do the time. How much time in *la pinta* they were going to throw at me, I didn't know. What I did know was that unless I wanted to become somebody's punk, I couldn't show weakness.

My strength was tested in the next few weeks when Annette, who I assumed would stay by my side forever, decided my wrongdoings were not her problem. Only seeing each other during visiting hours put a damper on our already strained relationship. I could see in her eyes that day in the courtroom that she had already decided to move on with her life. I had refused to believe it until I received a short note from her that said, among other things, *goodbye!*

Meanwhile, the public defender who I had grossly underestimated was working a deal with the D.A. that would give me twelve years for manslaughter. I do half of that and with good behavior I could be out in six. Man, I could have kissed the guy!

He explained to me that the *balas* from the *cuete* I got busted with were lodged in the *ranfla*. Lucky for me, Trigger's *balas* peppered the *ranfla*, but hadn't actually hit anybody. No one ever said Trigger was a good shot. Everybody just assumed, wrongly as it seems, from his *placaso* that he was a deadly shot. Isn't it strange how you can misjudge people?

In addition to the *cuete*, there were no witnesses, and apparently, the *juras* found a couple *cuetes* in El Gato's *ranfla* that had been fired as well. I hadn't even realized that El Gato and his homeboys had gotten off a few *balas*. Add to that piece of news my plea of self-defense and military experience, not to mention my clean record, and my lawyer was able to polish up the tarnished image the D.A. had tried to lay on me. When all was said and done, the D.A. was more than happy to work a deal for twelve years.

My joy, at learning this madness could possibly end after six years, was mixed with remorse. I was saddened over the fact that I had actually killed another human being. Like some brave on the warpath, a soldier in the battlefield, or a tough mobster who just unloaded his Tommy into someone's gut, there was no glory in killing. The fact that *El Gato* worshiped the same violence that had nearly consumed me didn't seem important now. I had taken the justice that belongs to Heaven alone and soiled my hands. Six years was a long time but only a pittance for such a sin against God.

Soon after I reached an agreement with the D.A. and the judge confirmed it a done deal, I caught the chain back to County and waited for my transfer to Chino. When it came through, I was shuffled into a small room, stripped of my clothing, and searched for contraband. They checked everywhere but found nothing. Then one of the *juras* threw me a clean set of county blues which I quickly put on, while another *jura* prepared a set of chains. I hated the sound of the chains as much as what they meant, but there was nothing I could do about it. The other *jura* gaffed me with a chain around my waist and each hand cuffed at my side.

We were lined up as they called out our names. One by one we entered the bus. When my name was announced, I headed into the bus, and once inside, I was directed by a *jura* with a chain in his hands to face the window and kneel on the seat that was in front of me. The *jura* fastened both of my ankles with a short chain. Suddenly, a wave of depression and loneliness sweep over me. This was the lowest point in my life. I felt that not only my manhood but any sense of humanity I had left had just been stripped away. I could barely move my feet as the chain tightened around my ankles and I was directed to a seat next to an older *vato* with glasses. I sat there feeling like a dog chained and forgotten in the backyard because nobody wants him around.

A few minutes later, the bus headed out with two guards in front and one in a wire-mesh cage in the back of the bus, with a loaded shotgun, keeping an eye on everything that moved. These *juras* were going to make certain we got where we were going.

During the trip, the *vato* next to me introduced himself as being from White Fence, a notorious gang in East *Los* dating back to the forties. He quickly sensed that I wasn't in the mood for conversation and left me alone.

About two hours later, the bus rolled through a gate in the tall chain-link fences topped with razor wire. I stared out at the massive stone block facility and I knew I had finally arrived. Like so many other homeboys before me, I, too, was now in Chino Central . . . *la pinta*.

For so many years, I had heard stories about homeboys who had done time here. Some had "graduated" while others were in for the long haul. They had all seemed special somehow, as if they were prisoners of war and had held their tongues in spite of all the enemy's coercive efforts and incentives to get them to implicate other homeboys. They were our heroes. And now I had also fallen into the hands of the enemy.

Inside, the guards pushed us through the processing line. I was going to be *torcido* for at least six years and these fools wanted me to hurry up. *Hurry up and do what? Feel lonely!* Realizing that I'd never see Annette again, and knowing that *mi jefita's* visitations would be limited, I was already lonely and feeling sorry for myself. It was hard to continually tell myself, *it's my fault, just deal with it!*

At Chino, I got to shed my county blues for some state issued jeans and a light blue shirt that fit just right. They took my shoes and gave me a pair of black slippers. All in all, the new wardrobe was a plus.

Since we had been on the bus all morning, the guards decided we might be hungry. We weren't ready to be turned loose in the general population yet, so they ran us through a hallway into a secluded courtyard. Wouldn't you know it, one of my homeboys was standing behind a table handing out box lunches. I hadn't seen Lazy in years. We weren't allowed to shake hands, so we just nodded in recognition of each other and he kicked me down with some extra oranges and cookies in my box. Suddenly, I didn't feel so lonely.

After everyone from the bus had received their lunches, homeboy Lazy strolled over and gave me the lowdown on what homeboys were there and where I would probably be assigned. He told me that after lunch they'd finish processing us, then kick us over to the gym. From there, I'd be assigned to a cell within a couple hours, at most a day.

I enjoyed kicking back out in the open air and was especially happy to see somebody I knew. It wasn't long before another line of prisoners filed into the courtyard. *De volada,* I saw four more homeboys that I recognized. A couple of them I hadn't seen in more than ten years. The guards kept them in line, so we couldn't chit-chat, but it was good to exchange a quick *"Q-vo?"* with them all the same. I knew there would be time later to catch up. Lots of time.

Lazy had to go back to work handing out lunches, so I strolled the courtyard alone, soaking up the warm rays of the sun, fresh air, and sounds of birds flying overhead. While I was happy to see some familiar *caras,* my feeling of sadness returned. What I really wanted was to hop into my *ranfla* and cruise through the *barrio* or out on the open highway. *Anywhere! I don't care. In here, I go where and when la pinta wants me to go.* I hated it, but I couldn't show weakness, especially not there!

As I circled the courtyard, I noticed the *veterano* from White Fence who had introduced himself to me on the bus was hanging by himself. For a moment, I thought about continuing the conversation with him but remembered the advice from the *veteranos* at County and decided I'd better keep to myself. No sooner than the thought popped through *mi mente,* he headed straight for the guard's station. He exchanged a few words with the guards and they quickly spun him around, handcuffed him, and carted him off through a heavy metal door that looked like it led into a cellblock. I wondered what he had said to the guards, but I knew enough to know it was something that was best left alone.

Suddenly, I heard a sound that reminded me of the Army. I'd recognize that sound anywhere. It was the cadence of *soldados* doing calisthenics and it was coming from the courtyard next door. A large canvas hung between our courtyard and the one next door, so I couldn't see who was making the noise, but I could see the attention of the guards on the watch tower shift from us to the source of the sound.

"*La Qlica, ese,*" a voice whispered behind me.

I quickly turned to see *Mosca* standing behind me. I could have soiled my state-owned jeans. I hadn't seen him in years. He was a couple years older than me. I'd usually see him hanging with *Conejo*. Last I heard he had gotten busted for a *movida* on Cherrieville in 1976, then caught some extra time on a few jailhouse murders. It was hard to believe he had been in here all that time.

"*Órale, Mosca,*" I said as we shook hands.

"I heard you was coming, *ese*," he said keeping the conversation subdued.

I wasn't sure how to answer him, so I just nodded and was glad the cadence from next door kicked in again momentarily distracting him so he didn't notice the sadness in my eyes.

"*La Qlica* runs this place, Homes," he added.

"*Sí mon,*" I agreed.

"Even the guards won't mess with them, *ese*. It's a mutual thing, Homes. *La Qlica* respects them and they let *La Qlica* do their thing. *Tu sabes?*"

Mosca wasn't telling me anything I didn't already know. I had heard enough stories about *la pinta* to understand that *La Qlica* had the *jugo* to do whatever they wanted. This was *La Qlica's* way of messing with everybody because they could. Everyone knew Chino Central was their headquarters. What was tripping me out was the impact the cadence had on everyone in our courtyard. It was as though a thick cloud of fear had descended. It didn't matter who you were—*chicano, gavacho* or *mayate*—and it didn't matter how tough you thought you were, *La Qlica* was tougher. I wasn't afraid to throw blows with anyone, or pull the trigger when necessary, but my knees were shaking at the sound of the cadence. I knew I wasn't more than *cucaracha* guts on the soles of their shoes if it came down to it. *La Qlica* was in control and they were letting everyone know it.

Homeboys who had been in *la pinta* used to tell us when we were youngsters, *if you want in La Qlica, just raise your hand. If you raise your hand, you'd better be willing to kill someone on their list. But if you ever plan to see the light of day outside the walls, ese, you'd better keep your hands in your pockets and don't have anything to do with La Qlica's business. Don't ask! Don't tell!*

The way I saw it, join *La Qlica* and you have a two-prong retirement program. They retire anybody that gets in your way and you retire in *la pinta*. I just got here and figured I had plenty of time to decide what to do.

I didn't know what kind of connections *Mosca* had. For all I knew he recruited for *La Qlica* and was testing my interest. On the outside, I had thought about joining *La Qlica*, but right now I didn't know if I wanted to retire in a prison cell. I also knew that *La Qlica* and homeboys respected those who decided to do their time and not step on anybody's toes. I didn't know what I wanted, so I kept my hands in my pockets and my mouth shut and let *Mosca* ramble on as though I didn't know anything about what went on in here.

"They call *gavachos:* 'Woods,' *mayates:* 'Terrones,' *Mexicanos* are called 'Border Brothers' and we're *'Eses,'* either *Sureños* or *Nortenos*," he explained with a look of darkness in his eyes that was similar to that cold stare that *Conejo* used when he was searching for signs of weakness. It was similar and yet at the same time, it was different. It scared me.

"You're going to eat, take a dump, and bunk with *Sureños*," he continued. "That way, anybody wakes up dead, they know it was done by a *Sureño*."

I got the sense that *Mosca* didn't care about strength or weakness. The dark, cold look in his eyes wasn't what scared me. What scared me was the sense that he didn't care about anything at all.

Just then, the guards decided that we'd had enough time for lunch. They lined us up and marched us back through the hallway, into a room that looked like a make-shift clinic. Several male nurses prepared to take samples of our blood to find out what kind of diseases we might have. I wasn't sure I wanted to know.

Just as a nurse started to slip a needle into a vein in my right arm, some guards rushed in with a Wood and two *Terrones* on stretchers. They each had severe stab wounds to the neck and blood was gushing everywhere. I immediately recognized the signature of *La Qlica*.

The guards must have decided they had enough blood without collecting ours, so we were hurried off to an old gymnasium that had been converted into a large dormitory filled with bunks and inmates. Four *vatos* waited by the door, watching everybody as they entered. Somehow I could tell they weren't there by chance. As soon as I strolled past, one of them approached me respectfully and said, "Where you from, *ese?*"

"*Calle Doce,*" I responded quickly with an equal measure of respect.

"*Órale*, three of your homeboys just got moved to the west yard, *ese*," he said, pausing for a brief moment before extending his hand. "Li'l Demon *de White Fence.*"

I shook hands with him.

"There's a bunk by us. You can kick it there if you want," he said.

"*Órale,*" I said not wishing to show any disrespect.

As we neared the bunks, Li'l Demon leans close to me and asks, "Was there any of my homeboys with your group?"

"*Sí mon*. One *vato* but I don't remember his *placaso, ese.*"

"*Órale*. Was he a *veterano* and wore glasses, tall and thin?"

"*Sí mon, pero* the *juras* gaffed him and took him away."

It suddenly dawned on me why the *veterano* had approached the guard's station in the courtyard.

Li'l Demon squinted his eyes as a frown spread across his *cara*.

"Can you believe it, Homes! We've been waiting for that *vato* for a week."

I didn't need to know any more about this, so I quickly shifted the subject by asking, "What homeboys from *Doce* are here?"

Li'l Demon's thoughts were still on his *movida*.

"What?"

Then my question seemed to soak in all at once and he blurted out, "Li'l *Flaco*, Goofy, and Blinks." *Man, last time I saw those vatos was before I joined the Army!* That seemed to end our conversation.

As I sat down on my bunk, I quickly realized how tired I was, so I leaned back while Li'l Demon and his *vatos* kicked off a game of Spades. As I lay there slowly fading, it hit me what homeboy Lazy had said about only being in the gym for a couple hours. Li'l Demon and those three *vatos had been lying in wait for that* veterano *for a week!* I suddenly didn't feel like I needed to close my eyes, so I kicked back and counted tiles on the ceiling. I was up to seven hundred and eighty-nine for the third time when I heard a guard over near the door call my name. I hopped out of the bunk and said *"al rato"* to Li'l Demon and his homeboys, then queued up behind the other inmates whose names had been called.

The guards headed us down a stone block hallway leading to a cell block. Instead of turning toward the cells, they marched us into a small cafeteria to the right. I hadn't done anything all day except wait, but all the same I was starved and this grub smelled good. Day-old *frijoles* would smell good next to the garbage they fed us at the County.

I grabbed a tray and plastic spoon. They didn't have any forks or knives for obvious reasons. I didn't give that a second thought as I followed the line toward the food. The Wood serving the food slopped some gravy over my potatoes, and I took my tray and slid in on the end of a bench with three other *vatos*. I didn't know any of them and they looked to be as hungry as I was, so we all ate in silence.

No sooner had I swallowed my last bite, the guards called my name again. I strolled over to a table at the far end of the cafeteria where they issued me a sheet and a gray, woolen blanket. The smell reminded me of the blankets we were issued in the Army. The only difference was that the Army gave us green blankets. A guard directed me to cell number 27 on the second tier.

I stood in front of the small steel door as the guard did a final quick inspection of the cell. My eyes followed him as he checked around the stainless steel sink in the corner, the toilet, and the mattress rolled up on the cement bunk. My eyes quickly darted to the other side of the cell. *Thank God! Just one bunk!* At last, I'll be able to get some sleep with both eyes closed. Satisfied that the last occupant hadn't left behind any contraband, the guard stepped out of the cell. I stepped inside, a buzzer sounded and the door slammed shut behind me sending an echo down the entire cell block.

I immediately spread the mattress out on the cement bunk then fixed the sheet and blanket, took a dump, washed *mi manos y cara*, then hit the bunk. As I laid there in solitude, drifting between consciousness and sleep, at the end of my first day, the cadence of *La Qlica's soldados* echoed in *mi mente*. I could see the three blood-soaked inmates that had been carted into the make-shift clinic on stretchers, and I couldn't escape the fact that I, too, had killed someone. Not with my bare hands, where I could feel a *filero* pierce his skin and smell warm life seeping from his body. I had killed from a safe distance, letting a *bala* do the dirty work, even though the Army had made certain that I knew how to kill a man while standing eyeball-to-eyeball with him. These hands could kill at close range. I drifted off thinking that I could easily be a *soldado* for *La Qlica*. All I had to do was raise my hand and I would be immersed in the *jugo* of *La Qlica*.

Later that night in my cell, I opened my eyes. Lights were out and everything was quiet. *Mi mente* hovered in that zone between sleep and awake. I looked around and couldn't believe what I saw. Trigger was standing at the end of my bunk. He looked exactly as I remembered him, with a twisted little smirk on his *cara*, when he strolled away from my *ranfla* right after our *movida* on *El Gato*.

"*Órale, Braso,*" he said. "Don't let me catch you slippin', *ese!*"

Then as quickly as he appeared, he was gone and I suddenly felt terribly helpless and alone. I was completely awake now. My whole body was trembling. There was no one I knew that I could turn to. Then for some reason, I remembered what Pastor Ramirez had told me about responsibility. That's what Trigger was trying to tell me, *take responsibility for your life!* I knew that I had gotten myself into this mess and I'd have to deal with the consequences however harsh they were turning out to be, but inside I always had someone else to blame. It was never my fault! If it weren't for those *vatos* from Cherrieville, the *juras,* the D.A., *El Gato*! *Always somebody else!*

At that moment, I threw myself on my knees and prayed to God for the strength to vanquish the demon that had plagued my life for as long as I could remember. The demon that was as close as my shadow and always waiting around the next corner, ready to seduce my soul with temptation, the demon that had guided me down the path of evil. I prayed to God for the strength to overcome my greatest enemy . . . *me!*

"Father, I'm sorry for what I have done." I pleaded. "I place my life in your hands. Please give me the strength to carry the burden that I alone have placed on my shoulders."

The words flowed from my mouth without conscience thought. It suddenly became crystal clear to me that there was one path to salvation, one road for this sinner to follow, one enemy for me to overcome, and God was the only one who could help me now.

This time *mi mente* was made up.

I don't recall when prayer relapsed into the arms of slumber, or whether I made the transition still leaning with bowed head against my bunk, but three thousand six hundred and forty-nine days later, those heavy iron doors slammed shut again. This time they were behind me. On April 27, 1994, the same day as my cell number, I stepped out of prison a free man and climbed onto a bus headed back home to Pomona with a new sense of who I was and what I could accomplish during my stay in this world.

It had taken me ten long years, four years longer than I had expected, to regain my freedom. During that time, I'd had the opportunity to think about my life and the terrible things that I had done. Not Cherrieville, not even the Chino Sinners or the *juras* or Annette, as hard as it was for me to admit, could be blamed for my insanity. As hard as it was for me to admit, it was all my fault.

With God's help, I found the key to my chains of bondage within myself and came to realize that being a *vato loco* was simply *loco*. It was madness destined to end in a coffin, either the one you're buried in, or the four-by-eight kind that lines the cell blocks in *la pinta*. When I finally came to my senses, I realized that *"vato loco"* was not the epitaph I wanted engraved on my headstone.

As violent and confused as life was in *la pinta*, it was the solitude and serenity of my cell that saved me. I thanked God that I had been given a cell to myself, where I had a chance to be alone with my thoughts that first night. I thanked God for letting me taste the turmoil in *la pinta* without becoming part of it, and I thank God most for sending Trigger to my cell on my first night to give me a message of hope.

I don't know what combination of events makes one man turn toward the darkness and another face the light. I only know that, for me, on my first night in *la pinta*, events came together in the right combination to unlock the possibility of a future that I had never even imagined. A future that I didn't know existed as long as I remained embroiled in the madness.

Somehow, *mi jefito* and *jefita* understood that madness, but were unable to explain to me where it would lead. My *jefito* had tried to tell me, but unfortunately I was too headstrong to heed his warnings. He knew, long before the iron doors of *la pinta* slammed shut on me, where my life was headed. I look back with regret now that it took me so long to figure it out for myself.

Now that I'm back in the world, the road isn't necessarily easy, but it's clear. I need to love myself as much as I love and respect others. It's a simple concept, but it had taken me so long to understand it.

As my bus rolls into Pomona, I see through the window a *veterano* strolling along the sidewalk with his *ruca* at his side. He is *pelón* with a tattoo on the side of his neck. A pair of dark shades covers his eyes. He's decked out in Khakis with a razor sharp crease down the leg and a Pendleton hanging open below the top button over a crisp white T-shirt.

I suddenly remember how carefully I used to press the crease into my Khakis before caravanning with my homeboys to the L.A. County Fair Grounds. I remember strolling in looking all *bonarood* and standing toe-to-toe with the *vatos* from rival *barrios* while throwing blows until the blood flowed in the "fun zone." I thought this demonstrated the love and respect I had for my homeboys and they had for me, but I know now that it was just an excuse to vent the hatred and anger that had built up inside me over the years.

The memories are as close and vivid as if I were there, only now, I know that the love and respect I thought I shared with my homeboys was nothing more than an illusion. None of us had the *huevos* to stand up and be the men we were without using violence, threats, and intimidation to try and prove how tough we were, because we didn't have the discipline and motivation to acquire an education, or the other tools necessary to make a successful contribution to the world on behalf of *La Raza*. All we could do is tear down what others were trying to build.

Suddenly the bus jerks to a stop in front of the bus station. I gather my things and move toward the exit. As I step off the bus and my feet once again touch down on the *calles* of Pomona, I gaze into the welcoming eyes of *mi jefita* and *mi hermana*. Suddenly, I feel ashamed for all the pain and suffering I have caused them, and so many other *madres* and their *hijas*, and I realize that all the things I thought I had done in defense of this *tierra* had been done because I was too weak to give my spirit and soul the freedom to follow another path.

None of these things, from getting jumped into *Calle Doce* to killing *El Gato*, had made me a man. They had simply made me a *matón* and landed me in *la pinta*. I couldn't believe it had taken me more than thirty years to discover that that's not who I wanted to be.

Epilogue

Around the time I checked out of Chino Central, homeboy Fat Joe passed through on a transfer to another *pinta* with one more year to do. Before he left he told me that he had had enough of the madness. I heard later that when he got out, he got married and raised a family.

Payaso, the clown who took life as one big joke, could have followed in the capable footsteps of Cheech Marin, Pablo Rodriguez, or George Lopez and been a popular standup comedian. Instead, homeboy is still gang-affiliated and has a lifetime gig in *la pinta*. No one's laughing about that,

Nite Owl happened to be at the wrong place, at the right time. Being forced to leave the *barrio* turned out to be a blessing for him and gave him the opportunity to taste a different lifestyle. He now lives and works back east where he takes care of his family.

Travieso finally freed himself from drugs and the gang life and married his *ruca*. Sadly, his *carnal* J-Bird couldn't shake the heroin monkey off his back and died in the early nineties due to a serious infection in his leg caused by years of slamming.

Black Crow served sometime after the death of Linda. He managed to shake heroin while in *la pinta* but couldn't break free of the gang mentality after his release. Six *balas* to the body and one to the head brought my close, and very much loved, homeboy down after he and another homeboy got into a power struggle for leadership of the *barrio*. Both homeboys wanted to call the shots, but the *jale* only required one candidate. Homeboys didn't appreciate the way it was handled, and put a hit out on the shooter, who wisely disappeared.

Homeboys Wicked and *Wesos* stayed true to their convictions and moved on with their lives without further gang involvement. Unfortunately, poor health brought down Wicked before his fortieth birthday. His older *carnal* Bad Boy, who ran interference for Wicked after he had decided gang life was too hazardous for his health, served his tour in the Marines, got married after an honorable discharge, and is doing well.

Conejo and Trigger enjoyed the luxury of retiring from gang life without having to do time in *la pinta*. They simply stepped back and let the youngsters take over. It didn't come as much of a surprise when I found out that the reason *Conejo* and Big Jerry green-lit my move toward Christianity was because they were involved in searching their own souls. *Conejo* didn't follow that path very far but did manage to stay free of gang activities. While I was in *la pinta*, Big Jerry and Evil fell victim to an overdose of heroin.

Homeboys *Malo*, Fish, and Slim remain committed to the gang mentality and, at the time of this writing, still stroll along the same path of self-destruction that I once tread.

*   *   *

Unlike many of the thousands of homeboys and homegirls that strolled the *barrios* of East L.A. before me, I survived long enough to escape the whirlwind of death and destruction. Not because I was smarter or tougher than everyone else; I helped bury homeboys that were both smarter and tougher. Not because I was salvaged by a mentor that intervened on my behalf; my parents tried and I wouldn't let them. Pastor Ramirez also tried; his faith was strong while mine was weak. I survived the madness because God graced me with a combination of coercions that resulted in my being safely sequestered in *la pinta* long enough to reflect on the choices I had made in my life. God granted me the opportunity to discover for myself that I could control the direction of my life by controlling the choices I made.

When I was jumped into *Calle Doce* at the age of fifteen, I didn't think to myself, *I want to end up dead or in la pinta when I grow up.* Joining *Calle Doce* was what the *niños* I hung out with did. It was no more unusual for me to join *Calle Doce* than it was for George W. Bush to go to Harvard.

To me, the *veteranos* represented the leadership of the *barrio* and I wanted to follow in their footsteps. It took me nineteen years, with ten of those in *la pinta*, to realize the dead-end nature of that path. The great irony is that the *veteranos* were not totally misguided. In the years following WWII, and for several decades thereafter, the *barrios* of East L.A. were under attack by savagely racist and corrupt forces of authority that brutalized Mexican-American populations living there. The *veteranos* formed gangs to defend the *barrios*.

Even so, gangs were not an invention of *Chicanos* in Southern California. They have frequently cropped up in populations that found themselves victimized when politically and morally corrupt officials subverted the rule of law to serve their own greedy interests. As far back as the 1830s, Irish immigrants in the southern reaches of New York City faced ruthless persecution which resulted in the formation of the Dead Rabbits, Bowery Boys, the Plug Uglies, and other street gangs which defended the rights of the Irish immigrant population and simultaneously abused them. Chinese immigrants, who built America's railroads, found themselves facing a similar situation in San Francisco. It is a puzzling contradiction that America which warmly welcomes immigrants in the popular poetry of Emma Lazarus, "give me your tired, your poor, your huddled masses yearning to breathe free," then treats them so harshly once they step foot on our shores.

Even *La Qlica* promoted the contradictory forces of unity and chaos among *La Raza*. While it is no secret that *La Qlica* employed violence to resolve conflicts, it is not commonly known that *La Qlica* single-handedly accomplished what *juras* and politicians alike had been unable to accomplish. *La Qlica* ended drive-by shootings, which in the mid-eighties were mushrooming out of control in the *barrios* of East Los Angeles.

The beginning of the end of drive-bys in East L.A. came about when some *vatos* from Cherrieville hit our *barrio* early one evening in an effort to kill homeboy *Malo*. They unloaded a volley of *balas* into a yard full of *niños* and *rucas*. One of our homegirls was hit and a baby was killed. The baby's *jefitos* were devastated. The *juras* apprehended the *vatos* from Cherrieville, but that didn't stop *Calle Doce* homeboys from retaliating. As the cycle of violence escalated throughout Southern California, more and more *niños* and innocent by-standers were getting shot. Meanwhile, greedy record company executives and marketing moguls motivated by easy profits prompted crop after crop of "instant" gangsters by encouraging youngsters to identify with the gangster image promoted by rap artists. With so many *veteranos* dead or away in *la pinta*, the youngsters coming up lacked a true understanding or appreciation of history, especially *Chicano* history, including the struggles endured through successive generations of Zoot Suiters, *Pachucos*, and *cholos*. Additionally, the youngsters lacked a code of respect or the leadership necessary to keep a lid on the violence which was boiling over. Each round of aggression and retaliations lacked balance and proportionality. Each successive *movida* seemed to escalate the level of violence. The collateral damage soon reached such proportions that *La Qlica* finally stepped up and issued a memo commanding *Chicano* gangs that had existed since the forties and fifties, as well as those "qlicked" up with *La Qlica*, to terminate all drive-bys. That included Cherrieville and *Los* Sharkies *Calle Doce*.

To enforce their order, *La Qlica* gave a green light to hit any *barrio* found guilty of a drive-by. This meant that all *sureños* in *la pinta* had a mission to take down the *vatos* from the offending *barrio*, until that *barrio* cleaned it up by killing any of their own homeboys involved in a drive-by. To put it bluntly, this memo was executed to a tee. Believe me it didn't take long for the youngsters out on the *calles* to get the message. As a result of *La Qlica's* bold action, drive-bys stopped almost overnight.

This is not intended to justify the choices I made or where those choices have led me. That responsibility lies squarely upon my shoulders. I have come to realize that there is no honor or glory in killing. I view what I did as the actions of a misguided coward who was too timid to face the truth. Ultimately, each homeboy must face his own reckoning. Therefore, it is useful to understand the situation which helped frame my choices and continues to guide thousands of young *Chicanos,* blacks, Orientals, and whites alike toward a maelstrom of death and violence. Until community leaders decide to quit winking at racism and poverty in all its ugly forms, I believe this march toward doom will continue to populate the prisons and graveyards of America with untold numbers of innocent and willing victims alike.

They say in *la pinta*, there are three ways to survive hard time: drugs, the crazy house, or religion. I'm not crazy. Throughout my entire sentence, I stayed away from *La Qlica* and the drug trade. Instead, I enrolled in art classes and studied computer repair to keep *mi mente* occupied and alert. It didn't matter where the system sent me; I tried to make the best of my circumstances. I took advantage of the programs and worked to prepare myself for the day I would walk out a free man.

During my term of incarceration, I had the opportunity for some deep soul-searching, which solidified my relationship with God, not as a means of escape from my responsibility for the wrongs I suffered upon others, but rather as a guide for the new direction that my life was headed. God's love brought me a greater understanding of myself and how my decisions can impact the lives of others for the good if I so decide.

I'm not perfect, but I try my best to thank God every day that I'm alive and free, and that I discovered, before it was too late, that my life is a precious creation which is continually evolving. I now know that my search for answers to the mysteries of life may lead me to many interesting places, none of which is more mysterious or more wonderful than those revealed when homeboy's soul strolls freely toward the light at the end of the storm.

Glossary

Abogado: Lawyer

Adelitas: Women who fought in Pancho Villa's army

Agua: Water

Al rato: Later

Alameda: Tree-lined avenue

Ay Dios mío: Oh my God

Ay: Gee

Ay te wacho: Se you later (slang)

Aztlan: Region of southwestern United States

Bala: Bullet

Balazo: Flying bullet

Barrio: Poor Latino neighborhood, ghetto

Basura: Trash

Bolas: Dollar bills (slang)

Braso: Gang name modified from *"brazo"* meaning arm

Brocha: Thick, bushy mustache (slang)

Buenos días: Good morning

Caiga: Come here (slang)

Caja: Box

Cajón: Dresser drawer

Caldo de res: Beef soup

Califas: California (slang)

Calle Doce: Twelfth Street

Calle: Street
Cantón: Pad, house (slang)
Cara: Face
Caras cobardes: Cowardly faces
Carnal: Brother (slang)
Carnala: Sister (slang)
Carne asada: Seasoned meat
Casa: House
Chale: No way
Chango: Monkey
Chavala: Young girl, sissy (slang)
Chica: Young girl
Chicana: Female Mexican-American(s) born in southwestern United States
Chicano: Male Mexican-American(s) born in southwestern United States
Cholos: Flashy dressed young Chicanos in the seventies and eighties who were influenced by the Pachuco and Zoot Suit era
Chones: Boxer shorts, underwear (slang)
Cinco de Mayo: May 5, 1862, mistakenly known as Mexican Independence Day, marked the defeat of French invaders by Mexican patriots in the Battle of Puebla which succeeded in expelling the invaders and postponed French support for the Confederacy during the American Civil War
Cobija: Blanket
Cochino: Pig, gross (slang)
Comida: Food
Cómo un animal: Like an animal
Cómo un: Like a
Con todo respecto: With all due respect
Conejo: Rabbit
Cora: Heart (slang)
Cucaracha: Cockroach
Cuete: Gun (slang)

Cuete'ad: Shot, shoot, shooting (slang)

Cuidado: Be careful

Cuñado: Brother-in-law

De aquellas: Cool, everything is cool (slang)

De dónde eres: Where are you from?

De volada: Hurry up, right now, immediately (slang)

Dispensa: Excuse me (slang)

Dónde esta mi pájaro: Where is my little bird?

Dónde vas: Where are you going?

Drapes: Describes the flashy clothes worn by Zoot Suiters in the forties

East Los: East Los Angeles

El otro: The other one

En la manaña: In the morning

Entiendes?: Understand?

Escuchame carnalitos: Listen to me little brothers

Escuchame: Listen to me

Ese: Dude, him (slang)

Esperate: Wait

Esposa: Wife

Estudiantil: Student

Familia: Family

Feria: Money (slang)

Filero: Knife or blade (slang)

Firme: Fine (slang)

Flaca: Skinny girl (slang)

Flaco: Skinny boy (slang)

Frijoles: Beans

Gacho: Bad, messed up (slang)

Gata: Female cat

Gato: Male cat

Gavacho: White man (slang)

Gente: People

Gordo: Fat boy, big (slang)

Gracias: Thank you

Grito: Yell or call

Hermana: Sister

Hermano: Brother

Hija: Daughter

Hijo: Son

Hito: Son

Homeboys: Boys from the neighborhood

Homes: Homeboy (slang)

Homies: Homeboys (slang)

Hoyo soto: Grave

Huevos: Referring to a man's bravery (slang)

Jackete: Bad reputation or image (slang)

Jale: Job (slang)

Jardin: Garden

Jefes: Parents (slang)

Jefita: Mother (slang)

Jefito: Father (slang)

Jugo: Juice, power, control (slang)

Jura: Cop, police (slang)

La Llorona: Legendary Hispanic crying witch

La Qlica: Mexican mafia (slang)

La Raza: Hispanic race

Le serio: Serious (slang)

Llave: Key

Lobo: Wolf

Loco: Crazy

Los Olivos: The olives

Los Santos de Noche: Night Saints

Los Sharkies Twelfth Street: The Sharkies Twelfth Street
Malo: Bad
Manaña: Tomorrow
Manos: Hands
Maravilla: Wonder
Mariachi: Mexican guitar player
Maricón: Gay person (slang)
Matar los: To kill them
Mateo: Grind
Matón: Killer
Mayate: Black person (slang)
Me la rayo: I swear it's true, putting everything on it
Mente: Mind
Menudo: Mexican soup
Mi: My
Mijo: My son
Mio: Mine
Mira: Look!
Molacho: Toothless (slang)
Mosca: Fly
Movida: Drive-by, hit (slang)
Movimiento: Movement
Nada: Nothing
Niños: Children
No hay pedo: No big deal
Noche: Night
Norteños: Chicanos from northern California (slang)
Nuestra: Ours, mine
Órale: Alright (slang)
Oso: Bear

Pachucos: Flashily dressed young Chicanos of the fifties and sixties who influenced by the Zoot Suit era
Payaso: Clown
Pelón: Bald
Pendejos: Good for nothing, stupid, idiot
Pero: But
Pinta: Prison (slang)
Pisto: Beer (slang)
Placaso: Nickname, alias (slang)
Pleito: Trouble, fight (slang)
Pollo: Chicken
Polvo: Angel dust (slang)
Porqué: Why, because
Primo: Cousin (slang)
Pues: Well, since
Puro: Pure
Q'vole: Hi (slang)
Q-vo: Hi (slang)
Que no: You know, yeah
Qué paso: What happened?
Que si: Yes
Qué: What
Ranfla: Car (slang)
Rata: Snitch (slang)
Ratón: Rat
Raza: Hispanic Race
Rifa: Rules
Rifamous: Rules
Rola: Song (slang)
Ruca: Girl, girlfriend (slang)
Sabes que? You know what?

Sangre: Blood
Sí mon: Yeah man (slang)
Sí: Yes
Soldados: Soldiers
Soldaderas: Female soldiers who fought during the Mexican Revolution
Solo: Alone
Sombrero: Hat
Somos Calle Doce: We are Twelfth Street
Soy Chicano: I am Chicano
Suegra: Mother-in-law
Sur: South
Sureño: Chicanos from southern California (slang)
Tac: Tattoo (slang)
Tacos: Meat served in a hard-shelled tortilla
También: Too, also
Te acuerdas: Remember or don't forget
Tecato: Heroin addict (slang)
Terrón: Black (slang)
Tio: Uncle
Todos son: All of us are
Torcido: Locked up in jail (slang)
Toro: Bull
Tortilla: Flat flour bread
Travieso: Naughty, mischievous, one who always get into trouble (slang)
Trucha: Watch out, be careful (slang)
Vamanos: Let's go
Vatito: Little dude (slang)
Vato loco: Crazy dude (slang)
Vato: Dude
Ven: Come here
Veteranos: Older men, veterans of the neighborhood (slang)

Vida loca: Crazy life
Wesos: Gang name modified from *"huesos"* meaning bones
Wila: Message, letter (slang)
Winos: Winos
Ya estuvo: That's it (slang)
Yesca: Marijuana (slang)
Yo soy: I am
Y-que: So what (slang)

Song List

Song titles listed alphabetically with chapter number in parenthesis.

Backstrokin': Fatback Band (20)
Baila, Simón: Tierra (9)
Ballero: War (5)
Be Thankful For What You've Got: William DeVaugh (6)
Bounce, Rock, Skate, Roll: Vaughn Mason & Crew (17)
Cisco Kid: War (9)
City Life: Blackbyrds (9)
Come and Get Your Love: Redbone (9)
Double Dutch Bus: Frankie Smith (17)
Duke of Earl: Gene Chandler (16)
Evil Ways: Santana (4)
Fencewalk: Mandrill (9)
Fight the Power: Isley Brothers (9)
Get Down Tonight: K.C. & The Sunshine Band (10)
Gimme Some More: Fred Wesley & The J.B.s (15)
Greetings, This Is Uncle Sam: Monitors (12)
Happy Feelin's: Maze and Franky Beverly (12)
I Heard It Through The Grapevine: Roger (18)
I Shot the Sheriff: Eric Clapton (4)

It's A Thin Line Between Love and Hate: Persuaders (11)
Lowrider: War (9)
Me and Baby Brother: War (4)
Might Mighty: Earth, Wind and Fire (4)
More Bounce To The Ounce: Zapp & Roger (14)
Nite Owl: Tony Allen (11)
Oogum Boogum: Brenton Wood (2)
Oye Como Va: Santana (4)
Papa Don't Take No Mess: James Brown (9)
Right Place, Wrong Time: Dr. John (7)
Run Through The Jungle: Credence Clear Water Revival (8)
Se Me Paro: Johnny Chingas (11)
Shoot Your Shot: Junior Walker and the All Stars (5)
Shot Gun: Junior Walker and the All Stars (5)
Slipping Into Darkness: War (6)
Smile Now, Cry Later: Sunny & The Sunliners (15)
Somebody Please: The Vanguards (8)
Soul Power: James Brown (10)
Take Me to The Next Phase: Isley Brothers (15)
Take Your Time (Do It Right): The S.O.S. Band (16)
Tell Me She's Lovely: El Chicano (11)
The Breaks: Kurtis Blow (18)
The Heat Is On: Isley Brothers (15)
The Payback: James Brown (8)
The Town I Live In: Thee Midnighters (14)
The World Is A Ghetto: War (11)
Together: Tierra (18)
Try Me: James Brown (18)
Viva La Raza: Zapata (4)
Viva Tirado: El Chicano (1)
Who's That Lady: The Isley Brothers (10)

311

Why Can't We Live Together: Timmy Thomas (8)
You're Still A Young Man: Tower of Power (14)

www.ingramcontent.com/pod-product-compliance
Lightning Source LLC
Chambersburg PA
CBHW071653160426
43195CB00012B/1456